SUSAN HAMPSHIRE'S

Easy Gardening

SUSAN HAMPSHIRE'S

Easy Gardening

HOW TO MAKE YOUR GARDEN TAKE CARE OF ITSELF

HAMISH HAMILTON · LONDON

Garden plans by Lynne Smith
Garden perspective (pp.78-9) by Mark Walker of Mia Design

Photographs by Christopher Cormack unless otherwise stated

Design by Annette Stachowiak

HAMISH HAMILTON

Published by the Penguin Group
Penguin Books Ltd, 27 Wrights Lane, London W8 5TZ, England
Viking Penguin, a division of Penguin Books USA Inc.
375 Hudson Street, New York, New York 10014, USA
Penguin Books Australia Ltd, Ringwood, Victoria, Australia
Penguin Books Canada Ltd, 2801 John Street, Markham, Ontario, Canada L3R 1B4
Penguin Books (NZ) Ltd, 182-190 Wairau Road, Auckland 10, New Zealand

Penguin Books Ltd, Registered Offices: Harmondsworth, Middlesex, England

First published in hardback under the title *Trouble Free Gardening* by Elm Tree Books 1989
Published in paperback under the title *Easy Gardening* by Hamish Hamilton 1991

1 3 5 7 9 10 8 6 4 2

Typeset by Wyvern Typesetting, Bristol

*Back cover: This rose was bred by Meilland in France and was named 'Susan Hampshire' in
1974. The reason for such an honour was that at the time I was on television a great deal and
also The Pallisers was in the pipeline. There was already a rose called 'Fleur' (of Forsyte fame)
so 'Susan Hampshire' was the next best thing. Its good points are its vigorous upright growth, old
fashioned fragrance, an unusual shade of pink; it is generally disease resistant.*

Contents

1:	*Introduction*	7
2:	*The right approach*	10
3:	*The conversion of two back yards*	12
4:	*Introduction to the designs*	20
5:	*Children's garden*	21
6:	*Town house garden*	30
7:	*Front garden*	37
8:	*Paved garden*	44
9:	*Cottage garden*	49
10:	*Wildlife garden*	59
11:	*Disabled garden*	70
12:	*Georgian garden*	76
13:	*The garden mistake*	85
14:	*Year-at-a-glance calendar*	88
15:	*Plant association*	90
16:	*Bulbs*	93
17:	*Alpines*	95
18:	*Ground cover*	97
19:	*Weeds*	100
20:	*The interest created by foliage*	101
21:	*Dividing plants*	103
22:	*Herbs*	105
23:	*Trees*	107
24:	*Roses and shrubs*	115
25:	*Tubs*	119
26:	*Planting on a slope*	125
27:	*Pruning*	127
28:	*Low-maintenance vegetables*	131
29:	*Compost*	134
30:	*Fencing*	137
31:	*Paving and hard surfaces*	144
32:	*Ornaments*	149
33:	*Lighting*	153
34:	*Pests*	155
35:	*Insurance*	160
36:	*Some final do's and don'ts*	162
37:	*Plant lists*	166
38:	*Glossary*	183
39:	*Recommended books*	187
40:	*Useful names and addresses*	188
41:	*Index of plants*	191

Acknowledgements

I should like to thank the many people who have, in their own special way, contributed to this book.

Firstly, my special thanks goes to Tom La Dell, Landscape Consultant, for his enthusiasm and encouragement and for so splendidly compiling the plant section at the back of the book; Lynne Smith for her excellent designs and Mark Walker for his drawing of the Georgian garden. I am also extremely grateful to Bridget Garms, Maureen Defries and Janine Fischer for their resilience when coping with my spelling as well as the Latin plant names.

I must take the opportunity to add how much I appreciate the kindness of the many exceptional 'expert' friends, including David Austin, Peter Beales, the Harkness family and Fred Whitsey, who have generously answered my questions and shared their wisdom.

I am very grateful too to World's End Nurseries for lending plants to be photographed and also the numerous garden centres who have welcomed me over the years.

Thanks too must go to Ernie Rees, who has tirelessly worked with me to help create our low maintenance garden in the country. Thanks also to Philip Allan for his contribution.

Almost last, but not least, Caroline Taggart, my editor whose idea the book was, and who so diplomatically restrained me from abandoning the book in despair each time I was faced with rechecking the spelling of Latin plant names. Finally my husband, Eddie, who patiently comforted me when I woke in the night worried by the fact that my personal experience and knowledge of this garden did not always coincide with the experts. 'Write a personal book,' he would say, and so I did.

1: *Introduction*

My earliest memory of the garden was when I was still in my sister's hand-me-down dungarees. I recall sitting in the wheelbarrow watching my father planting asparagus. The fact that I was sitting on a mixture of farmyard manure and compost did not seem to worry me in the least. Even at such an early age I enjoyed being close to nature, and was fascinated by the plants and insects around me.

I remember that I relished being pushed up and down the garden in the wheelbarrow at great speed and, needless to say, occasionally landing up in the rose bed! But this sort of adventure did not prevent me from loving the garden or indeed rose beds. I would wander round the garden with crushed rose petals between my palms, inhaling their glorious fragrance and marvelling at the silky texture of their petals.

'What are you doing?' my mother would ask.

'Eating the smell,' I would say, and very lovely it was too. To this day roses remain my favourite flower.

The thought of those crushed rose petals almost purée in my hands brings back memories of days when a border overgrown with weeds did not worry me. Stress was a word I had never heard and a sensation I had never experienced, and no one was ever late due to a traffic jam.

My love of the garden didn't end at adolescence or diminish in my twenties, although once I was earning my own living I was too busy to spend much time gardening.

Then in 1967 Fred Whitsey, the delightful gardening authority and great plantsman, suggested that the gardening magazine he edited would like to convert my two back yards into a garden and design 'A Garden for Fleur' (I had just played Fleur in *The Forsyte Saga*). Despite this generous offer, I was reluctant to accept at first, because I was working about fourteen hours a day on a long television series (wig and costume fittings included) and the last thing in the world I imagined I would have time to do was take care of a garden of my own.

But Fred assured me that the garden he envisaged would not need more than one hour a week spent on it. Unbelievable though this seemed, the two back yards behind my terraced cottages, which were an appalling eyesore, were duly transformed, and my love of gardening in adult life, and my interest in trouble-free gardening, was born.

As it transpired, the garden was so easy to manage that I sometimes spend less than one hour in ten weeks on caring for it, yet it still looks interesting and presentable all year round. In fact, there is a photograph of the garden in the book after I have neglected it for *a year*.

The pleasure this walled haven in London has afforded me has added a very special dimension to my life. Inhaling the scent of the lime trees or night-scented stocks after returning home from work in the theatre; watching the wrens, robins, thrushes and jays from the kitchen window while doing the washing up; eating outside on a summer's day; sitting and writing in the garden; or just the therapeutic benefits of half an hour passed watering the plants, weeding or dead-heading the climbing roses, have enriched and improved the quality of my life beyond all measure.

So encouraged was I by this easily maintained small London garden that I decided to convert a two acre field around our cottage on the Surrey/Hampshire border into a low maintenance wild garden, and asked Tom La Dell, old school friend, landscape architect and landscape scientist, and now technical consultant on this book, to design the garden for me and very brilliantly he did it too.

I had mistakenly imagined that converting the garden would be easier and less expensive than enlarging the house. It was certainly more enjoyable, but I had not taken into consideration that two acres is a very large area to convert from scratch. After the contractors had laid two herring-bone brick terraces, boundary fences had been erected, wells built, trellises constructed, and earth-moving machines had worked for ten days reshaping the land, the cost of the garden conversion to date exceeded the estimate for the proposed and not-to-be-built extension to the house!

So in the interest of economy I decided to finish the garden myself. Shifting hundreds of wheelbarrows full of top soil and spreading lorry-loads of cow manure and mushroom compost became everyday tasks. With the help of my son Christopher and my nephew Jeremy, I planted ninety trees and thousands of shrubs and daffodils.

The man who came once a week and who could do everything from laying paving stones to digging land drains, constructed and erected two wooden rose arbours and four trellises to surround the second terrace. He dug the trenches, hammered in the pressure impregnated wood and remarked earnestly, 'Plants are strange animals.' So the process was not without its laughs.

It is only the constructing and establishing of a low-maintenance garden that is the hard part; from then on it becomes easier and easier. Knowing I would have such a large area to maintain, getting it right at this stage was all important.

By the time the garden was completed, I had spent roughly six hundred hours on my knees and made four thousand holes for planting. In order to have the beds completely weed-free, I had battled with yard upon yard of ground elder, pulled up hundreds of shoots of bracken and dug out root after root of stinging nettles. My life had been spent ankle deep in mud and I felt as though calcified seaweed and bonemeal were almost coming out of my ears.

Added to which I pulled what seemed like every muscle in my arms, suffered from painfully stiff joints and strained my back, working for hours in the cold and rain. My hands were so rough that I was ashamed to show them and they felt like a nail brush to anyone shaking my hand. Yet none of these complaints seemed important: I was as happy and as proud as if I had built the whole of Rome myself.

When I woke each morning I felt the excitement of a child at Christmas and rushed to the window to look out on the result of my endeavours. Each night I went to bed dreaming of the plants still waiting to be planted or transplanted to make my low-mantenance haven complete. The rose-eating deers, the rabbits who confined their nocturnal diet to my shrubs, and the ongoing battle with the weeds were not able to extinguish my happiness. The joy was total.

When finally the garden was finished, the house of course remained too small, so alas we had to move, to a farmhouse with six acres of high-maintenance garden. I left behind my garden labour of love for someone else to enjoy its low maintenance.

Happily all gardening improvements do not need to be quite so back-breaking, ambitious or large. The progress made in the art of trouble-free gardening has been enormous. No longer is it a problem if people are too busy to spend much time caring for a garden, as careful planning, clever planting and the right plant combinations can produce a fair-sized garden that virtually takes care of itself. So the days of longing to have a garden yet worrying it would be impossible to find time to take care of it are past.

A great many gardens, such as the magnificent old kitchen gardens, are extremely labour-intensive. Lots of carpet bedding is also a tremendous example of what love and labour can do, but hopeless for busy people, unless they are lucky enough to have a gardener or three.

Not so long ago, an extremely well-known garden expert announced to me, 'I *loathe* low-maintenance gardens, they are so *boring* and so *predictable* – never exciting or beautiful.'

I disagree, they don't have to be predictable or boring and they certainly *can* be beautiful. As a point of interest the expert in question's garden looked *abandoned*, probably as there wasn't enough labour around to be intensive!

My two-acre conversion was as low-maintenance as can be: a weekly mow on the main lawn, biannual cut of the long grass in the wild section and pruning of roses once a year. As I have said, my much smaller London garden can be neglected for months on end and still look good.

It is odd that I, who was and is happy to garden eight hours at a stretch, should find low-maintenance gardening so interesting. Now, disease-resistant plants, evergreens that need minimum pruning, ground cover to keep out the weeds, plants that divide, all hold a place in my heart. The amazingly rare plant that flowers for a day, has to go in and out of the greenhouse and needs constant attention is not for me (or for most of us). I read recently about a survey which showed that only 24% of people in Britain enjoy gardening, while 42% find it a chore or worse.

The discovery that a full-time career and a garden can be enjoyed and go hand in hand was a turning point in my life. So, anxious to show others how simple it is to have both, I have written this book.

2: *The right approach*

Try to look upon the garden as another room, and spend as much or as little money as you would on any other main feature of the house.

It is against most people's instinct to spend money *outside*. One imagines that outside, nature, which costs nothing, will provide and take care of everything. This, alas, at least in the initial stages, is not the case. A garden, even a natural wild garden, costs money at the outset. But with good planning, economies can be made. For instance some plants and trees create problems, others are obliging and easy. To avoid heartache there are lists of trouble-free plants and trees from which to choose at the back of the book.

But if you are as financially generous to your garden as you would be to your kitchen or dining room, then it's a comfort to know that with a pleasant garden you are not only improving your property, you are enhancing the whole fabric of your life. There are no electricity, gas or rates bills for the garden, and hopefully the good Lord will provide sun, wind and most of the water to keep the garden flourishing once it is there.

The sort of hefty expenses that occur through wear and tear inside the house – recovering the sofa, making new curtains and redecorating – won't crop up outside once the garden has been constructed and planted. While the fabric of a house deteriorates with time, a garden, especially a low-maintenance garden, improves with age. There will be small expenses each year like summer bedding plants for the tubs and window boxes, organic fertiliser for feeding the plants and the odd plant replacement. But if you stop to consider how often, without objecting, you may buy a plant or flowers for the sitting room, furniture polish or even a hoover for the house, why shouldn't a garden warrant the same love, maintenance and treatment?

Taste and style are very individual. You or I may not like to see a bed full of marigolds or pansies, or Municipal Gardens choice of bedding plants, but that doesn't stop it being a joy to behold in someone else's eyes.

So it is important to do what *you* like. You will have to live with it. If you see a feature or plant scheme that pleases you, by all means try it. Gardening books are only there to inform, give suggestions, ideas, short cuts and guidance, not impose taste or style on the individual.

Colour

Cottage gardens are enhanced by the use of as many coloured flowers as can be planted in them. But if you are planning a small town garden, the thought and consideration given to *colour* at planning stage, *before* buying a single plant is of great importance.

When my garden in London was planned, I was disappointed to be told that none of the existing plants in the back yard could be saved because they would not fit into the new colour theme.

Before you are initiated into the wonders of horticulture, it's easy to imagine that any plant, even if it only has one green leaf, or if it flowered once two autumns ago, must be preserved at all cost. But I have since learnt that it is not worth keeping plants that don't fit into the scheme of things, as *all* the plants in a trouble-free garden need to work towards presenting a year-round display.

So the colour of plants, along with the site in which they are to be planted, should be considered at planning stage. It is pointless to have plants that will not flourish in a certain position. For instance, if you want to have a light grey effect and plant small lavender and senecio in a damp shady corner, they will not survive as they both prefer full sun. So choose the right plant for the site. There is usually a choice of plants for sun or shade with either dark or light leaves. Some hostas, for example, have a creamy, variegated leaf, love the shade and make a wonderful display to brighten up a dark spot from spring to autumn. Although they die back each winter, they are ideal for creating a light effect.

Vibrant colours in a small space can often overpower the more subtle pinks and whites. So to achieve a pleasing effect limit your choice of colour to ones which will blend harmoniously together.

Fred Whitsey selected a pastel theme for my garden and advised me to discard the violent yellow and orange flowers that were already there. This pastel choice was perfect for the garden, and the subtle theme of light and dark pink, white and a little blue, married together beautifully.

Buying and Care Cards

Some camellias, roses or geraniums have lovely gentle pinks, other strong strident reds. So look at the *care card* (if there is one) carefully before buying – especially if the flower is not in bloom – to check if the colour will fit in with your plans for your garden.

On the other hand it is easy to be tempted by the 'pretty picture' on the care card and buy a plant that is totally unsuitable for your garden. So however nice a plant looks, don't buy it without first finding out its colour, what conditions it likes, what size it will grow and so on. A low-maintenance garden needs trouble-free perennials and evergreens. Otherwise you will be forever planting new plants to fill up the gaps made by plants, bought on a whim, that have now died down, as they turned out to be annuals or unsuitable for your soil or site.

The pictures on care cards usually show only the flower, not the whole shrub or plant; this can be very deceptive, so find out about the *whole* plant before buying.

3: The conversion of two back yards

This first design which the old *Popular Gardening* have graciously allowed us to show is the very reason I became seriously interested in low-maintenance gardening. I was impressed by the ease with which the garden took care of itself (rather than my taking care of it), and overwhelmed by the year-round fragrance, colour and variety it offered in exchange for so little work. It was all these qualities that contributed to my obsession with gardens that are planned, built, laid out and planted with the correct choice of flowers and shrubs, in such a way that they do not rule your life.

Not many garden lovers can sit outside and just enjoy the garden for long without being tempted to jump up and do some small job that they feel needs to be done, but for those who are not addicted to gardening a 'little work' garden is there to be *enjoyed*.

My garden was laid out in 1969 and it has deteriorated very little over the years, considering it has only had the odd plant replaced and often been neglected cruelly for months on end.

Apart from a good organic feed in March, pruning, watering and seasonal planting of the tubs in May, it has been left year in year out to struggle or flourish as it will.

I confess that some of this neglect is due to my involvement in the as yet untamed six acre (2.5 hectare) garden outside London, which has meant that this garden has seen less than six hours of my love and attention a year and has been forced to take care of itself. Yet it has proved unquestionably that it is a successful 'trouble free' garden. But that goes without saying as it was so *well thought out and planned* in the first place.

The Original Garden

Years ago when I was working on one long classic television series after another I had two dingy back yards behind the two Victorian artisan's cottages in which I live. The yards were on three different levels, with poor soil, a variety of straggly and unsuitable plants, and shaded by huge overhanging lime trees which not only took the goodness from the soil, but also produced an aphid excretion in the summer which made everything beneath sticky and black. There was no area in which to sit and there were slugs and snails everywhere. At one time there had been a 'privy' in the garden and a bicycle shed, the remains of which were falling down in one corner.

I had bought the second cottage in the early sixties from my neighbours, a couple who were pensioners and whose family had lived in the street since the cottages were built over a hundred years ago. In the old days there were vegetables, chickens, outside loo and a clothes line in the back yards, before developers bought the cottages and converted them.

So I was very fortunate when Fred Whitsey suggested his magazine would design a garden for me and asked Bill Brett, consultant landscape designer of William Wood and Son, to do the design.

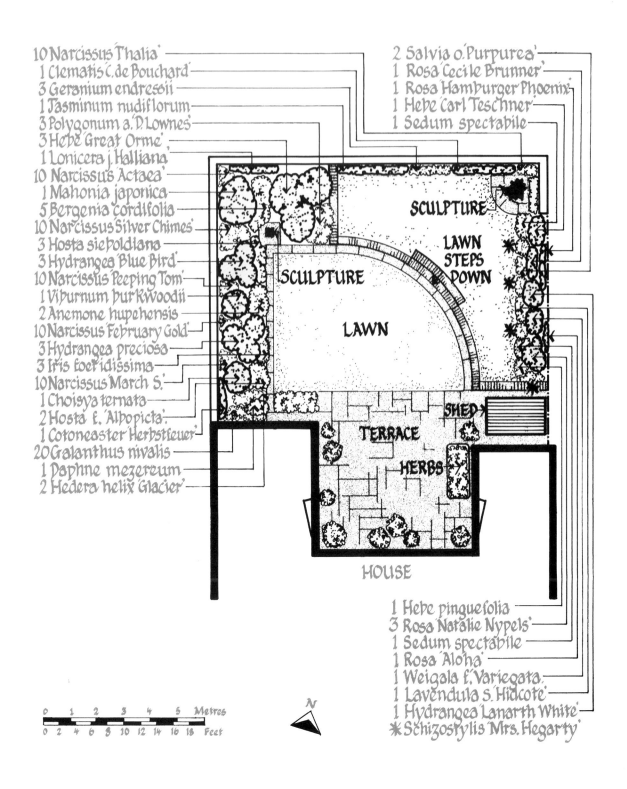

10 Narcissus 'Thalia'
1 Clematis 'C. de Bouchard'
3 Geranium endresii
1 Jasminum nudiflorum
3 Polygonum a. 'D. Lownes'
3 Hebe 'Great Orme'
1 Lonicera j. 'Halliana'
10 Narcissus 'Actaea'
1 Mahonia japonica
5 Bergenia cordifolia
10 Narcissus 'Silver Chimes'
3 Hosta sieboldiana
3 Hydrangea 'Blue Bird'
10 Narcissus 'Peeping Tom'
1 Viburnum burkwoodii
2 Anemone hupehensis
10 Narcissus 'February Gold'
3 Hydrangea preciosa
3 Iris foetidissima
10 Narcissus 'March S.'
1 Choisya ternata
2 Hosta f. 'Albopicta'
1 Cotoneaster 'Herbstfeuer'
20 Galanthus nivalis
1 Daphne mezereum
2 Hedera helix 'Glacier'

2 Salvia o. 'Purpurea'
1 Rosa 'Cecile Brunner'
1 Rosa 'Hamburger Phoenix'
1 Hebe 'Carl Teschner'
1 Sedum spectabile

SCULPTURE

LAWN STEPS DOWN

SCULPTURE

LAWN

SHED

TERRACE

HERBS

HOUSE

1 Hebe pinguefolia
3 Rosa 'Natalie Nypels'
1 Sedum spectabile
1 Rosa 'Aloha'
1 Weigela f. 'Variegata'
1 Lavendula s. 'Hidcote'
1 Hydrangea 'Lanarth White'
✳ Schizostylis 'Mrs. Hegarty'

0 1 2 3 4 5 Metres
0 2 4 6 8 10 12 14 16 18 Feet

N

My Garden

The Obstacles

The problems presented to the designer were the mature overhanging lime trees and the varying levels of the garden – although the cottages were on the same level, the back yards had in places a discrepancy of 12 in to 18 in (30 to 45 cm). There were patches of crazed concrete, and low brick walls that had fallen down. The dilapidated shed, permanent puddles on compacted poor soil, ill-assorted trellis, builders' debris, bricks and slates didn't help either. The area, which was 30 ft (9 m) deep and 60 ft (18 m) wide, was an unsightly mess.

Priorities

I wanted a garden that demanded very little time, as I was often away working or working round the clock at the studio. I wanted a place to sit. I didn't want to have to put in different plants in the summer, then replace them in the autumn or have to do a lot of digging. My dream was to spend less than an hour a week on it and still have a beautiful garden.

Only during the establishing years was I obliged to devote a certain amount of time to weeding. But ultimately the garden demanded less than an hour a month and yet was still interesting and pleasant the year round.

One of my first requests for the garden, apart from the fact that I wanted it to be easy, was *roses*. I love roses, but unfortunately in such an enclosed area, with little or no breeze being able to circulate, roses tend to struggle for life rather than flourish in the garden.

Time has shown that climbing roses, which can get their heads above the wall and into the air and light, do extremely well providing they are fed with Top Rose or bonemeal each year. So a number of climbing roses were added to the original planting plan. In the early stages, climbing roses need training and cutting, two jobs that at the beginning were not on my list of things I was prepared to do in this 'little work' garden. But for the *very* little effort they have cost me, twenty years later, I am still enjoying their beauty and am delighted they were planted.

The Design

This simple, elegant design has brilliantly married the two levels of the walled garden together and banished completely the desolated look of neglected back yards.

As you look from the terrace at the back of the house over the two-tier garden, the sweeping raised crescent moon in the corner cleverly exploits the change of levels, and thus this built-up area is transformed into a pleasant sitting arbour, which has the sun in the summer until at least seven or eight o'clock and is a perfect place to enjoy a quiet read or late tea.

The wooden trellis on two sides of the arbour provides strong support for the

left: My garden after a year's neglect – all I've done is water, feed, and sweep up the leaves. The ivy has grown about 3 feet (90 cm) (photo by Susan Hampshire)

above: After about three hours spent trimming and planting up terracotta pots, and below: two months later after no work at all.

Jasminum officinale and *Clematis montana* 'Rubens', plus some welcome shade to cool this sun trap on sunny days. On the opposite side the densely planted lush foliage and statue complement the sun-filled sitting area.

Walking across the grass to the house from the arbour you go down two brick steps to the second grass area. The interesting outline of the grass is emphasised by bricks laid on the edge making a flat 'mowing stone' to facilitate cutting the grass.

The small shed for garden implements, lawn mower and dustbins on the right of the terrace is camouflaged by the tubs in front. Utilities such as a barbecue and clothes line were not required so a space didn't need to be found for them.

Practicalities

One of the first moves we made before moving or levelling the soil of the back yards was to ask the local council to reduce the canopy of the overhanging lime trees growing in the grounds behind the terrace. In my case it was an essential step to let in both rain and light.

Trees are sometimes the cause of problems but the principles behind these are reasonably well defined in law. If a tree overhangs a neighbouring property, the neighbour can cut the branches or the roots back to the boundary. The cut off parts still belong to the tree's owner, as do the fruits, apples, and so on, on a fruit tree! In the interests of neighbourly relations, it is advisable to tell the tree's owner your intention to cut it, but this is not a legal duty.

Trees in the street and in adjoining council property are the council's responsibility. But a tree in your own garden may have a preservation order on it, so make enquiries before starting work on the garden. Make sure you use an experienced tree surgeon to do this sort of work.

The Importance of a Paved Area

We have so few fine days in England that when they do come it's nice to be outside but not, needless to say, on grass that is soaking wet from rain the day before. So a paved terrace is essential. Chairs and tables need to stand on a hard surface as no one (not even the lawn) wants to have heels and chair legs sinking into the grass.

Development

Like every garden, this one has evolved with time. Jardinières have been added, plants that have died in the frost have been replaced, a sculpture removed, and a conservatory built, greatly reducing the size of the original terrace.

The years have seen climbing frames, portable sand pits, children's parties and picnics on the grass, to say nothing of tents, caged rabbits and wandering tortoises.

At one time the little grass lawn was used for football and swingball to such an extent that it had to be paved over with York stone to avoid the muddy shoes treading in and out of the house. I came by my York stone in a curious way. Many years ago when the council were sadly ripping up the York stone paving slabs outside the stage door of the theatre where I was working, the workmen told me the smaller pieces were to be discarded and if I wished I could take them home. So each night I loaded the boot of my car – ruining the suspension in the process – and took home small sections of York stone which now cover the lower grass area as well as the brick 'mowing stone', which was destroyed by youngsters trying to play football.

But none of these changes has been fatal. They have left their mark, which is as it should be, as gardens are there to be used as an extension of the house.

MY GARDEN

The plants listed below are the plants that have flourished despite neglect over the past 20 years in my pink, white and blue garden, and not had to be replaced. See back of book for more details.

T = *Trouble free*

Climbers

Lonicera japonica 'Halliana' *Height 25–30 ft (7.5–9 m) Sweet-smelling cream flowers from June to October. Semi-evergreen, mid-green leaves. Good camouflage climber and will grow anywhere.*

T Hydrangea petiolaris *Self-clinging hardy deciduous climber. In the wild it can grow to 60 ft (18 m) but is easily pruned. Attractive picturesque plant to clothe walls or fences and will grow on north- and east-facing walls without complaining. Flat heads of cream-white flowers in June. Dark green leaves, flaky brown stems. Prefers damp wall and shade, and needs a few ties as it grows: if the wall is too dry it may fall away.*

T Jasminum nudiflorum *(Winter jasmine). Hardy deciduous climber that needs training and support. Grows to 10 ft (3 m). Yellow flowers which make a dazzling display in winter on naked green branches. Tiny oval three-fingered dark green leaves. Prune after flowering to keep it tidy. Tolerates sun or shade.*

T Jasminum officinale *Hardy deciduous vigorous climber. Grows to 30 ft (9 m). Mid-green leaves. Sweet-smelling clusters of small white star-like flowers from June to October. Best in sunny position for more flowers.*

Climbing Rose Aloha *Height 7–10 ft (2.25– 3 m). Rich pink, very full flowers with strong perfume from June onwards. Shiny green leaf. (Also good as a large shrub).*

Shrubs

T Mahonia japonica *Evergreen shrub, happy in sun or shade. Long dark green holly-like leaves. Height 6–8 ft (2–2.5 m). Spread 6–8 ft (2– 2.5 m). Long pendulous clusters of lemon yellow flowers with lily of the valley scent. Wonderfully easy and dramatic shrub. Don't be afraid to cut it back after flowering to keep it bushy. But I haven't cut mine more than twice in 20 years!*

T Hebe 'Great Orme' *Evergreen shrub. Grows to 4 ft (1.2 m). Spread 3–4 ft (90 cm–1.2 m). Dark green fleshy leaves, pink flowers on spikes from May to July. Tolerates all conditions, even maritime, but not extreme cold. Hebe pinguifolia has white flowers on spikes in May.*

continued over page

A pleasing contrast of greens in the leaves of a variegated hebe.

MY GARDEN (*continued*)

T Daphne mezereum *(Mezereon) Deciduous shrub. Height 5 ft (1.5 m) spread 2 – 4 ft (60 cm – 1.2 m). Sweet-smelling pink/purple flowers from February to March, followed by poisonous scarlet fruit. Light green leaves with grey/green underside.*

T Cotoneaster 'Autumn Fire' *Evergreen shrub. Grows to 15 ft (4.5 m) if supported, or 3 or 4 ft (90 cm – 1.2 m) as ground cover. Dark green leaves, tiny white flowers in May, red fruits (loved by the birds) in autumn. Tolerates shade or sun.*

T Choisya ternata *(Mexican orange blossom) Wonderful evergreen bushy shrub with aromatic shiny dark green leaves. Height 6 – 8 ft (2 – 2.5 m) and spread 6 – 8 ft (2 – 2.5 m), but it has grown to almost 18 ft (5.5 m) in this garden. Sweet-smelling white flowers in May and sporadically throughout the summer and autumn. Tolerates both shade and sun – a most obliging shrub. Doesn't like soggy soil.*

T Viburnum burkwoodii *Evergreen shrub. Height up to 8 ft (2.5 m). Spread 8 – 12 ft (2.5 to 3.5 m). Sweet-smelling clove-scented white flower clusters (pink when in bud) from January to May. Excellent hardworking shrub. Dark green leaves with brown/grey felt underside. Tolerates shade or sun. In this garden it is trained as a climber.*

T Hydrangea 'Blue Bird' *Deciduous shrub. Height up to 2 ft 6 in (75 cm). Spread 2 ft 6 in (75 cm). Delightful blue lace-cap flowers in July. This shrub prefers shade but tolerates some sun. Mid-green leaves. All hydrangeas make excellent dried flowers and do need plenty of moisture.*

T Hydrangea 'Lanarth White' *Deciduous shrub. Height about 3 ft (1 m). Nice compact habit. White lace-cap flowers from July to October. Pale green leaves. Unlike many hydrangeas this variety flowers best in sun.*

Hosta ventricosa

MY GARDEN (*continued*)

T Weigela Florida 'Variegata' *Deciduous shrub. Height 4–5 ft (1.2–1.5 m). Spread 4–5 ft (1.2 m–1.5 m). Mid-green leaves with broad cream/white margins. Attractive and obliging shrub with pale pink foxglove-like flowers May and June.*

Herbaceous

Bergenia cordifolia *(Elephants' Ears). Excellent evergreen ground cover. Pink and red flowers in spring. Large flat dark green leaves. Handsome ground cover, except once twelve years ago when it was attacked by snails.*

T Hedera helix 'Glacier' *(Ivy) Ground cover or for a shady wall. Silver grey leafed ivy. This variety will grow to 5–10 ft (1.5–3 m).*

T Sedum spectabile *Hardy herbaceous plant. Height 12–18 in (30–45 cm). Spread 15 in (37.5 cm). Pink head of flowers 3–5 in (7.5–12.5 cm) across from September to October. Fleshy silver/green leaves. Brings welcome autumn colour.*

T Salvia officinalis purpurea *(Sage) Evergreen small shrub. Purple leafed sage, obliging ground cover. Height 18 in (45 cm), spread 18 in (45 cm). Blue purple flowers in June and July. Prefers sun.*

T Hosta sieboldiana *Herbaceous perennial. Excellent low-growing late spring and summer ground cover plant. Broad silver/blue leaves, pale lilac flowers in July to August. Can grow 2 ft by 2 ft (60 by 60 cm). Both shade and sun-loving.*

The deciduous shrubs are underplanted with snowdrops and miniature cyclamen and spring flowering bulbs.

4: *Introduction to the designs*

Oh the beauty of the small garden! The garden that doesn't send you to sleep worrying about what still needs to be done, a garden that is easily maintained and in which a luscious and inspiring show is all the more dramatic as its impact is seen at one glance.

This section is devoted to a series of garden designs aimed to give you ideas for the kind of garden you may require. There is a choice of garden for anyone ranging from the young mother, disabled person, nature lover, to high flyer – each with its own charm and characteristics. Whether you wish to economise or splash out there is a garden for you.

All these designs are for gardens of a limited size and that is the joy. I have both a large and a small garden and I would sing the praises of the small any time. A well-planned and planted garden such as these is not going to send you rushing in despair for a gin and tonic, as it should be easy to manage and be planted in such a way that it never gets out of hand.

If among these garden designs you see one for a south-facing garden and yours faces north, the design can easily be adapted. The shade-loving plants on the design can be put into your shady area and the seating area can be reversed so as to catch the sun in your garden. If you have a north wall and acid soil, you can enjoy the 'no trouble' azaleas and camellias which love that position, and so on.

You may not wish to remake a garden from scratch, but should some of the aspects of the garden designs be similar to your own (for instance, if your garden slopes up away from the house), you can incorporate the ideas for that garden into your own. If you have a cottage garden and you prefer the plan for the wildlife garden, you can adapt those ideas to fit your own space. A garden is part of you: text book gardens may be perfect on paper, but not nearly so interesting or personal if you do not feel strongly about them yourself.

Loving what *you* have is all important. So these designs are here to offer as little or as much as pleases you. The planting plan will offer some choices for making up planting schemes. Marry those ideas with your own and you should have the right combination.

Detailed planting suggestions are given for half of each garden. To design your own planting for the other half, refer to the plant lists on pp. 166–182. Numbers on the plans, highlighted in green, refer to specific lists of suitable plants e.g. 6A refers to the list of evergreen trees on p.179.

5: Children's garden

(Multi-coloured, slopes up)

This practical garden is ideal for people with young children, although later it can easily be adapted into an interesting and pleasant garden for an all-adult household.

The view from the kitchen window as the garden slopes up away from the house is a pleasing one. The rectangular patio joins the main circle of the garden which is grassed over and surrounded by a hard surface outer circle. These two shapes married together make an unusual and exciting combination.

The grass area is suitable for parents and young children to sit and play in, and a perfect spot for watching small children circling round on a tricycle on the hard outer surface designed expressly for that purpose. As the children grow up, the grass can be used for swingball or sunbathing.

Behind the main circle the garden opens out into a semi-circular space for a climbing frame and small swing. The raised earth behind is held back by 2 ft 6 in (75 cm) logs placed upright and butt-jointed in the soil. Chip bark, shredded bark or bark flakes covering the earth provides a reasonably softened surface should the children fall off the swing or climbing frame. 6 in (15 cm) of pea shingle is also an effective surface under children's climbing frames, swings and see-saws, but it is not as effective as shredded bark.

Grass in this area beneath the swing would have been tiresome to maintain as small feet constantly walking on it would wear it away; besides which muddy feet going in and out of the house would not be welcome. The grass in the centre ring need only be cut each week with a small rotary mower.

Between the main circle and the swing area another half-circle is reserved for the sand pit. This can be converted into a paddling pool providing the correct type of liner is used in the first place. Suitable fibreglass liners can be bought in many shapes and sizes at most large garden centres. Behind the swing area an *Acer palmatum* (Japanese maple) tree breaks up the line of the fence; on hot days it provides some shade and is a safe tree for children as it has no poisonous berries.

Behind the sand pit the earth is again held back by logs with periwinkle or similar resilient low-growing evergreen flowering plants planted at the base of the retaining wall (see *Planting on a Slope*).

The sand pit area gets full sun until well after tea time. It can be seen clearly from the kitchen window and is easily reached from the kitchen door should there be a mishap. It is important that children's play areas are built in sight of the house and in the sun, not in dark, damp and uninviting corners. But remember that very small children need protection against the sun.

On the opposite side of the garden the retaining log wall and closely planted evergreen shrubs behind the seat catch the late afternoon sun and conceal the path to the rotary clothes line. This space could alternatively be used as a secluded sitting area or opened out for a Wendy house if the family prefer the laundromat or have a

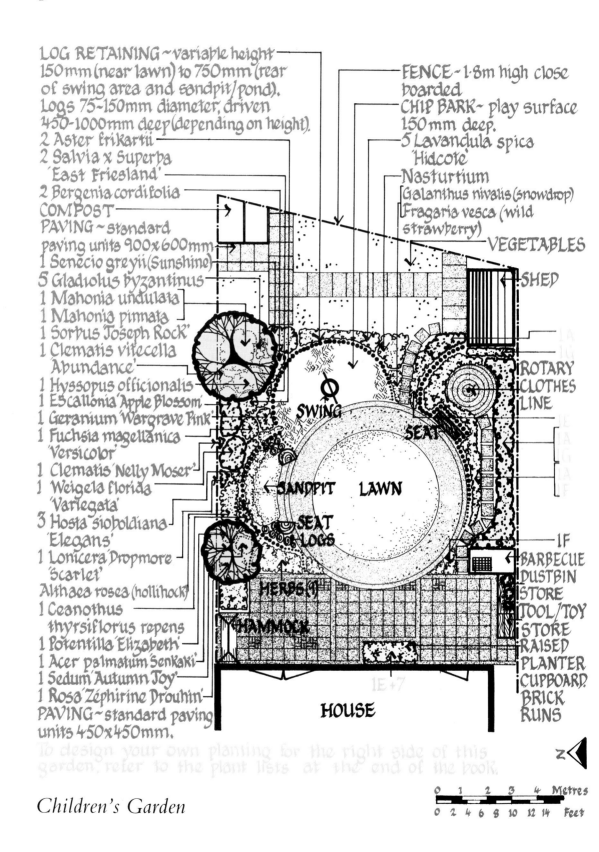

LOG RETAINING ~ variable height
150mm (near lawn) to 750mm (rear
of swing area and sandpit/pond).
Logs 75~150mm diameter, driven
450-1000mm deep (depending on height).
2 Aster frikartii
2 Salvia x Superba
  'East Friesland'
2 Bergenia cordifolia
COMPOST
PAVING ~ standard
paving units 900x600mm.
1 Senecio greyii (Sunshine)
5 Gladiolus byzantinus
1 Mahonia undulata
1 Mahonia pinnata
1 Sorbus 'Joseph Rock'
1 Clematis vitecella
  'Abundance'
1 Hyssopus officionalis
1 Escallonia 'Apple Blossom'
1 Geranium 'Wargrave Pink'
1 Fuchsia magellanica
  'Versicolor'
1 Clematis 'Nelly Moser'
1 Weigela florida
  'Variegata'
3 Hosta sieboldiana
  'Elegans'
1 Lonicera 'Dropmore
  'Scarlet'
Althaea rosea (hollihock)
1 Ceanothus
  thyrsiflorus repens
1 Potentilla 'Elizabeth'
1 Acer palmatum 'Senkaki'
1 Sedum 'Autumn Joy'
1 Rosa 'Zéphirine Drouhin'
PAVING ~ standard paving
units 450x450mm.

FENCE ~ 1·8m high close
boarded
CHIP BARK ~ play surface
150mm deep.
5 Lavandula spica
  'Hidcote'
Nasturtium
(Galanthus nivalis (snowdrop)
Fragaria vesca (wild
  strawberry)
VEGETABLES
SHED

ROTARY
CLOTHES
LINE

SWING
SEAT
SANDPIT   LAWN
SEAT
& LOGS

HERBS (I)
HAMMOCK

1F
BARBECUE
DUSTBIN
STORE
TOOL/TOY
STORE
RAISED
PLANTER
CUPBOARD
BRICK
RUNS

HOUSE

To design your own planting for the right side of this garden, refer to the plant lists at the end of the book.

Children's Garden

0   1   2   3   4 Metres
0 2 4 6 8 10 12 14 Feet

22

tumble drier.

At the end of the garden is a sunny space for vegetables plus a little shade by the boundary wall for such vegetables as lettuce. A second shed for storing prams and bicycles, plus a compost pen for grass cuttings, leaves and kitchen waste, are situated on the right and left.

It is never too soon to introduce children to plants and a little simple gardening. So this space would also be ideal for children to have their own garden and grow easy vegetables like courgettes, broad beans, calabrese, spinach, shallots, radishes, potatoes, beetroot, leeks and nasturtium flowers if the vegetable patch is not needed for adults. Children can be encouraged to grow plants in pots, then, should they become neglected, they can be transplanted into the beds by the parents.

But if you do not want the space for vegetables or children, each area including the terrace can be slightly enlarged, or taller-growing evergreen shrubs such as choisya or rhododendrons can be planted instead, screening the end and giving the impression the garden goes on for ever! Bamboo can also make a dramatic and interesting feature in a garden and in full sun *Arundinaria viridistriata* is stunning with its green and gold stripe. It grows to 3 ft (90 cm) but must have full sun otherwise the leaves will just be shades of pale green.

Herbs and Fragrance

Soft herbs, of which you can eat everything that you cut from the plants, such as parsley, mint, fennel, basil and chervil, are useful to have as near to the kitchen as possible. Plant these herbs outside the kitchen window in a raised planter at window-box level, with a cupboard for garden tools and children's garden and sand pit toys below. To cover the wall a rose can be planted in the ground on either side of the planter: choose a sweet-smelling rose whose perfume can be enjoyed through open patio doors and the kitchen windows, or while sitting outside; *Kathleen Harrop* is a lovely *thornless* climbing rose, safe for children and ideal for such a spot. *Jasminum officinale* would be another good choice.

The hard herbs, which grow on twiggy stems which you cannot eat, such as sage, thyme and rosemary, can grow on the left of the kitchen door where they will get full sun. A rowan tree which has non-poisonous berries, safe for children, is growing behind, so even if it is raining they can still be picked with a quick sprint across the terrace before the hair loses all its curl!

Seating

Couples with young families seldom have time to sit down for long until after the children have gone to bed or are grown up. Therefore there is all the more need for several easily accessible seating areas to rest weary limbs for a few moments while occupying children or watching them play.

European hardwood armchairs or log seat on either side of the sand pit and a wooden bench on the opposite side of the circle set back into the plants are pleasant places to sit and observe youngsters.

The patio lends itself happily to a variety of positions for tables and chairs for eating outside – including, if desired, a space for a garden hammock on the left of the patio window where it will get the afternoon sun.

A barbecue may not be needed but, if it is, a convenient place for it is opposite the kitchen door, handy for taking the food from the fridge, collecting the mustard and throwing rubbish into the dust bin on the right.

The patio itself is in three square sections and can be made up of simple flag stones, riven concrete paving slabs, bricks or large terracotta tiles, according to taste and budget.

Although much in demand for paving areas of small formal town gardens, York stone is very expensive and does tend to go very dark with time. But more important it is not advisable for a young family as it is *very slippery when wet*. Young children may skid and hurt themselves on the hard surface, to say nothing of the hazard to the visiting older generation.

If you choose brick, make sure it is a *paving* brick *not* engineering brick which is smooth and also very slippery when wet (see *Bricks and Paving*). A tinted concrete paving slab would be a good choice.

Boundaries

The question of how little or how much the property is already overlooked is of prime importance when deciding what fencing to choose. If you want privacy, you must have an adequate barrier between your property and the next (see *Fencing*).

In a garden where there will be small children the fence needs to be a solid 6 ft (nearly 2 m) high timber fence to prevent youngsters wandering out of the garden. A section of the fence can be painted with blackboard paint (obtained from educational suppliers or school or play groups), ideal for outdoor murals done with chalk.

Important Notes for Children

1. Children should keep shoes on when the lawn is being mowed.
2. Use an electric circuit-breaker on all electrical garden tools for safety in the home with children and pets.
3. Do not water if electric lawn mower is in use.
4. Do not let children play with the mower.
5. Do not leave glass or garden tools on the ground especially when children have bare feet.
6. Use perspex tumblers and mugs in the garden.
7. Tools and machinery should be stored out of children's reach.
8. Store garden chemicals out of reach or lock them away as they could be mistaken for food and may be poisonous.
9. Do not use *identifiable drink and food bottles and jars* to store chemicals. Always store chemicals in their original containers.
10. Do not use slug pellets as they are dangerous to children and pets.
11. *Garden light fittings*, except those that are well above 4 to 5 ft (about 1.5 m), are *not recommended* in gardens where there are children.

CHILDREN'S GARDEN **SOME POISONOUS PLANTS TO BE AVOIDED**
Before listing poisonous plants to be avoided where there are children, it is important to point out that it should be explained to children that although the plants in their garden are not poisonous, there may be poisonous plants in other people's gardens. Therefore they should *never* eat leaves of unfamiliar plants or berries. Laburnum (tree) and oleander (flowering shrub) are only two of the many popular yet poisonous species that can be found in many gardens.

Trees
Fagus sylvatica (*Beech*)
Laburnum
Prunus × amygdalo – persica 'Pollardii' (*Ornamental Almond*)
Quercus (*Oak*)

Shrubs
Buxus
Cotoneaster
Daphne mezereum
Hedera (*Ivy*)
Hippophae rhamnoides (*Sea Buckthorn*)

Perennials
Aconitum (*Monkshood*)
Aquilegia (*Columbine*)
Avena (*Oat grass*)
Caltha (*Marsh Marigold*)
Helleborus (*Christmas rose*)
Iris
Polygonatum (*Solomon's seal*)
Pulsatilla (*Pasque flower*)

Conifers
Juniperus (*Juniper*)
Taxus (*Yew*)

above: Senecio 'Sunshine', *a reliable low-maintenance shrub (photo by Pamla Toler).*

opposite: The hardy fuchsia with its unusual shaped flowers gives striking autumn colour (photo by Pamla Toler).

Water and Safety

Each year there are accidents in the garden. Toddlers fall into fish ponds, bog gardens and little pools. The shock of the water can stop the youngster's heart. This and not the depth of the water is often the cause of tragedy. So do fence off or cover over or drain away any water if there are *very young* children in the house or visiting. The paddling pool should be drained or covered if it is not in use. Always make sure there is an adult present if a toddler is near water.

Bonfires and Fireworks

Fireworks are dangerous, so always follow the firework code printed on the box. There are thousands of accidents involving children and fireworks each year.

Keep bonfires well away from house, trees, sheds and fences. Do not make the fire too big. Keep children well away from flames. Do not light bonfires in a strong wind in a small space near property and remember smoke from bonfires can be extremely annoying to other people, especially in summer: it is civil to check with neighbours before lighting a bonfire. Do not leave a smouldering fire; make sure it is properly put out.

CHILDREN'S GARDEN
Bright colourful planting scheme. See back of book for more details.
T = *Trouble free*

Trees

T Sorbus 'Joseph Rock' *(Yellow berries) or S. 'Embley'* (..ed berries) *(Mountain ash or Rowan). Excellent and interesting tree for a small garden. Grows to 15–25 ft (4.5–7.5 m) and has a neat upright habit. Mid-green divided leaves, white flowers in May and June and red or yellow berries in August. Splendid yellow/orange autumn foliage offsets the berries if the birds don't get them first!*

T Acer palmatum 'Senkaki' *(Japanese maple) Slow-growing coral bark maple. Height 15 ft (4.5 m). Spread 8 ft (2.5 m). Yellow/green leaves becoming pale green in summer and brilliant cream autumn colour. Coral coloured bark, really striking in winter. A most beautiful tree.*

Shrubs

T Senecio greyii 'Sunshine' *Excellent evergreen shrub. Height 3 ft (90 cm), spread 4–6 ft (1.2–1.8 m), grey/green leaves with silver underside. Yellow star-like flowers from June to July. Extremely tolerant and reliable plant. Prefers sunny position but will do well in shade. Prune hard in spring if you want a neat shrub.*

T Mahonia (Oregon grape) 'Undulata' and 'Pinnata' *Evergreen shrub. 'Undulata' yellow pendulous scented flowers early spring followed by bluish black berries with bluish bloom. Lovely dark green wavy and glossy leaves. 'Pinnata' flowers late winter and has grey/green leaves. Excellent plants under trees or in the sun or shade. Height up to 5 ft (1.5 m), and nice and bushy.*

T Hyssop officinalis *Evergreen bushy shrub. Aromatic dark green leaves and blue flowers on spikes June to August. This is a delightful herb and safe for children. Clip it over in spring. There are also white and pink flowered varieties.*

T Skimmia *Another trouble-free evergreen shrub which provides interest in summer and autumn. This has tiny pinkish white flowers in spring and bright red autumn berries which last all winter and are not poisonous. Nevertheless, children should be taught never to eat any berries from trees and shrubs. Height 3–4 ft (about 1 m). Spread 3–4 ft (about 1 m). Needs shade or the leaves may 'bleach' in the sun.*

T Escallonia 'Apple Blossom' *This bushy evergreen shrub is also ideal for adding colour and interest. It has small shiny mid-green leaves and delightful pale pink and white flowers, born freely from June to October. Prune in spring. Prefers sun.*

T Weigela florida 'Variegata' *An attractive compact shrub with lovely broad cream-white leaf margins on the light green leaves and an abundance of pale pink flowers growing in clusters from each stem in May and June. Prune to keep in shape.*

T Potentilla Elizabeth *Yellow flowers. 3–4 ft (about 1 m) high and wide. Nice long-flowering hardy deciduous shrub which looks like dead twigs in winter (so do not pull it out!). Just trim in early spring to keep in shape.*

Ceanothus thyrsiflorus 'Repens' *(Californian lilac) Wonderful shrub once established. It has beautiful display of bobbles of small blue flowers in May and June. Shiny dark evergreen leaves. Grows to 3 ft (90 cm). Spread 5–6 ft (1.5–1.8 m) and perfect as a mound near the front of a border. Some branches may die back in a cold winter and should be cut off in spring.*

Fuchsia magellanica Versicolor *Hardy shrub. Height 3–4 ft (about 1 m). Slender pink flowers July to October. Grey-green variegated leaf, rose-tinted when young. Fuchsias, which are often overlooked, are now back in fashion and can be relied upon to give splendid autumn colour.*

CHILDREN'S GARDEN *(continued)*

Climbers

Lonicera 'Dropmore Scarlet' *(Honeysuckle) Height 10–15 ft (3–4.5 m) A deciduous climber. From June to August drooping red unscented flowers with cream insides.* Lonicera Periclymenum Serotina *flowers from July to October, and is a variety of the native honeysuckle.* Lonicera 'Gold Flame' *has fragrant yellow flowers 1½–2 in (4–5 cm) long from July to September. If the two are planted side by side there will be a nice show of yellow and red flowers climbing up together. These two are not quite as vigorous as 'Dropmore Scarlet'.*

Clematis 'Nelly Moser' *A popular and spectacular twining climber with mid-green deciduous leaves and lovely pale pink with purple/red stripe flowers from May to September. Height about 12 ft (3.5 m).*

T Clematis viticella 'Abundance' *Double pompom flowers in summer. Deciduous dark green leaves.*

Climbing Rose Zephirine Drouhin *A reliable Bourbon rose ideal on a north-facing wall which helps to prevent its one failing, mildew. It has stunning, bright magenta pink, sweet-smelling semi-double flowers throughout the summer. A thornless rose, grows to 9 ft (nearly 3 m). Excellent in a garden where there are children. Is prone to black spot if it does not get a good root run.*

   Kathleen Harrop, *a sport of the above rose, has pale pink flowers, no thorns, sweet scent but is a little less vigorous.*

Herbaceous Plants

Herbaceous plants die back in winter and all the plants chosen for these gardens are perennials.

T Sedum 'Autumn Joy' *Height 2 ft (60 cm), spread 2 ft (60 cm). Flat, pink heads, tiny flowers 4–8 in (10–20 cm) across in September. Fleshy pale green leaves. Fairly hardy, sun-loving plant. Butterflies love it.*

T Hosta sieboldiana 'Elegans' *Good low-growing summer plant. Broad-leafed hardy herbaceous perennial. Silver/blue leaves, pale lilac flowers in July to August. Can grow to 2 ft by 2 ft (60 cm by 60 cm). Sun or shade tolerant.*

T Geranium Wargrave pink *Hardy herbaceous perennial, flowers all summer and brings colour and interest to a border. Fresh green leaves that make excellent summer ground cover. Happy in sun or shade.*

T Aster frikartii *(Michaelmas daisy) Hardy herbaceous perennial. Height 2 ft 6 in (75 cm). Dark green leaves, orange centred soft blue flowers from July to October. Sun loving.*

T Bergenia cordifolia 'Purpurea' *(Elephants' ears). Obliging hardy evergreen ground cover. Large leathery flat mid-green leaves which go purple in autumn. Striking deep pink flowers in the spring. This reliable plant is more effective planted next to a spiky or feathery plant as a contrast. Sun and shade tolerant.*

Salvia Superba 'East Friesland' *Hardy perennial. Evergreen sub shrub. Height and spread 2 ft (60 cm). Bushy clump-forming plant with mid green leaves and an abundance of bright blue/purple flowers from July to September. As well as being extremely good ground cover, it is also a useful herb for cooking.*

Gladiolus byzantinus *Height 2 ft 6 in (75 cm). Magenta flowers on spikes in June. Long spiky mid-green leaves. This gladiolus is hardy in most gardens.*

For the end of the garden, either: Herbs and vegetables; Bulbs, snowdrops; Wild strawberries; Nasturtiums
   or Choisya *(Mexican orange blossom),* Rhododendrons, Arbutus *(Strawberry tree)* and Arundinaria viridistriata *(Bamboo)*

6: *Town house garden*

(Grey, silver, blue and white)

This delightful if slightly extravagant plan is designed for a garden that slopes up away from the house. It is fairly traditional and formal in its concept and offers everything from a *trompe l'oeil* trellis arch to a fountain and small pond. The simple shape is enhanced by interesting planting (see *Planting on a Slope*).

From its wide terrace you can sit and enjoy the sweep of the steps lined with terracotta pots as it stretches along the terrace and joins the retaining wall. The view up the steps through the arch of New Dawn roses across the circular path with its turfed inner circle is finished with the classical *trompe l'oeil* trellis arch on the far wall and in front of it is a statue. This gives an added dimension to the garden.

On either side of the statue there are two sitting areas, each with its own individual character. On the right of the terrace is a lush arbour, a perfect foil for the statue at the back of the paved three-quarter moon sitting area, which faces south and makes a delightful afternoon resting place. On the opposite side beneath the birch tree is a European hardwood bench to catch the morning sun, with planted tubs placed on either side to add a stylish finish. Beneath the tree, shade-loving hostas and *Euphorbia wulfenii* are planted and make a perfect place for reading the Sunday papers and drinking morning coffee.

The garden is full of surprises. As you look directly in front of the 'morning' seating spot, your eye is drawn to the fountain and pond, behind which a mirror framed by an arch of ivy and passion flowers helps to create the illusion that this water garden leads to another and goes on for ever.

The substantial brick walls with trellis above are covered with evergreens and climbers, and on the right, which is the sunny side, are sweet-smelling flowering shrubs and climbers, with perennial herbaceous plants planted in front.

The functional aspects of the terrace are cleverly disguised and the simple bay trees in tubs at the bottom of the steps make an ideal gateway. On the right there is a 2 ft 6 in (75 cm) barbecue shelf surrounded by pots. The 3 ft (90 cm) high retaining wall has trailing plants cascading down the front and behind it hard herbs such as thyme and low-growing sage planted in the high bed, all adding to the aroma and interest of the terrace and making the retaining wall a pleasing feature. It is important to plant *low*-growing flowers and shrubs in the bed above the retaining wall so as not to enclose the terrace too much and make it claustrophobic.

In the far right hand corner is a dust bin store, nicely concealed in the corner cupboard hard by the climber-covered pergola which leads along the side of the house to the road. This pergola offers another opportunity to grow climbers, a delightful addition to any garden as they grow effortlessly towards the sky.

Birds are always fascinating and to encourage them in front of the herbs and perennial herbaceous plants a bird bath is placed on the retaining wall to enhance the view from the kitchen window. But do not have the bird bath too low or the cats will get the birds.

The kitchen door is surrounded by low troughs, sinks and jardinières filled with soft herbs and seasonal colour. There is no garden shed as the lawn mower can go in the garage.

The garden is never dull, always interesting and delightful, and will need very little work other than cutting the grass, tying up the climbers and watering the containers.

Alternative

The second design for a town house is an alternative for those who do not wish to have grass. It consists of a two-tiered terrace, with the steps leading from the first square terrace up to the second. This paved area is enclosed by trellis with the planting area behind: it is a secluded and pleasant place for sitting and eating, and more relaxing as it is placed away from the house.

The pleasing irregular shape of the lower terrace surrounded by the retaining walls (holding back the higher level soil) gives the impression that the area is much larger than it is. The pots, urns and statues, plus the square water fountain and pool on the right of the lower terrace make this area also an interesting and exciting place to sit, altogether an imaginative and striking design.

TOWN HOUSE GARDEN
See back of book for more details
T = *Trouble free*

Plants to **surround the seating area**, a difficult corner, east facing and quite shady.

Trees
T Betula jacquemontii *(Himalayan birch).* *Ascending habit. Grows to 24 ft (7 m). Mid-green leaves turning gold in autumn. Dazzling white trunk and branches. Peeling bark.*

East corner shrubs (beneath tree)
T Garrya elliptica 'James Roof' *(Silk tassel bush). Evergreen shrub with grey/silver green leaves. Male form has abundant catkins 9–12 in (22.5–30 cm) long in February and March. Likes half shade. Vulnerable to cold winds. Grows 8–15 ft (2.5–4.5 m), width 6–12 ft (1.8–3.5 m). James Roof gives you extra long catkins.*

T Hydrangea petiolaris. *Deciduous self-clinging climbing hydrangea. Prefers shade, excellent clothing for walls. Delicate sprays of white flowers in June. Give it a few good ties as it grows or it may alarmingly peel off the wall; it needs a damp wall in order to cling properly. Grows to 15 × 15 ft (4.5 × 4.5 m).*

T Euphorbia wulfenii. *Dramatic evergreen sub-shrub. Grows 2–4 ft (60 cm–1.2 m), width up to 4 ft (1.2 m). Wonderful bushy habit which has a tremendous impact when its green leaves and dense terminal panicles of green/yellow bracts appear each year in late winter.*

continued on p. 34

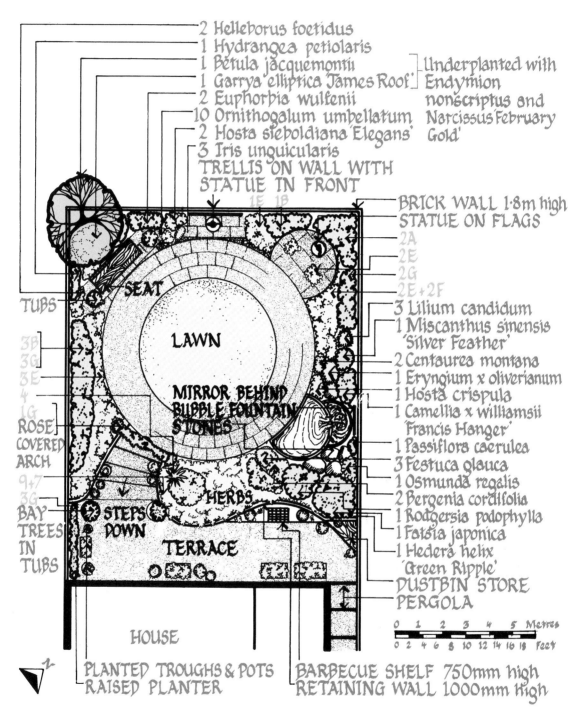

2 Helleborus foetidus
1 Hydrangea petiolaris
1 Betula jacquemontii
1 Garrya elliptica 'James Roof'
2 Euphorbia wulfenii
10 Ornithogalum umbellatum
2 Hosta sieboldiana 'Elegans'
3 Iris unguicularis

Underplanted with
Endymion
nonscriptus and
Narcissus February
Gold'

TRELLIS ON WALL WITH
STATUE IN FRONT

1E 1B

BRICK WALL 1·8m high
STATUE ON FLAGS
2A
2E
2G
2E+2F

TUBS

SEAT

LAWN

3B
3G
3E
4
1G

MIRROR BEHIND
BUBBLE FOUNTAIN
STONES

3 Lilium candidum
1 Miscanthus sinensis
  'Silver Feather'
2 Centaurea montana
1 Eryngium x oliverianum
1 Hosta crispula
1 Camellia x williamsii
  'Francis Hanger'
1 Passiflora caerulea
3 Festuca glauca
1 Osmunda regalis
2 Bergenia cordifolia
1 Rodgersia podophylla
1 Fatsia japonica
1 Hedera helix
  'Green Ripple'
DUSTBIN STORE
PERGOLA

ROSE
COVERED
ARCH

9+7
3G

HERBS

BAY
TREES
IN
TUBS

STEPS
DOWN

TERRACE

0 1 2 3 4 5 Metres
0 2 4 6 8 10 12 14 16 18 Feet

HOUSE

PLANTED TROUGHS & POTS
RAISED PLANTER

BARBECUE SHELF 750mm high
RETAINING WALL 1000mm high

To design your own planting for the remainder of the garden,
refer to the plant lists at the end of the book.

Town House Garden

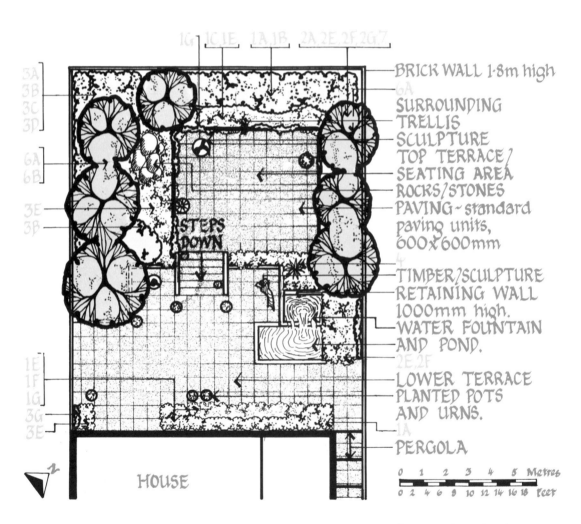

3A
3B
3C
3D

6A
6B

3E
3B

1E
1F
1G
3G
3E

1G   1C,1E   1A,1B   2A,2E,2F,2G,7

BRICK WALL 1·8m high
6A
SURROUNDING
TRELLIS
SCULPTURE
TOP TERRACE /
SEATING AREA
ROCKS / STONES
PAVING ~ standard
paving units,
600 x 600mm
4
TIMBER / SCULPTURE
RETAINING WALL
1000mm high.
WATER FOUNTAIN
AND POND.
2E,2F
LOWER TERRACE
PLANTED POTS
AND URNS.
1A
PERGOLA

STEPS
DOWN

HOUSE

0   1   2   3   4   5 Metres
0 2 4 6 8 10 12 14 16 18 Feet

To design your own planting for this garden, refer to the plant
lists at the end of the book.

Alternative Town House Garden

TOWN HOUSE GARDEN (*continued*)
Herbaceous and Bulbs
Iris unguicularis *An evergreen beardless iris. Height 9 in (22.5 cm). Long, dark green strap-shaped leaves. Soft lilac flowers with yellow blaze from October to March. Flowering starts later after a bad summer.*

T Hosta sieboldiana 'Elegans'. *Hardy perennial with large rather rounded silver-blue leaves and lilac flowers in June, July and August. Sun and shade loving. Height and width 2 ft (60 cm).*

T Ornithogalum umbellatum (*Star of Bethlehem*). *The bulbous hardy plants grow up to 12 in (30 cm). Profusion of white flowers on corymbs in April to May. Easy and spreads well. Pretty when in flower. Generally trouble-free.*

T Endymion nonscriptus (*Bluebell*). *Bulbs. Blue flowers in spring. 10 in (25 cm) high. Excellent for keeping down the weeds in spring. (The Spanish bluebell E. hispanicus is easier to find but not so elegant as our native bluebell.)*

T Helleborus foetidus. *Yellowy cream flowers with magenta stripe in February to March. Strong shiny evergreen deep-cut leaves. Height 2 ft (60 cm). Spread 2 ft (60 cm). Splendid ground cover under shrubs. Tends to seed itself. These seedlings can be dug up and planted together and will soon form a large clump.*

Astilbe arendsii. *Most attractive perennial providing it is planted in shade and has moist soil. Ideal for planting round a pond. If the soil is not moist astilbes will need regular watering in dry spells. Ferny mid-deep green foliage and long-lasting feathery flowers in late June. When established it divides well.*
    'Bressingham Beauty' *has pink flowers, grows to 2 ft 6 in (75 cm)*
    'Deutschland' *has white flowers and grows to 2 ft (60 cm).*

'Faval' *has dark red flowers and grows to 2 ft (60 cm).*

Summer bedding
Nicotiana (*Tobacco plants*) *in tubs on either side of the seat, with trailing* Lobelia (*annual*) *planted in between to give an elegant blue and white summer show.*

Plants to grow round the small pond and fountain. This does not mean these plants are bog garden plants or need especially damp soil. They are just decorative plants suitable for the site.

Shrubs
Camellia williamsii 'Francis Hanger' *Delightful evergreen shrub. Likes lime-free soil and benefits from a yearly top-dressing of peat. Height 6–8 ft (1.8–2.5 m), spread 4–6 ft (1.2–1.8 m). Glossy dark green leaves and single white flowers which shed as they fade – true low maintenance! Erect upright habit. Camellias do not like early morning sun, so are ideal for a west-facing wall.*

Fatsia japonica. *Handsome evergreen shade tolerant shrub. Large glossy dark green leaves which make a striking contrast to other foliage. Height and spread about 8 ft (2.5 m). Can grow to 15 ft (4.5 m). White flowers in panicles in October, but this plant is really grown for its foliage.*

Climbers
T Passiflora caerulea (*Passion flower*). *Vigorous evergreen (in mild conditions). Fragrant blue flowers with yellow centres (up to 4 in/10 cm across) from summer to autumn. Can grow to 20 ft (6 m).*

Hedera helix 'Green Ripple' (*Common Ivy*). *Hardiest of all evergreen climbers. Shiny evergreen leaves with a wavy edge. Can grow to 100 ft (30 m) on a wall, but in this garden it will not get the opportunity.*

continued over page

top: Astilbe 'Bressingham Beauty', *ideal for a shady, moist spot.*
above: A young Fatsia japonica *in a small, walled town garden.*
right: The variegated ivy Hedera helix 'Gold Heart' *spreads itself over a stone arch (photo by Susan Hampshire).*

TOWN HOUSE GARDEN (*continued*)
Herbaceous
T Rodgersia podophylla. *Hardy perennial. Height 3–4 ft (90 cm–1.2 m). Rough, horse-chestnut-like leaves with a jagged outline, mid-green colour often with a reddish sheen. Buff-coloured, feathery plumes of flowers in June and July.*

T Bergenia cordifolia 'Silberlicht' *(Elephants' ears). Hardy evergreen. Large, round, flat mid-green leaves, about 10 in (25 cm) long. White flowers faintly tinted with pink in the spring, excellent spreading ground cover. Tolerates sun and shade.*

T Festuca glauca *(Grass). Hardy perennial grass. Height 6–9 in (15–22.5 cm). Bristly hedgehog-like blue/grey spikes rise from thick central tuft. Typical grassy flowers in small spikes in June and July.*

T Osmunda regalis *(Royal Fern). Hardy fern. Pea-green fronds with broad leaflets. Reddish 'flowering' leaves appear in summer.* Needs to be kept moist all through the summer, *so do not plant if this is not possible. Height and spread 4–5 ft (1.2–1.5 m).*

T Miscanthus sinensis 'Silver Feather'. *Another strong grass worthy of space. Hardy perennial. Narrow mid-green leaves with a white stripe down the middle. Silky reed-grass heads in autumn. 'Silver Feather' can grow to 6 ft (1.8 m). Likes sun.*

Lilium candidum *(Madonna lily). Lovely hardy lily which can be difficult to get established but worth a try. It must have full sun and can get botrytis disease. Height 4–5 ft (1.2–1.5 m). Pale green leaves, large white trumpet-shaped fragrant flowers in June and July.*

Eryngium × oliverianum *(Sea holly). Most unusual and attractive herbaceous perennial. Perhaps not used more frequently because of its prickly and spiky greyish holly-like leaves. Height 2 ft–2 ft 6 in (60–75 cm). Round blue thistle-like flower heads in July and August. Sun loving.*

T Centaurea montana *Perennial. Height 18 in–2 ft (45–60 cm). White, hairy, mid-green oblong leaves. Masses of open-faced daisy-like blue flowers in May and June. Likes sun or shade.*

T Hosta crispula *Hardy perennial. Height and spread 2 ft (60 cm). Useful shade-loving plant. Dark green broad pointed leaves with definite white margins. Lilac blue flowers in August. Sun or shade.*

Helleborus foetidus *(Stinking hellebore). Hardy evergreen perennial. Shiny dark evergreen leaves and yellow-green flowers March to April. Attractive obliging plant which seeds itself. If the plants are dug up and planted together within a year they will form an impressive clump. Height and width 18 in (45 cm). Generally trouble-free.*

7: Front garden

(Bright pink, purple and strong colours)

A front garden often appears to be a statement of what the owners would like the outside world to think of them. And indeed the appearance at the front of the house does make passers-by curious about the rear garden. If it is attractive, they will imagine that the back is better, even if it happens to be a jungle.

Very sociable gardeners may enjoy being exposed to the world at large as they cut back the flowering shrubs but, for those who don't, it's worth considering investing in 'low maintenance' in the area in the front of your house. If you want to be seen outside your front door in your shirt sleeves or pinny with your rear to the sky, on your hands and knees pulling out the weeds as the neighbours pass you by, fine. But, if not, an attractive front garden that is not time-consuming is highly desirable.

Apart from its competitive aspect an attractive front garden also greatly enhances the visual appeal – and the value – of the property. When you are trying to sell a house, the first impression is obviously very important.

The Design

The design offers two alternatives, both based on the same principle, either two large squares and one smaller square in the middle, or two large circles with a small one between; each version is in a completely different price range. (A third alternative could be a simple paved area on each side of the path with a large jardinière in the middle planted with a dramatic plant such as cordyline or a clipped bay. Very severe and smart.) And as many front gardens of semi-detached or terraced houses are half the size of the main design, a smaller alternative has also been drawn up. Very little change is required, only the detail in the runs of brick which will now have to splay out from the path to the main circle; also the runs of brick on the outer part of the circle will no longer encroach into the brickwork of the path.

The Garden

As you come through the front gate which has a low picket fence on either side, you are presented with two large circles of brick with plants growing in between and a sundial, bird bath or plant featured in the centre of each circle.

Round the perimeter of the garden, the planting areas are broken up with runs of brick, so the plants can be contained, and don't grow into each other and get out of hand. The advantage of this is that only the plant or shrub fills the area between the bricks, and bricks alone occupy the space the weeds would otherwise try to dominate.

Around the two main circles, low perennial plants such as thyme, camomile and campanula break up and soften the area, while at the same time highlighting and drawing the eye to the circles of lavender or geraniums with the bird bath, plant, jardinière, urn or statue chosen for the centre.

The path going up to the front door has a small circle of brick in the middle, an elegant luxury and one of the features that makes the design so special. Instead of the path going in a straight line to the house, you walk through a pattern of ever-decreasing brick circles until you reach the front step.

Brick

Should you decide to use brick rather than paving slabs, you will not be disappointed. Brick paving is to my mind one of the most beautiful paving surfaces. Providing you choose a suitable brick, it is long lasting and mellows superbly. On the other hand, brick will be more expensive than paving slabs, and should you be considering laying the bricks yourself, you should bear in mind that the preparation and the laying of bricks is hard work.

In Bangladesh bricks were used a great deal for roads and there are many well-worn herring-bone brick roads, some of which were laid many years before the British left in 1949. Driving over them in a rickshaw is one thing, but the pure delight of their smooth, rounded surface under bare feet is never to be forgotten. Yes, brick is beautiful. It has so much texture and warmth and, if it is within your budget, it is a wonderful addition to any property. Frost-proof, *non-slip* brick and *not* engineering bricks should be chosen. (See *Paving*.)

Paving: Easy and Economical

The alternative paved version is not as unusual or pleasing as the brick but the advantage is that it is easy to lay yourself. You lay standard paving units of 18 in × 18 in (450 × 450 mm), 9 in × 9 in (225 × 225 mm) or 18 in × 9 in (450 × 225 mm) on to a flat bed of sand, or, for true low maintenance, it is more satisfactory to lay them on a bed of concrete. With sand, the paving can often become uneven and slippery after heavy rains because the slabs retain the moisture that seeps up from the sand below, and also there is the danger that weeds will grow in the sand between the slabs.

The procedure for laying slabs is reasonably straightforward. Level the space, then:
1. Check the surface is even with string and a spirit level, with a fall to take the water away from the house.
2. Spread sand or concrete over the whole area except areas required for planting, and again check the level.
3. Lay the standard paving slabs, leaving the squares you wish to fill with plants without either concrete or sand in them, ready for earth and compost for planting.

It's important to remember when putting sand beneath the slabs that it should be under the whole slab and not just under the corners, otherwise when the temperature beneath the slab changes it will crack. The paving slabs will stop the more vigorous shrubs and plants from spreading too much.

Cordyline australis *is an effective accent plant (photo by Susan Hampshire).*

FRONT GARDEN
Pink, purple and white colour scheme
T = *Trouble free*

Trees
T Cercis siliquastrum *(Judas tree). Spring flowering purple-pink pea-like flowers. An ideal tree for this corner but it is not suitable for cold or clay gardens. It likes full sun so do not plant it if the garden is north-facing. Grows to 15–20 ft (4.5– 6 m). Bright green rounded leaves. An attractive ornamental tree with flowers growing directly off even quite old branches.*
or
Pyrus Salicifolia 'Pendula' (Willow-leaved pear) *Dome-shaped weeping branches make this delightful ornamental tree an attractive feature. Masses of tiny silvery green leaves and cream flowers in spring. Height 8–12 ft (2.5–3.5 m), spread 6–8 ft (1.8–2.5 m).*

To use for the **focal point** in the centre of each circle or square there is the choice of:
T Rose Albertine *(Rambler). Weeping standard. With its strong fragrance and coppery pink flowers developing from salmon red buds it is a popular and pleasing standard rose. A spectacular centrepiece when in flower. It has glossy green leaves and flowers freely in June and July. Sunny position.*
or
T Bay tree *(in tub). Planted in a tub or in the ground this tree clipped into a formal pompom shape is another elegant alternative for the centrepiece. The dark evergreen leaves are trouble-free and make a stylish feature. Not hardy in very cold areas. Tolerates shade or sun. Bay trees in tubs should be treated with systemic spray (to prevent disease) every few years.*

continued on p. 42

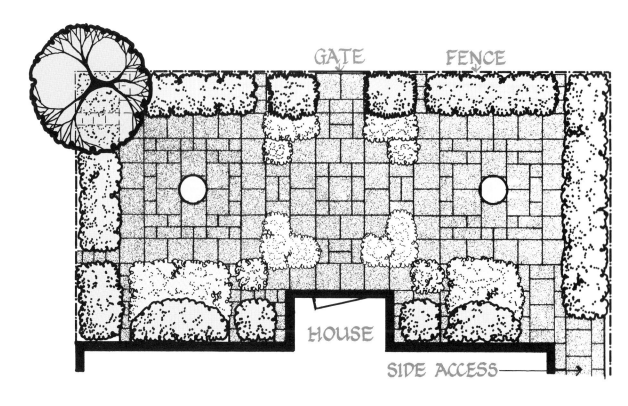

GATE FENCE

HOUSE

SIDE ACCESS→

The Front Garden – unit paving alternative

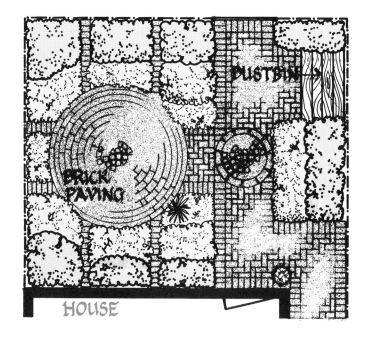

DUSTBIN→

BRICK
PAVING

HOUSE

ABOVE~design based
on standard paving
units of 450x450mm,
225x225mm and
450x225mm.
LEFT~very little
change is required
from the 'Brick paving
alternative'. This design
is suitable for a semi-
detached or terraced
house.
ABOVE AND LEFT~
To design your own
planting refer to the
garden opposite.

The Front Garden – half size

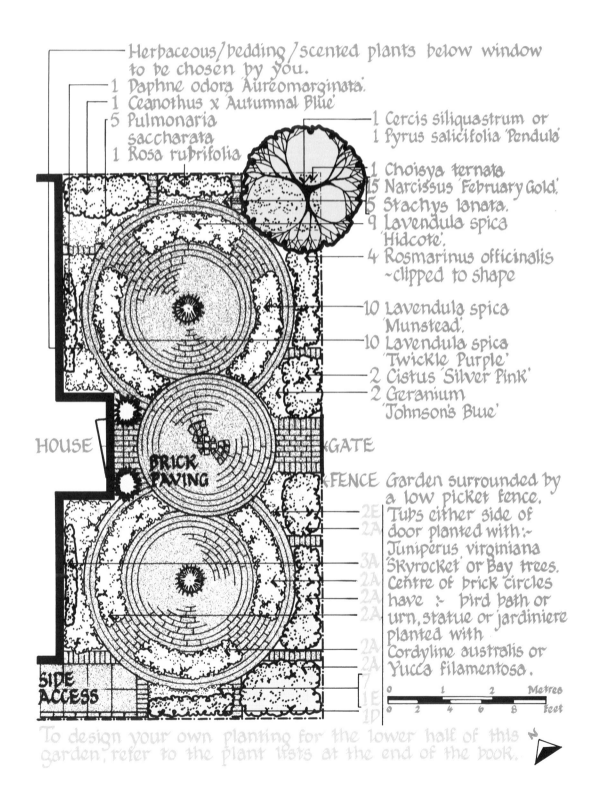

Herbaceous/bedding/scented plants below window to be chosen by you.
1 Daphne odora 'Aureomarginata'.
1 Ceanothus x 'Autumnal Blue'
5 Pulmonaria saccharata
1 Rosa rubrifolia

1 Cercis siliquastrum or
1 Pyrus salicifolia 'Pendula'

1 Choisya ternata
15 Narcissus 'February Gold'.
5 Stachys lanata.
9 Lavendula spica 'Hidcote'.
4 Rosmarinus officinalis ~clipped to shape

10 Lavendula spica 'Munstead'.
10 Lavendula spica 'Twickle Purple'
2 Cistus 'Silver Pink'
2 Geranium 'Johnson's Blue'

HOUSE

BRICK PAVING

GATE

FENCE Garden surrounded by a low picket fence.
2E Tubs either side of
2A door planted with:-
Juniperus virginiana
3A Skyrocket or Bay trees.
2A Centre of brick circles
2A have :- bird bath or
2A urn, statue or jardiniere
planted with
2A Cordyline australis or
2A Yucca filamentosa.
7
1E
1D

SIDE ACCESS

0	1	2	Metres
0	2 4	6 8	feet

To design your own planting for the lower half of this garden, refer to the plant lists at the end of the book.

The Front Garden – brick paving alternative

FRONT GARDEN (*continued*)
In an **urn** the choice of:

T Yucca filamentosa *Hardy stemless evergreen shrub. Good in poor conditions. Attractive long spiky erect leaves with wispy filaments peeling off the edges. Striking centrepiece. Ivory coloured, bell-shaped flowers in erect panicles 3 ft – 6 ft 6 in (90 cm – 2 m) tall in July to August.*

T Cordyline australis *With its straight, long, spiky green leaves, it also makes an elegant centrepiece for any urn or focal point but it is vulnerable to frost in winter and is best tied up with string to protect its 'heart' in November.*

Alternatively, the centrepiece could be a bird bath, sundial or sculpture (an interesting piece of wood or stone).

Plants in circular beds
T Lavender *Hardy evergreen shrub. In the summer this will make a stunning display of purple scented flowers round the centrepiece. Height 1 – 2 ft (30 – 60 cm). Spread 18 in – 2 ft (45 – 60 cm).*
Lavandula spica 'Hidcote' *flowers July to September*
Lavandula spica 'Munstead' *blue flowers July to September*
Lavandula spica 'Twickel Purple' *flowers July to September. Long spikes. Prefers sunny position.*
or
Geranium pratense 'Johnson's Blue' *Hardy herbaceous perennial – but not the same as a pot plant geranium (Pelargonium) that grows in window boxes. Height 12 in (30 cm). Delicate blue flowers all summer long, prettily divided leaves. Excellent summer ground cover.*

Other small plants to go round the side or between the paving slabs are camomile, thyme, campanula and vincas.

Boundary Plants
T Cistus 'Silver Pink' *Height and spread 2 – 3 ft (60 – 90 cm). Grey/green leaves above and grey beneath. Silver/pink flowers in June and July. Fairly hardy evergreen. Sun-loving.*

Pulmonaria saccharata *Hardy herbaceous perennial. Its unusual foliage makes it a good accent plant. Large flat green leaves with silver grey blotches. Pink flowers turning to blue in March and April. Height and spread 12 in (30 cm).*

Rosmarinus officinalis *Rosemary to form part of the hedge along the front fence line. Hardy evergreen shrub. Tiny silver/grey aromatic leaves. Small purple flowers March to April and then on and off until September. Sun-loving.*

T Choisya ternata *(Mexican orange blossom). Dark shiny aromatic evergreen leaves and clusters of white flowers spring and autumn. Height 10 – 20 ft (3 – 6 m) (to grow along the fence). Shade and sun-loving. Most useful and undemanding shrub.*

T Rosa rubrifolia *Perfect choice to create a boundary on each side of the garden. It is undemanding, grows to 7 by 5 ft (just over 2 m by 1.5 m) and has unusual coppery mauve leaves with a grey tinge, light pink flowers in summer and attractive hips in autumn but it is its foliage that makes this a special plant. The thorns are small and not very troublesome. Sun and shade tolerant. Seeds itself.*

T Stachys lanata *(Lambs' tongues) Herbaceous perennial. Soft furry long slim grey/silver leaves, woolly blue flower spikes June and July. Grows to 1 ft (30 cm), spread 2 ft (60 cm) or more. Good summer ground cover.*

Ceanothus 'Autumnal Blue' *A lovely vigorous hardy evergreen shrub. Height 8 – 10 ft (2.5 – 3 m). Spread 6 – 10 ft (1.8 – 3 m). Glossy large green leaves and delightful haze of blue flowers from July to September/October. Sun-loving.*

Geranium 'Kashmir White', *a delightful summer
flowering perennial.*

FRONT GARDEN *(continued)*
Daphne odora 'Aureomarginata' *(under window)*
*Fragrant evergreen shrub. Grows to 4 ft (1.2 m).
Will easily follow the line under the window. Green
leaf with creamy white variegation. Powerfully
scented rose pink flowers from January or February
through to April. Prefers shade.*

Below the window there is room for some
summer bedding such as night-scented stocks
and *Nicotiana* (tobacco plant).

Tubs
In tubs on either side of the front door *Juniperus
virginiana 'Sky Rocket' (Pencil cedar). Slow-
growing evergreen conifer. Will only grow to 8–10 ft
(2.5–3 m) in a tub. Pale grey foliage and very slim
and upright growth.*
or
Bay Tree *(see above).*
Muscari 'Heavenly Blue' *(Grape hyacinth) can be
planted round the edge of the tub. Deep blue flowers
appear in April/May. Height 8–10 ft (2.5–3 m)
and Ivy (variegated) or Vincas or Fuchsia 'Lady
Thumb', a hardy shrub which may be cut by cold
weather. Delightful pink flowers in July. Light green
leaves, height about 2 ft (60 cm).*

8: *Paved garden*

This paved garden is both interesting and exciting for someone who is fascinated by shape and texture, and who doesn't want to touch a trowel or think about working in the garden once it is laid out and planted.

The garden of this terraced house faces east and is designed in such a way that it is particularly attractive to admire from the first floor window. The amazing swirling path leading to the three brick circles shown on the plan indicates each brick that is needed. Its busy detail is very much in fashion, and good luck to the householder who intends to lay it himself.

As the bricks, stone, paving and cobbles are concentrated in such a small area, the initial outlay will be expensive, but the advantage is that it will be very inexpensive and easy to maintain.

The brick and stone paving can be laid in two different ways. One is to point between the brick or slabs with mortar to keep out weeds; the other is to brush sand between the bricks so that rockery-type plants such as campanula, *Aubretia deltoidea* and *Alyssum saxatile* can be encouraged to grow in the cracks and break up the stone work with plants. The disadvantage of the second method is that weeds too can grow between the stones.

The Garden

Looking along the garden from the house, an archway against the rear wall surrounded by trellis is deliberately placed to the left of centre, so that the focal point is in front of the house rather than the path which is to the right.

On either side of the second circle is a pleasant sitting arbour surrounded by *Jasminum officinale affine* and the New Dawn rose. Opposite the sitting arbour is the pleasing view of a statue with *Artemisia Powis Castle* planted on either side.

Throughout the garden, large pots or containers can be placed to vary the height of planting and break up the paving with colour. Despite the small space, the garden is exciting, interesting and very undemanding.

Practicalities

A built-in barbecue in such a small garden would become too important a feature and take up too much of the planting area around the side. But a portable barbecue can easily be stored round the side of the house on the existing paving area near the dust bins.

Although a shed is always useful, a space has not been allocated for one as garden implements such as a spade and mower will not be necessary in this garden; just a trowel kept in the kitchen drawer should be enough!

The rotary washing line can be fixed into a hole prepared in the centre of the third circle, away from the eating area.

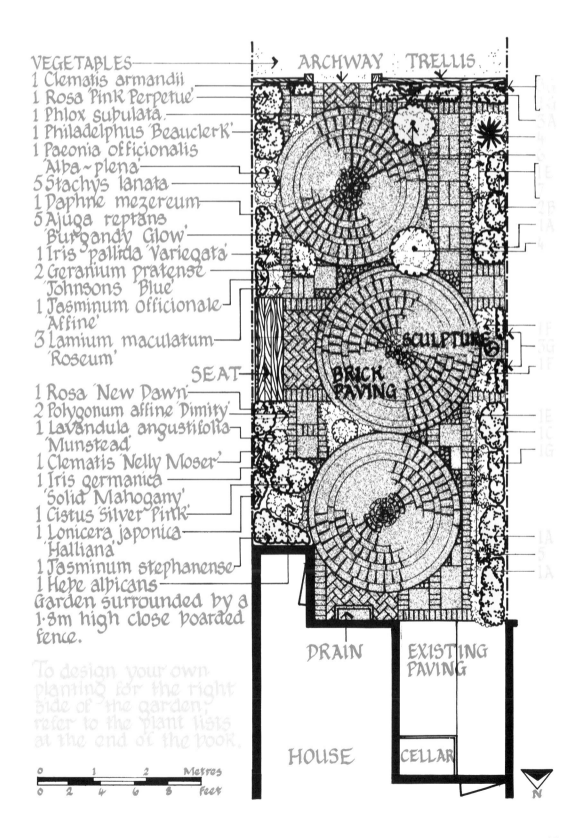

VEGETABLES
1 Clematis armandii
1 Rosa 'Pink Perpetue'
1 Phlox subulata
1 Philadelphus 'Beauclerk'
1 Paeonia officionalis
  'Alba~plena'
5 Stachys lanata
1 Daphne mezereum
5 Ajuga reptans
  'Burgandy Glow'
1 Iris pallida 'Variegata'
2 Geranium pratense
  'Johnsons Blue'
1 Jasminum officionale
  'Affine'
3 Lamium maculatum
  'Roseum'

SEAT

1 Rosa 'New Dawn'
2 Polygonum affine 'Dimity'
1 Lavandula angustifolia
  'Munstead'
1 Clematis 'Nelly Moser'
1 Iris germanica
  'Solid Mahogany'
1 Cistus 'Silver Pink'
1 Lonicera japonica
  'Halliana'
1 Jasminum stephanense
1 Hebe albicans
Garden surrounded by a
1·8m high close boarded
fence.

To design your own
planting for the right
side of the garden,
refer to the plant lists
at the end of the book.

ARCHWAY   TRELLIS

SCULPTURE

BRICK
PAVING

DRAIN   EXISTING
        PAVING

HOUSE   CELLAR

0   1   2   Metres
0 2 4 6 8 Feet

N

Philadelphus *(mock orange) is a hardy deciduous flowering shrub with many varieties. Most (but not all) have sweet-smelling white flowers (photo by Pamla Toler).*

The flower of 'lambs tongues' (Stachys lanata). *This useful edging plant is recommended for several of the gardens in this book.*

Newly planted variegated jasmine, a hardy and vigorous climber (photo by Susan Hampshire)

Herbs

Herbs are a welcome addition to any garden. If planted in the correct position, they are trouble-free plants, and grow in terracotta pots on the first circle immediately in front of the house where they'll get the most sun; behind them the larger herbs such as rosemary, hyssop and sage can be planted in the beds, along with thyme, which is a low-growing 'woody' herb.

Flowers and Shrubs

Despite the fact that this is such a small garden, the varying shapes of beds and planting areas between the paving and along the perimeter of the garden give you plenty of opportunity to plant interesting climbers, shrubs and flowers to break up the stone quality of the garden and bring a lush variety of plants and colour into the space. The planting itself becomes a pattern related to the paving and all the more interesting if a colour scheme of say blue and pink is used.

Fencing

It is not unusual for small, period terraced houses to be surrounded by 4 ft (1.2 m) brick walls. These can be extended upwards by hard wood trellis or sections of plastic covered wire squares fixed between solid wooden posts set 5 ft (1.5 m) apart, an ideal structure for the climbers, and will quickly make an excellent screen between one property and another. (For other ideas see *Fencing*.)

PAVED GARDEN
See back of book for more details
T = *Trouble free*

Shrubs
T Philadelphus × Beauclerk *(Mock orange) Delightful, hardy deciduous summer flowering shrub. Grows to 8 ft (2.5 m). Spread 5–6 ft (1.5–1.8 m). Milk white sweet-smelling flowers in June and July. Midgreen leaves. Prune after flowering to keep compact.*

Daphne mezereum *Deciduous shrub. Grows to 5 ft (1.5 m). Spread 2–4 ft (60 cm–1.2 m). Light green leaves. Sweet-smelling purple/pink, red/violet flowers from February to April followed by scarlet berries, which are poisonous. Prefers sun.*

T Lavendula spica 'Munstead' *Hardy evergreen shrub. Height 1–2 ft (30–60 cm), spread 18 in–2 ft (45–60 cm). Lavender blue flower spikes in July to September. Needs to be replaced every 5–10 years. To keep bushy cut back last year's growth only each spring. Do not cut back into old wood. Prefers sun.*

T Cistus 'Silver Pink' *(Sun rose). Evergreen shrub. Height 2–3 ft (60–90 cm). Spread 2–3 ft (60–90 cm). Thick green leaves with grey underside. Silver flowers in June–July. Hard-working shrub which earns its place in the garden.*

T Hebe albicans *Hardy evergreen rounded shrub. Height 2 ft (60 cm), spread 2 ft (60 cm). Slightly fleshy grey/blue leaves, white flowers in June and July.*

continued over page

PAVED GARDEN (*continued*)

Climbers for sunny positions

Clematis armandii *Dark evergreen leaves. White flowers April to May. Grows to 30 ft (9 m). Very open-growing climber that will try to find its way off the wall on to a tree or shrub. Needs shaded roots.*

T Rosa Pink Perpétue *(Climbing rose). Grows to 15 ft (4.5 m). Has deep to light pink flowers in July and September. Easy and reliable.*

Jasminum stephanense *Vigorous semi-evergreen (in mild winters) climber. Grows 10–15 ft (3–4.5 m). Dull green leaves and lovely clusters of pale pink flowers appear in June.*

T Jasminum officinale affine *(Common white jasmine). Hardy and deciduous vigorous twining climber. Mid-green leaves. Cluster of white sweet-smelling flowers from June to October. Can grow to 30 ft (9 m) if you let it.*

T Rosa 'New Dawn' *Climbing rose. Grows to 10 by 10 ft (3 by 3 m). Repeat flowering, large clusters of pale pink delicate fragrant flowers from June onwards. One of the most disease-resistant roses.*

Clematis 'Nelly Moser' *Deciduous clematis. Height about 12 ft (3.5 m), mid-green leaves. Stunning, pale pink/mauve flowers with central carmine strip from May to November.*

Lonicera japonica 'Halliana' *Rampant semi-evergreen twining climber. Height 25–30 ft (7.5–9 m), mid-green leaves. Fragrant pale pink flowers June to July, often creamy when young. Needs training otherwise it soon becomes matted.*

Herbaceous

Phlox subulata *Hardy, herbaceous, dense mat, low-growing plant. Grows no more than 4 in (10 cm), spread 18 in (45 cm). Lavender flowers May and June. Mid-green leaves.*

T Paeonia officinalis 'Alba Plena' *Hardy herbaceous perennial. Very pale pink flowers May and June. When in flower height about 2 ft (60 cm). Large dark green leaves. Divides well. Dies down in winter, but is certainly impressive when in flower.*

T Stachys lanata *(Lambs' Ears). Hardy low-growing herbaceous perennial. Soft grey/green woolly/furry leaves. Good summer ground cover, easily divided and excellent for the edge of a border or bed. Purple flowers on woolly spikes in July. Height 1 ft – 18 in (30–45 cm). Prefers sun.*

T Ajuga reptans 'Burgundy Glow' *Wonderful evergreen ground cover. Oblong green/burgundy leaves. Blue flowers in June and July. Grows between 4 in (10 cm) and 1 ft (30 cm). Likes shade.*

T Iris pallida 'Variegata' *Tall, hardy bearded iris. Prefers sun. Can grow to 3 ft (90 cm). Lavender blue flowers May and June. Good plant to vary foliage.*

T Lamium maculatum 'Roseum' *Excellent ground cover. Herbaceous perennial. Good in shade. Grows to 9 in (22.5 cm). Mid-green leaf with silver stripe and pink flowers in May. Prefers shade.*

T Geranium 'Johnsons Blue' *Hardy herbaceous perennial – not the same as pot plant geranium (Pelargonium) that grows in pots on window sills! Grows to 1 ft (30 cm). Delicate blue flowers throughout the summer and prettily divided leaves. Good summer ground cover in sun or shade.*

T Polygonum affine 'Dimity' *Height 6–9 in (15–22.5 cm), spread 18 in (45 cm) or more. Narrow dark green leaves. Dainty pink flower spikes from July to September, which turn deep red as they mature.*

Iris germanica 'Solid Mahogany' *(Bearded iris) Evergreen foliage, height 2–3 ft (60–90 cm). Mid-green leaves. Unusual, deep red/brown mahogany scented flowers in early May. Likes sun.*

9: *Cottage garden*

One of the sights that makes England so breathtakingly beautiful in summer is the traditional cottage garden. There is nothing lovelier in June and July. Usually a cottage garden has no formal strucure and needs attention twelve months of the year. So a design for a 'trouble-free' cottage garden which still looks like a cottage garden is ingenious and unusual.

This design, which divides the garden into four, is based on an old Eastern concept representing the four rivers of life. This theme has been used in gardens since Biblical times.

The View

Looking out from the cottage and towards the end of the garden, its circular form is divided into four by the plants and paving slabs. The sundial in the centre makes a pleasant and interesting focus of this outlook. On the right honeysuckle and jasmine grow up the fence, flowering shrubs make a delightful sitting arbour in the far right hand corner, and on the left and at the end of the garden a mixed hedge encloses hawthorn trees growing in the far corner.

One of the pleasures of this garden is that there is no grass to be cut each weekend in the summer. Therefore, it is a suitable garden for old and young alike and will not demand time once it is established (see *Year-at-a-Glance Calendar*).

Paving

Gravel is an attractive alternative to paving slabs. Not only is it in keeping with cottage tradition but it looks warm, welcoming and mellow from the day it is laid (see *Bricks and Paving*). But it is *not suitable* for wheelchairs or older people and weeds will grow in gravel unless it is in constant use.

The circular brick path draws your attention to the main ring which is also divided into four, enhanced by the sundial or bird bath in the middle. Inside the brick circle the design can be defined by selective colour planting, i.e. the cross through the circle can be in nepeta or lavender, a true old cottage garden plant, forming a good grey-green evergreen cross. (Nepeta is vulnerable to hard winters and cats! It is also called cat mint: cats love to roll in it if they get the chance.) Then you could choose, say, yellow sage or purple sage, or other coloured evergreen herbaceous perennials to punctuate the spaces between. If you choose nepeta rather than lavender, its silver-green foliage and blue flowers in summer and autumn can be underplanted with early and later flowering spring bulbs. Once this area has been planted, it is unlikely that it will need any attention except yearly cutting back and eventually the odd plant replacement.

Lavender should be replaced every six to eight years and needs to be cut back every spring to keep it bushy. But remember *not* to cut back all the old wood, as lavender

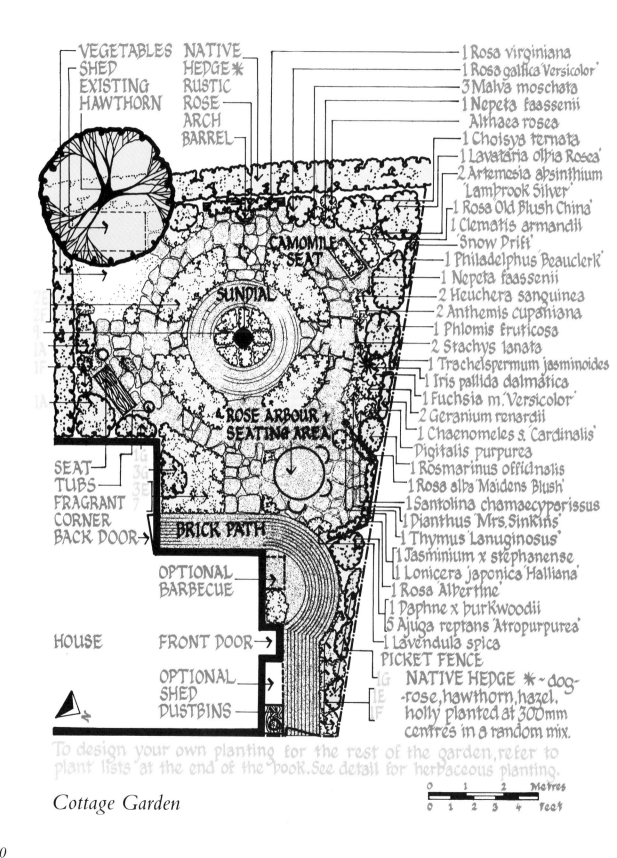

VEGETABLES
SHED
EXISTING
HAWTHORN

NATIVE
HEDGE ✲
RUSTIC
ROSE
ARCH
BARREL

1 Rosa virginiana
1 Rosa gallica 'Versicolor'
3 Malva moschata
1 Nepeta faassenii
Althaea rosea
1 Choisya ternata
1 Lavataria olbia Rosea
2 Artemesia absinthium 'Lambrook Silver'
1 Rosa 'Old Blush China'
1 Clematis armandii 'Snow Drift'
1 Philadelphus 'Beauclerk'
1 Nepeta faassenii
2 Heuchera sanguinea
2 Anthemis cupaniana
1 Phlomis fruticosa
2 Stachys lanata
1 Trachelspermum jasminoides
1 Iris pallida dalmatica
1 Fuchsia m. 'Versicolor'
2 Geranium renardii
1 Chaenomeles s. 'Cardinalis'
Digitalis purpurea
1 Rosmarinus officinalis
1 Rosa alba 'Maidens Blush'
1 Santolina chamaecyparissus
1 Dianthus 'Mrs. Sinkins'
1 Thymus 'Lanuginosus'
1 Jasminium x stephanense
1 Lonicera japonica 'Halliana'
1 Rosa 'Albertine'
1 Daphne x burkwoodii
5 Ajuga reptans 'Atropurpurea'
1 Lavendula spica
PICKET FENCE
NATIVE HEDGE ✲ ~ dog-
-rose, hawthorn, hazel,
holly planted at 300mm
centres in a random mix.

CAMOMILE SEAT
SUNDIAL
ROSE ARBOUR
SEATING AREA

SEAT
TUBS
FRAGRANT
CORNER
BACK DOOR →

BRICK PATH

OPTIONAL
BARBECUE

HOUSE

FRONT DOOR →

OPTIONAL
SHED
DUSTBINS

To design your own planting for the rest of the garden, refer to
plant lists at the end of the book. See detail for herbaceous planting.

Cottage Garden

0   1   2   Metres
0 1 2 3 4 feet

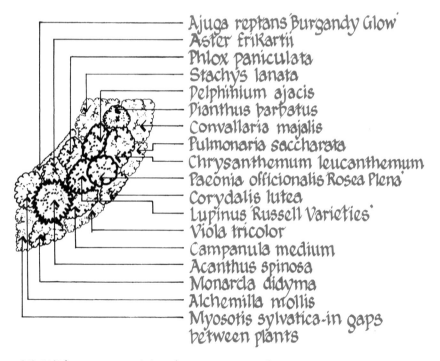

Ajuga reptans 'Burgandy Glow'
Aster frikartii
Phlox paniculata
Stachys lanata
Delphinium ajacis
Dianthus barbatus
Convallaria majalis
Pulmonaria saccharata
Chrysanthemum leucanthemum
Paeonia officionalis 'Rosea Plena'
Corydalis lutea
Lupinus 'Russell Varieties'
Viola tricolor
Campanula medium
Acanthus spinosa
Monarda didyma
Alchemilla mollis
Myosotis sylvatica-in gaps
between plants

ABOVE ~ a typical herbaceous border.

flowers on its old wood rather than growing up again from the ground like many other plants.

Beyond the central ring, at the far end of the garden, the paving and plants lead to another delightful feature, a rustic arch with an old English rose climbing over it; beneath is a large wooden barrel or terracotta pot planted with summer bedding plants. This adds depth and interest to the garden. From every angle, no matter where you choose to stand or sit, the view before you is pleasing.

Hedges and Fences

The screen or fence between the garden and the outside world is a question not only of taste but also of budget. Brick and stone walls, alas, are very expensive. But in a small garden the boundary is as important as the garden itself, so the choice must be right and in keeping with the property.

A mixed hedge of rose, hawthorn, field maple, dogwood and guelder rose on two sides offers variety and seasonal colour, and encourages wildlife. A hedge of this kind is not expensive, but it is extremely attractive and eminently suitable for a cottage garden. Once established it is resilient and only needs to be cut once every other year. If you wish to be very secluded you can let it grow and be surrounded by a 20 ft (6 m) hedge (but this could make the garden a little dark and claustrophobic).

Dog rose, hawthorn and hazel mixed are also an excellent traditional choice for a hedge, and holly could be planted in between to add the interest of its shining dark evergreen leaves and pillar-box red winter berries. A few ivies planted in the hedge also helps give it substance in the winter.

On the side nearest the house a picket or plain timber fence are both reliable options. A fence treated with *Saddolin* (obtainable from building merchants) will save the maintenance needed on a white painted fence. Saddolin, like other wood stain manufacturers, provides a choice of shade of stain. Climbers are easily trained to a timber fence and it makes an attractive structure on which scented honeysuckle, jasmine or even clematis can grow.

Seating

Selecting a suitable seating area is dictated by the position of the sun and the possibility of seclusion and shelter. So if the opportunity presents itself it is wise to have two alternatives; one for having lunch outside not too far from the cottage, and an afternoon spot to catch the late sun ideal for tea or early evening contemplation.

The nearest site opposite the cottage is a perfect place to pave and use for table and chairs for lunch or coffee as it has full midday sun. Sweet-smelling flowers and shrubs or the June-flowering *Buddleia alternifolia* with its heady summer aroma can form part of the fence, and make this an enchanting place to sit. Surrounded by jasmine, roses and other aromatic plants, you can enjoy the view across the whole of the garden, from the corner where large flowering shrubs provide shelter and background for the afternoon sitting area, to the large hawthorn trees in the far corner.

The second choice – in the near left hand side corner which gets sun until late afternoon – is an ideal place for a bench. On either side of this sheltered and secluded corner, large tubs help to vary the height of the flowers and add definition.

I think there are few pastimes more enjoyable and relaxing than lying back and letting the soft cushions in a garden hammock swing envelop you. It is a great pleasure to rock to and fro in a garden that isn't crying out to be tended. Should you not want a bench and low table in this evening corner, it would be ideal for a swing. (Cushions need to be brought inside from autumn to spring).

On the opposite side of the swing or bench corner is a camomile seat made with a trough planted with camomile (see directions p. 55), a delightful place for a short sit-down. On the right of the camomile seat is a partial-shade vegetable patch suitable for lettuces and spinach. This space could be used for old English rose bushes, roses that do not need full sun such as Maiden's Blush, *gallica officinalis*, *Felicité Parmentier* and *Louise Odier*, if vegetables seem like too much work (which on the whole they are: but see *Low Maintenance Vegetables*). Should you not want roses, bergenias are trouble-free and shade-loving and would do well, and hostas would be ideal beneath the trees should you wish the shed to be in the alternative position near the cottage on the right of the front door. If this is the case, there is plenty of space for a large variety of hostas which die down in the winter, but are extremely attractive in spring and summer with charming lilac-coloured flowers in June and July.

Positions for the Shed

In days gone by when men did the garden and women were confined to the kitchen, the shed was a special place, deliberately placed well away from the house where it couldn't be seen and where a man could enjoy a little privacy, odd jobbing and a smoke. But now with male and female roles less clearly defined, neither party wants to be rushing out in slippers or high heels to the far end of the garden to collect a trowel.

If you have to cross damp grass or soil to get to the shed, it will tend not to be used except as a store, and as a shed is easily camouflaged it can be built near the house without being an eyesore. In this garden there is a choice: the conventional spot at the far end under the hawthorn trees or on the right of the front door. Here there is room for a small, quickly reached shed, which can be covered in clematis or jasmine.

Planting

Close planting, indeed very, very close planting is the key to a successful trouble-free cottage garden. (See *List of Plants*.)

With close planting, the weeds don't get a chance, so if you plant from the choice provided, there should be plenty of colour and interest. In addition, the large paving slabs between the plants enclose the herbs and herbaceous perennials so they can't get out of hand. If they do, prune the more vigorous plants to stop them taking over. The under-planting of bulbs ensures spring colour and interest.

Conventional cottage garden planting is a question of mixing plants together and close planting, but this is not so reliable as low maintenance planting. If your choice of plants does not work, be ruthless and change it.

Practicalities: Dust Bins and Barbecue

Dust bins need to be near the house, but unfortunately the cupboards they are placed in are easily identified and often unattractive. The fact that it is a cupboard is hard to disguise but it can be made into an interesting feature by putting a selection of terracotta pots or a large shallow terracotta dish planted with alpines or *Sempervium tectorum* (house leek) on the top. Should this cupboard be put next to the shed in the alternative position on the left of the gate as you walk up to the front door, the two eyesores can be married together and camouflaged by a single vigorous *Clematis montana* 'Rubens'.

A barbecue is something that should only be built if you really want to use it a lot, otherwise, for our climate, portable barbecues are quite adequate. It is best to live in a house before deciding on the permanent site for the barbecue. In this garden it could be situated near the lunch seating area against the side of the house sharp left from the front door.

COTTAGE GARDEN
See back of book for more details.

The majority of the flowers and shrubs for this section of the cottage garden have been chosen for their aromatic quality or sweet-smelling perfume, thus creating a 'heady' aroma in both the eating area and the afternoon seating area.

Shrubs
Rosa gallica 'Versicolor'. *This very bushy, old variety will look good on the right of the main sitting arbour in the far corner. Height and spread 3 ft (90 cm). Dark green leaves and semi-double fragrant, rose red flowers with white stripes in June, followed by red hips.*

T Choisya ternata *(Mexican Orange Blossom). Height 6–8 ft (2–2.5 m). An excellent evergreen shrub. Shiny dark aromatic leaves, especially when crushed. Clusters of sweetly scented white flowers in May and off and on until the autumn. Very easy plant but does not like soggy soil.*

T Lavatera olbia 'Rosea'. *Height 6 ft plus (2 m). Vigorous sub-shrub, which has a fine grey down growing over the entire plant. Pink mallow-like flowers throughout summer. For best results cut back hard in spring.*

Rosa 'Old Blush China'. *Another delightful fragrant rose which smells like a sweet pea. Dainty mid-pink flowers throughout summer and sometimes up to Christmas after a mild autumn. Mid-green leaves. Height and spread 3–4 ft (90 cm–1.2 m). An excellent garden shrub.*

Philadelphus 'Beauclerk' *(Mock Orange). Reliable deciduous shrub. Height 6–8 ft (1.8–2.5 m). Spread 5–6 ft (1.5–1.8 m). Charming fragrant single white flowers in June–July. Mid-green leaves.*

T Fuchsia magellanica 'Versicolor'. *Height 4–6 ft (1.2–1.8 m). Spread 3–4 ft (90 cm–1.2 m). A bushy fuchsia with narrow grey/green and white or yellow variegated leaves. Red/purple pink-tinged flowers from July to October. Fuchsias, with their unusual flowers, provide excellent mid-to-late summer colour.*

Chaenomeles speciosa 'Cardinalis' *(Quince). Deciduous, early-flowering shrub. Crimson saucer-shaped flowers with yellow stamens January to April. Fragrant green yellow fruits. Height 6 ft (1.8 m). Spread 6 ft (1.8 m). Dark green glossy leaves. Excellent on banks or against walls.*

continued on p. 56

How to make a Camomile Seat

Should you possess an old stone sink or trough, it could be put to good use and made into a camomile seat. In order to turn the trough into a bench, it needs to be raised up on bricks or large stones, so that it stands about 2 ft 6 in (75 cm) from the ground.

If you haven't got a trough lying around, and not many people have, you can use a 2 ft (60 cm) wide and 3 ft (90 cm) long wooden plank. Take the plank and place the bricks on their side round the edge of it. Cement the bricks securely on to the wood, then fix the whole structure together with wire mesh. When the cement has set, mix up 'fake' stone (peat mixed with cement) and cover the whole surface inside, outside and round the edges, to give your 'trough' a 'stone' finish. This mixture will protect the trough and stop the wood from rotting.

When dry (leave at least twenty-four hours depending on the weather), drill two drainage holes. Next fill the trough with a layer of shingle, then moist *sandy* soil level with the top of the trough and plant non-flowering camomile. Keep well watered until it has established.

Once the camomile 'lawn' on the bench has established, it will start to grow over the sides of the trough and form a spongy surface on which to sit. Trim it every month or so in summer and water if it gets too dry.

A camomile seat will add an unusual and old world touch to a cottage garden – not forgetting the unique sensation and delightful aroma this comfortable seat will provide. It is well worth the trouble, if only for its novelty value.

PLANTING A CAMOMILE SEAT

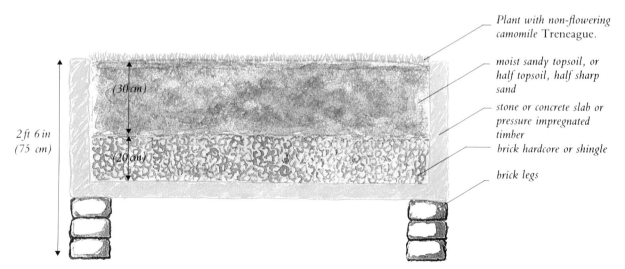

Plant with non-flowering camomile Treneague.

moist sandy topsoil, or half topsoil, half sharp sand

stone or concrete slab or pressure impregnated timber

brick hardcore or shingle

brick legs

2 ft 6 in (75 cm)

(30 cm)

(20 cm)

COTTAGE GARDEN (*continued*)

T Santolina chamaecyparissus *(Cotton lavender).*
A most useful evergreen, sun-loving shrub. Height
and spread 1ft – 18 in (30 – 45 cm). Mound-forming
leaves and silver dissected felty branches covered in
tiny leaves. Lemon pompom flowers July. Needs a
trim in spring to keep it neat.

Rosmarinus officinalis *(Rosemary). Another*
aromatic evergreen shrub. Height 4 – 6 ft (1.2 –
1.8 m), spread 4 – 5 ft (1.2 – 1.5 m). Narrow mid-
green leaves, white underside. Mauve flowers in
March and on and off until September. Excellent
herb for cooking. Needs pruning to keep it in shape.

Lavandula spica *(Lavender). Height and spread*
18 in – 3 ft (45 – 90 cm). True cottage garden plant.
Silver grey leaves, pale blue flowers on spikes from
July to September. Needs pruning back to old wood
once a year and replacing every 6 years or so.

Daphne burkwoodii. *Height 3 ft (90 cm), spread*
4 ft (1.2 m). Semi-evergreen, leaves light green.
Delightful clusters of light pink fragrant flowers May
to June and a few in later summer.

Rosa alba 'Maiden's Blush'. *Charming rose with a*
delicate fragrance. Height and spread at least 5 ft
(1.5 m). Grey/green foliage. Neat double blush pink
flowers in June and a few red hips in autumn. An
old rose that probably dates back to the sixteenth
century.

T Rosa virginiana. *Another old favourite and ideal*
for gardens in which it will not receive much
attention. This rose (dating from 1807) can survive
quite happily in any soil, even sandy, providing it
has a good yearly feed. It has attractive foliage – fat
orange hips – and will not grumble if left unpruned.
It has fragrant, rich, clear pink flowers all through
the summer. Grows to about 3 ft (90 cm), with pink
flowers June to August.

Climbers
Clematis armandii 'Snow Drift'. *Height 30 ft*
(9 m). Vigorous evergreen climber with dark glossy
green leaves, white fragrant flowers in April.

Trachelospermum jasminoides *('Touch-me-*
not'). Evergreen climbing shrub, height to 12 ft
(3.5 m). Leathery dark green leaves. White sweetly-
scented flowers with wavy edges July to August.

T Jasminum × stephanense *(Jasmine). Height 10*
to 15 ft (3 – 4.5 m). Semi-evergreen, twining climber.
Dull green leaves above with light green below and
clusters of pale pink scented flowers in June.

T Lonicera japonica 'Halliana' *(Japanese*
honeysuckle). A strong camouflage climber which
will soon take over and grow to the height of 25 ft
(8 m) if you let it. Light green leaves. White
sweetly-smelling flowers, changing to yellow from
June to October.

T Rosa 'Albertine'. *Height 18 ft (5.5 m).*
Vigorous climber. Highly scented double coppery
pink flowers. Good healthy leaves and splendid plant
to help create a sheltered eating corner.

T Phlomis fruticosa *(Jerusalem Sage). Evergreen*
bushy sub-shrub. Grey/green felted leaves, yellow
flowers mid-summer. Height 3 – 4 ft (90 – 1.2 m).
Spread 2 ft (60 cm).

Herbaceous
Malva moschata *(Musk mallow). Easy,*
undemanding perennial. Height 2 ft (60 cm). Mid-
green deeply cut leaves, rose-pink flowers June to
September.

Althaea rosea *(Hollyhock). Another traditional*
cottage garden plant. 6 – 9 ft (2 – 3 m), biennial or
may live a few years. Rough light green hairy
leaves. Single or double flowers, pink shades July to
September.

COTTAGE GARDEN *(continued)*

T Nepeta × faassenii *(sometimes listed as mussinii) (Catmint). Wonderful perennial for the edge of a border. Height 12–18 in (30–45 cm). Rounded grey/green leaves. Lavender-blue flowers May to September. Providing you haven't got cats (which will roll in the plant) it will give a splendid show all summer. Cut back in winter. 'Six Hills Giant' grows to 2 ft (60 cm) or more.*

T Artemisia absinthium 'Lambrook Silver'. *(Wormwood) Height and spread 3–4 ft (90 cm–1.2 m). Sub-shrubby perennial, silvery finely cut leaves, dull yellow flowers July–August.*

Heuchera sanguinea *(Coral flower). Height 1 ft–18 in (30–45 cm). Evergreen ground cover beneath deciduous trees. Dark green heart-shaped leaves. Bell-shaped bright red flowers in light airy plumes, June to September. Pleasing as cut flowers.*

T Anthemis cupaniana. *Height 6 in–1 ft (15–30 cm). Mat-forming plant. Finely dissected aromatic grey leaves. White daisy flowers June to August.*

T Stachys lanata *(Lambs' tongue). Height 1 ft–18 in (30–45 cm). Soft silver/grey leaves, covered in silver hairs. Purple flowers July in woolly spikes. Good summer ground cover, easily divided and replanted perennial. Prefers sun.*

Iris pallida dalmatica *(Tall bearded iris). Height 3 ft (90 cm). Long, slim, blue/grey leaves, lavender-blue flowers May–June.*

T Geranium renardii. *Clump-forming perennial. Height 9 in (22.5 cm). Spread 1 ft (30 cm). Handsome sage green rounded veined leaves. Lavender/white flowers with purple veins from May to July. Delightful easy plant, will grow anywhere.*

T Dianthus 'Mrs Sinkins'. *Old-fashioned pinks. Height 10–15 in (25–37.5 cm). White double flowers June. Grey/green evergreen leaves. Very strongly clove scented. Slugs and snails like the young shoots of pinks so if invaded by slugs surround the plant with gravel to protect it.*

Thymus lanuginosus *(Thyme). Height 3 in (7.5 cm). Mat forming. Mauve flowers June–August. Grey/green hairy leaves. Good herb for cooking.*

Ajuga reptans 'Atropurpurea'. *Excellent evergreen shade-loving ground cover. Oblong green/purple leaves. Height 4 in–1 ft (10–30 cm).*

Digitalis purpurea *(Foxglove). Height 3–5 feet (90 cm–1.5 m). Felted green leaves in rosettes. 3 ft (90 cm) high spikes, purple/red or white spotted flowers June to July. Biennial but they seed themselves so once you have one you will have many!*

T Paeonia officinalis 'Rosea-plena'. *This obliging hardy herbaceous perennial is good value and surprises one with its size (2 ft (60 cm)) and beauty as it grows up from nothing each spring. Deep pink flowers May and June. (Prefers not to have early morning sun.)*

TRADITIONAL COTTAGE FLOWERS
Acanthus spinosus (Bears' breeches)
Aster
Apple Trees
Alchemilla mollis (Ladies' Mantle)
Borage
Camomile
Campanulas
Clematis
Climbing Roses
Forget-me-nots
Foxgloves
Fuchsias

continued over page

Two good value cottage garden plants: campanula latifolia *(photo by Pamla Toler, left) and* acanthus *(bears' breeches) (photo by Susan Hampshire).*

TRADITIONAL COTTAGE FLOWERS
(*continued*)
Geraniums
Hellebores
Hollyhocks
Honeysuckle
Hostas
Iris
Larkspur
Lavender
Lilies
Lily of the Valley
Lupins
Marigolds
Michaelmas Daisies
Nepeta
Oxeye daisies
Pansies
Pinks
Phlox
Poppies
Primulas
Quince (*suitable behind bench or swing*)

Rosemary
Roses – 'Maiden's Blush', *gallica 'officinalis'*, *'Félicité Parmentier'*
Sage
Santolina
Sedum
Solidago (Golden Rod)
Stachys lanata (Lambs' Ears)
Stocks
Sweet Peas
Sweet William
Tobacco Plants
Thyme
Verbascum
Violets

For hedge:
Dogwood
Field Maple
Guelder Rose
Hazel
Holly
Hawthorn

10: *Wildlife garden*

There is unlimited joy to be gained from a wildlife garden. It is a great pleasure to know that jays and thrushes have a place to nest and breed, and there's a haven where kestrels and field mice, voles and hedgehogs can roam without being poisoned by insecticide or fertilisers.

To watch a hedgehog move swiftly over the grass in the moonlight or know a fox has threaded his way through the garden at dawn are just some of the thrills of having a wildlife garden, where *no chemical fertilisers*, *weed killers* or *pesticides* are used to destroy the work of nature. Instead organic fertiliser (see *Fertilisers*), love of nature and careful planning encourage all within the garden's boundaries to flourish.

In the last forty years we have destroyed as much woodland as our ancestors destroyed in the previous four hundred years. The twentieth century moved in and wildlife was squeezed out, mainly by farmers cutting down the hedgerows and spraying fertilisers and insecticides. Between 1947 and 1974, 140,000 *miles* (225,000 km) of hedgerow were lost. Nearly all was attributable to agricultural expansion. This so called 'progress' wiped out the natural habitat and with it much of the wildlife of the country. Instead we have, here and there, small pockets of wildlife dotted across the land. But the wildlife is trapped, unable to travel up and down the country due to the large stretches of barren ground between, where there is no food or shelter for the wildlife, other than along some of the old railway tracks where the wild flowers and plants have been left undisturbed and not been destroyed.

In Britain there are over a million acres (400,000 hectares) of garden and although a wildlife garden can never provide a home for the otter, the curlew or salmon, it can house many plants and mammals that may otherwise become extinct.

It's sad to think that if the present rate of destruction continues many of the small creatures that we grew to love in our story books as children will soon be creatures of the past.

The Garden

Looking down the 100 ft (30 m) garden from the house, the garden turns from quiet civilisation into an area that develops progressively into a wild garden. It's nice to think that with each foot of natural garden (no matter if it is as small as 30 ft by 30 ft) (9 m square), you are making a contribution to the preservation of wildlife and at the same time the hard work of digging and planting of the cultivated garden are left behind. Admittedly, you'll need to mow the meadow grass twice a year with a rotary mower at three inches (8 cm) off the ground so the grass is not cut too short, or with a scythe in March and July, and mow a path through the long grass in late spring, but apart from replacing the odd bog plant, it's one of the most satisfying and undemanding gardens *when*, and only when, it is well and truly established.

All the functional requirements and practical aspects are near the house. But once

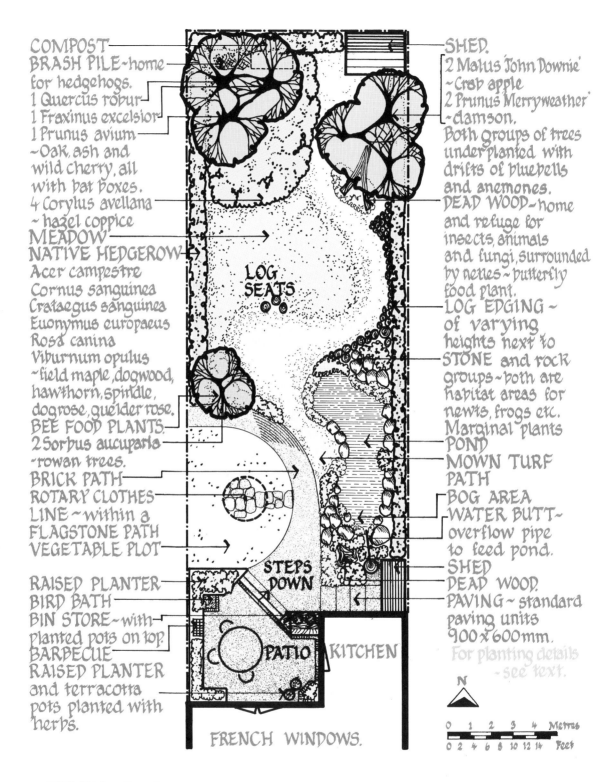

COMPOST
BRASH PILE~home
for hedgehogs.
1 Quercus robur~
1 Fraxinus excelsior~
1 Prunus avium
~Oak, ash and
wild cherry, all
with bat boxes.
4 Corylus avellana
~ hazel coppice
MEADOW
NATIVE HEDGEROW~
Acer campestre
Cornus sanguinea
Crataegus sanguinea
Euonymus europaeus
Rosa canina
Viburnum opulus
~field maple, dogwood,
hawthorn, spindle,
dogrose, guelder rose.
BEE FOOD PLANTS.
2 Sorbus aucuparia~
~rowan trees.
BRICK PATH
ROTARY CLOTHES
LINE~within a
FLAGSTONE PATH
VEGETABLE PLOT

RAISED PLANTER
BIRD BATH
BIN STORE~with
planted pots on top.
BARBECUE
RAISED PLANTER
and terracotta
pots planted with
herbs.

LOG
SEATS

SHED.
2 Malus 'John Downie'
~Crab apple
2 Prunus 'Merryweather'
~damson.
Both groups of trees
underplanted with
drifts of bluebells
and anemones.
DEAD WOOD~home
and refuge for
insects, animals
and fungi, surrounded
by nettles~butterfly
food plant.
LOG EDGING~
of varying
heights next to
STONE and rock
groups~both are
habitat areas for
newts, frogs etc.
Marginal plants
POND
MOWN TURF
PATH
BOG AREA
WATER BUTT~
overflow pipe
to feed pond.
SHED
DEAD WOOD.
PAVING ~ standard
paving units
900 × 600mm.
For planting details
~see text.

STEPS
DOWN

PATIO   KITCHEN

FRENCH WINDOWS.

N

0 1 2 3 4 Metres
0 2 4 6 8 10 12 14 Feet

Wildlife Garden

you leave those behind you move into another world, surrounded by a native mixed hedgerow of hawthorn, field maple, guelder rose, spindle, dogwood and dog rose, all perfect nesting places for small birds, and ideal for attracting bees and other insects.

On the right is the pond and bog area for small fish, frogs, frog spawn and newts and on the left two rowan trees with bird feeders and suitable bee and butterfly plants below.

As you move further down the garden to the meadow area the grass gets longer but the mown path makes walking easy and leaves the meadow area undisturbed to generate its own magic.

At the end of the garden there's a group of apple and damson trees. Below them a dead log is sprawled across the ground, a perfect habitat for snails, wood lice, mice and other small mammals, and in the spring bluebells and wood anemones can grow under the trees in drifts.

On the left hand side a hazel coppice is planted beneath an oak, ash and cherry tree, each with bat boxes in their branches. Bats are endangered species and it is a criminal offence to harm or disturb them.

Years ago we had bats nesting in the roof and I was naive enough to think they were vermin and should be removed. Luckily I didn't have the wherewithal to do it, and the bat family is still nesting there quite happily to this day.

But to get a wildlife garden established takes time and needs as much careful planning as any other garden. It's easy to imagine that it will all just happen and look wonderful on its own.

Not so, if you do nothing but wait. The art is to nudge things into the right direction rather than use the strict control of digging and pruning.

It's taken me over five years to get the correct mix of meadow grass and wild flowers established in my country garden. My soil was too good, and therefore the grass too vigorous, so ox-eyed daisies, cowslips, poppies and buttercups wouldn't grow. What I should have done was strip off the top soil, so that the wild flowers could easily have seeded themselves in the poor soil beneath. It has been exasperating to watch the wide selection of beautiful wild flowers growing on the builders' rubble – the ideal conditions for them – and not in my meadow.

To establish a meadow in a new garden, it is best to sow a wild flower mix from a reputable seedsman such as John Chambers or Emorsgate Seed (addresses at the back), then follow the maintenance procedure *exactly*. In an established lawn the only solution is to buy the plants of suitable flowers for meadows and plant them in the grass. This is a very effective way to establish them.

I was photographing this pyracantha when a voice from the other side of the lane asked, 'Would you like me to photograph that for you?' I turned around and to my astonishment saw one of the world's greatest photographers, Norman Parkinson, standing there. He was travelling around the country photographing English villages under threat for the Council for the Protection of Rural England. He duly and kindly took the photograph for me.

opposite: Nepeta (catmint, with the purple flowers) in a bed of herbaceous perennials where the weeds have no chance at all. I haven't given this bed more than two hours attention since I planted it two years ago. The other plants are Santolina chamaecyparissus *(bottom left),* Phlomis fruticosa *(top centre),* Felicia rose *(top right),* Tolmiea menziesii *('pig-a-back plant', bottom centre) and* Dorycnium hirsutum *(bottom right).*

Patio

The back of this house faces north so there is no sun on the small terrace in the afternoon. Nonetheless, it is an attractive morning-to-lunchtime area. Surrounded by its raised planter, barbecue and bird bath on the left and the terracotta pots and soft herbs on the right, it has a pleasing and practical feel.

Just outside the kitchen door on the right, the bin store is concealed in a slatted wooden cupboard with plant pots on top. Alternatively, this could be made into the barbecue, which at the moment is situated on the left of the terrace. Then the dust bin and kitchen waste container (destined for the compost heap at the bottom of the garden) could be constructed by the shed situated against the back wall of the house, handy for tools and the vegetable patch.

The main shed now at the bottom of the garden could also be incorporated with the shed at the back of the house; then it would not be necessary to walk through the long wet grass to collect the garden tools or calcified seaweed to feed the vegetables.

Vegetable Patch and Rotary Clothes Line

Although the vegetable space is near the house, for practical reasons, it is not too conspicuous as it is partly concealed by the attractive wooden container filled with flowers at the bottom of the steps. It can also be screened by another large container with a flowering shrub at the top of the steps.

The path round the vegetables in this design is brick, which makes easy, unmuddy access. Riven paving slabs are less expensive but not quite so suitable in a natural garden where concrete would be out of place.

The rotary clothes line is set up a path in the middle of the vegetable area in a circle of flag stones, again to make access easy. So from the moment you leave the kitchen door to pick a lettuce or hang up the washing, you need never leave the path.

The vegetable patch and clothes line are not the most beautiful items to gaze upon, but the neat semi-circular path encloses the vegetables attractively. Vegetables don't have to be unsightly and can look very presentable in a well-organised layout surrounded by ornamental cabbages to add a touch of colour. It is important in this garden that all the areas that are in constant use should be near the house so as not to disturb the part of the garden which is to develop naturally. Also near the house there will be fewer slugs and snails to find their way to the vegetables! (See *Low Maintenance Vegetables*.)

But should the idea of vegetables present too much trouble, then plants that attract butterflies such as Michaelmas daisies, *Sedum spectabile* (a favourite of the Painted Lady butterfly), spring flowering primulas (attract Orange Tip), grape hyacinths (attract the Comma butterfly) and of course *Buddleia davidii* (the butterfly bush) can be introduced in their place and they would certainly be pleasing to observe from the terrace.

Plant Association: The Natural Structure of Woodland

The trees and shrubs at the end of the garden should be encouraged to imitate the natural structure of woodland: trees, then beneath them smaller young trees, then shrubs, then sprawling shrubs, then flowers and bulbs. In this way a balance is created by the change in the mix of plants, so you always have plants that do not lose their leaves before the next plant is ready to come into leaf. If the change is gradual there will be less room for weeds.

Beneath the oak and ash trees, hazel trees should be planted. These hazels can be coppiced after five to ten years to keep them in hand and the oak, ash and cherry can be coppiced after twenty years if necessary.

Coppicing: Cut the hazel down to a height of 6 in to 12 in (15 to 30 cm) from the ground. Slope the cut up and outwards from the centre of the stump. Hazel is coppiced, then used for woven fencing. For generations, a large proportion of *ash* has been coppiced after eight years for tool handles and firewood. It is still excellent for both.

Oak trees can be pollarded but a good tree surgeon thinning the tree's canopy is often sufficient.

Bog Garden and Pond

Water is always fascinating and a wildlife pond or bog garden is no exception. Although there is only just enough space available, its presence is a valuable contribution to conservation since so many ponds round the country have disappeared.

But it is very important that the pond is laid out correctly and is the right size and depth, otherwise it will require a lot of work to maintain it, especially if it is too shallow. The trouble-free quality of a pond comes from *correct construction in the first place*. If it is too shallow the weeds will take over. There must be three different levels (see diagram).

The deepest section should be 3 ft (90 cm) deep and *at least* 7 ft (over 2 m) long and 4 ft (1.2 m) wide. The same membrane or plastic liner must cover the bottom of all three sections of the pond as well as coming up over the edges to lie under the large stones and rocks securing it round the side.

If the overflow is not correctly positioned (see diagram), the pond will never take care of itself and there will be too much bog surrounding it.

At the edge of the pond there should be large stones and rocks for newts, and marginal plants in the shallow water near the overflow.

The big plants can be sunk into the pond in clay pots; this way they won't become too big and get out of hand and also they can easily be replaced. 9 in (22.5 cm) terracotta pots placed in the water prevent the plant from spreading.

Around the edges in the bog, plant *Acorus calamus*, *Butomus umbellatus*, *Primula florindae* and *Primula candelabra* (this romantic and pretty plant will enjoy the moist surroundings, seed itself and look lovely growing between the grass and stones).

The tree stumps designed to be placed upright round the outer edge of the pond will blend well with the surroundings and make an ideal site to sit and watch the wonders of the water world beneath.

Apart from the pond membrane, all the materials in a wildlife garden should be *natural* and not man-made like plastic; synthetic materials will be obtrusive and alien to wildlife.

WATER BOG GARDEN

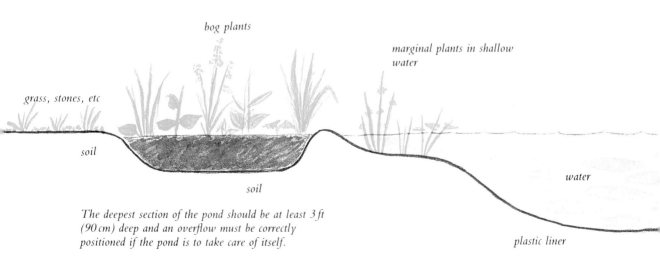

bog plants

marginal plants in shallow water

grass, stones, etc

soil

soil

water

The deepest section of the pond should be at least 3 ft (90 cm) deep and an overflow must be correctly positioned if the pond is to take care of itself.

plastic liner

Bird and Mammal Aids

Bird feeders in the rowan trees and bat boxes in the oak and ash trees will encourage wildlife. The tree stump for small mammals and brush wood pile habitat for hedgehogs at the end of the garden are to welcome the small creatures who are too often blinded by headlights and become victims of the overloaded roads.

In a wild garden where there are nettles, coarse grass and thistles, it is easier to attract butterflies than in a manicured garden without 'pernicious weeds'. The caterpillars of many of the common butterflies feed exclusively on these weeds. The nettles for laying eggs have to be in the sun as the small tortoiseshell won't lay its eggs on nettles in the shade.

Garden Butterflies

There are fifty-eight species of butterfly that occur in Britain, of which sixteen regularly visit gardens. These are listed below, together with the months when you are most likely to see them.

Brimstone, March–May, July–August
Comma, March–October, only in the South and Wales
Common Blue, May–June, August–September, only where bird's foot trefoil and clover grow in short grass
Gatekeeper, July–August, only in the South
Green-veined White, May–July
Holly Blue, April–May, July–August
Large Skipper, June–August
Meadow Brown, June–September

Orange Tip, April–June
Painted Lady, May–October
Peacock, March–May, July–August
Red Admiral, May–October
Small Copper, May–October, only where sorrel grows
Small Tortoiseshell, March–October
Small Skipper, July–August
Small White, April–October
Wall Brown, May–June, August–September

opposite: A mature hebe spreads its purple flowers along a sunny edge.

above: Sedum spectabile, *a herbaceous perennial which gives excellent autumn colour (photo by Susan Hampshire).*

left: The 'butterfly bush', Buddleia alternifolia. *It has a wonderful heady perfume in June.*

WILDLIFE GARDEN
See back of book for more details

Deciduous Trees
Suitable trees for this garden include:
Malus spp 'Golden Hornet' (Crab Apple Tree). *Excellent for attracting bees. Pretty white blossoms in spring. Height 15–20 ft (4.5–6 m). Spread 10– 15 ft (3–4.5 m). Bright yellow fruits which persist long after the leaves have fallen.*

Malus sylvestris (Crab Apple Tree). *Height 12– 15 ft (3.5–4.5 m). Spread 10–15 ft (3–4.5 m). There is quite a large choice of crab apples with varying blossoms. They all grow to about the same height except M. eleyi and M. 'John Downie' which grow to 25–30 ft (7.5–9 m). Spread 15– 25 ft (4.5–7.5 m). White blossoms in May followed by yellow/red fruits good for crab apple jelly.*

Salix caprea (Pussy Willow). *This pretty tree grows to 15 ft (4.5 m). Spread 15 ft (4.5 m).*

Sorbus aucuparia Rowan (Mountain Ash). *Height 15–20 ft (4.5–6 m). Spread 8–12 ft (2.5– 3.5 m). Excellent tree for any garden. White flowers in May/June followed by orange berries. Not good in shallow alkaline soils.*

Corylus avellena (Hazel nut). *Grows to 20 ft (6 m). Spread 15 ft (4.5 m). Mid green leaves. 2 in (5 cm) yellow male catkins in February.*

Quercus robur (Common English Oak Tree). *300 insects are associated with the oak tree, so an oak is an excellent choice for a wildlife garden. Height 12–18 ft (3.5–5.5 m). Spread 6–10 ft (1.8–3 m). Hardy, slow-growing, but eventually forms a substantial tree. Mid green leaves.*

Prunus avium (Wild Cherry Tree). *There are 430 species in the Prunus family which gives plenty of choice! Avium has a height of 30–40 ft (9– 12 m). Spread 20–30 ft (6–9 m). White flowers in pendulous clusters in April. Mid green leaves.*

Prunus domesticus (Damson Tree). *Grows to 20 ft (6 m). Dull dark green leaves. Edible plum-like fruit in summer.*

Buddleia alternifolia (Butterfly Bush). *This large and wonderfully sweet-smelling deciduous shrub grows to 12–20 ft (3.5–6 m). Spread 15–20 ft (4.5–6 m). The lilac-blue flowers have an intoxicating perfume in June and the tree looks a dazzling sight when it is completely covered by these clusters of small flowers all over its pendulous branches. Not native.*

Crataegus (Hawthorn). *This tree is much admired for its dense small white, pink or red blossoms. It has colourful fruit and rich autumn colour. C. monogyna, the common hawthorn, is used for hedging. Can grow to 15 ft (4.5 m).*

Acer campestre (Field Maple). *Native British tree useful as a hedgerow shrub. Height 15–20 ft (4.5– 6 m). Spread 10 ft (3 m). Mid green leaves, yellow in autumn. When not used as a hedge it makes a pleasant round-headed tree.*

Viburnum opulus (Guelder Rose). *Bushy deciduous shrub. Grows to 15 ft (4.5 m) (for hedge). Maple-like dark green leaves. Strong-scented flat-headed white flowers in May and June followed by clusters of bright red berries.*

Cornus sanguinea (Dogwood). *(For hedge). Height 10–15 ft (3–4.5 m). Spread 15–20 ft (4.5– 6 m). Deciduous large-branched shrub. Dark green leaves turn brilliant orange and red in the autumn. Small white flowers May, followed by clusters of black berries. Suckers, so keep it away from small plants.*

Euonymus europaeus (Spindle). *Height 6–10 ft (2–3 m). Spread 4–10 ft (1.2–3 m). Deciduous shrub. Mid green leaves. Small green flowers in May followed by wonderful orange/red waxy seeds, which are poisonous.*

WILDLIFE GARDEN

Plants to encourage wildlife (food and shelter)
Blackthorn, Buckhorn, Hebe, Pyracantha, Ribes odoratum, Syringa (Lilac), Viburnum opulus, Viburnum lantana, Erica, Cotoneaster.

Bog garden: Plants to go round the edge
Arocus calamus,
Butomus umbellatus,
Primula florindae; P. candelabra,
Marsh Marigolds *Calthia palustris,*
Malva sylvestris *(Common Mallow – relieves toothache!)*

Plants to encourage Bees
Alyssum, Crocus, Campanula carpatica, Chives, Borage (the best bee plant), Candytuft, Dianthus (pinks), Digitalis foxglove, Larkspur, Sage, Wallflower, French Marigold, Yellow Archangel, Thyme, Nasturtiums, Phlox, Campion, Rose.

To encourage Moths
Bladder Campion, Sweet Rocket, Evening Primrose, White Jasmine, Soapwort *and* Honeysuckle.

Plants to encourage Birds
Chickweed, Coltsfoot, Fat hen, Groundsel, Shepherd's Purse, Teasel, Betony, Knapweed, Cow Parsley, Burdock, Dandelion, Field Forget-me-Knot, Lesser Burdock, Meadowsweet, Michaelmas Daisy, Thistles

Plants to encourage Butterflies
Buddleia (Butterfly bush), Solidago, Hebe, *Sedum Spectabile,* Lavender, *Ligustrum* (Privet), Lilac, Michaelmas Daisy, Aubretia, Yellow Alyssum, Wallflower, Sweet Rocket, Honesty, Red Valerian, *Nepeta* (catmint), *Achillea,* Aster, *Centranthus,* Erigeron, *Helenium,* Scabious

Meadow plants
(*in order of size*)
Sweet Vernal Grass, *the tallest*
Yorkshire Fog
Ox-eye Daisy
Field Scabious
Sheep's Sorrel
Knapweed
Yellow Rattle
Yarrow
Red Fescue
Harebell
Cat's ear
Sheeps Bit
Lady's Bedstraw
Speedwell
Cowslip
Daisy, *the shortest*

Wild Flowers
Thrift
White Clover
Hawkweed
Vetch
Field Scabious
Wild Marjoram
Campion
Greater Knapweed
Ox-eye Daisy
Poppies

Other flowers for wildlife garden
Spring flowering Primulas
Bulbs
Herbs (both soft and woody)

11: Disabled garden

This attractive garden is suitable for those who are confined to a wheelchair. Its interesting layout and aesthetically pleasing shape are one hundred per cent practical, with consideration given to all the wheelchair gardener's requirements.

The elegant layout is formal yet this garden is as rewarding for the garden lover who is able-bodied as for the garden lover who is not.

The View

As you look out across the wide smooth paved garden from the bungalow, the main body of the garden is divided into four by four raised planters so the gardener can be surrounded by plants. The first quarter of these geometric-shaped raised planters to catch the eye is a welcoming seat with a rail to lean on and hold. The seat adjoins the raised planter, the back of which makes a small six-sided pond gracefully angled towards the house.

This geometric pond is mirrored on the opposite side of the wide obstacle-free path by another raised planter at a slightly higher level. This time a sundial makes an interesting feature in the corner of one of the four corners which point towards the centre. The yellow, cream and gold plants chosen for the planting plan will make this a bright and unusual garden.

The last two sections at the rear which make up the last two quarters of the square are wonderfully enveloping. The planters are 2 ft 4 in (70 cm) high, suitable for driving the wheelchair right into the plant area with plenty of room for knees and feet. This enables the gardener to get in among the plants, as the 'shelf' bed at the 'drive in' point is designed so beds are literally over the gardener's lap.

On the far side of the garden, nicely in view of the patio area, and catching most of the day's sun, are two ornamental trees – *Gleditsia Triacanthos 'Sunburst'*, which has delicate golden yellow leaves to enhance the garden with its burst of beautiful colour from spring to autumn, and *Prunus 'Pandora'*. There is enough space between the trees for a bench if required, ideal for a quiet rest in the shade. The raised planters opposite the bench with their overhanging plants provide plenty to admire, or long to get one's hands on, as the case may be.

Herbs

The joy of having herbs in salads or sauces is well worth the little trouble involved. Nearly all herbs are trouble-free. The soft herbs such as chives, mint and parsley can be kept in pots on the kitchen window sill, or fairly easily reached in the raised planter on the left of the patio doors.

Hard herbs such as rosemary and sage can afford to be further away as they can be picked and dried and do not *have* to be fresh. So they are located in the sunnily positioned raised planter opposite the small pond.

above: Purple sage: a resilient, trouble free herb in a sunny well-drained position.

left: A five-year-old Mermaid rose climbing up a wall in the courtyard of my country garden. The tub beneath is planted with variegated euonymus (photo by Susan Hampshire).

Cordon fruit trees in a ground level planter trained against 1·8m high close boarded fence. Mulch soil to keep weed growth down. Planted pots on 590mm high plinths.
1 Gleditsia triacanthos 'Sunburst'
1 Prunus 'Pandora'

RAISED BEDS on both sides of garden, 590mm high, 600mm wide.

Standard paving units 450x450mm, with brick delineation runs

1 Choisya ternata
2 Fritillaria imperialis 'Lutea'
1 Vinca minor 'Albo-plena'
10 Crocus speciosus 'Albus'
1 Jasminum nudiflorum
3 Tropaeolum majus
1 Hedera helix 'Glacier'
5 Viola tricolor
2 Tiarella cordifolia
1 Forsythia suspensa
1 Vinca minor 'Albo-plena'
DUSTBIN STORE - optional.
RAISED PLANTER 590mm high, planted with alpines around a sun-dial as a centrepiece.
TWO WAY DUSTBIN STORE

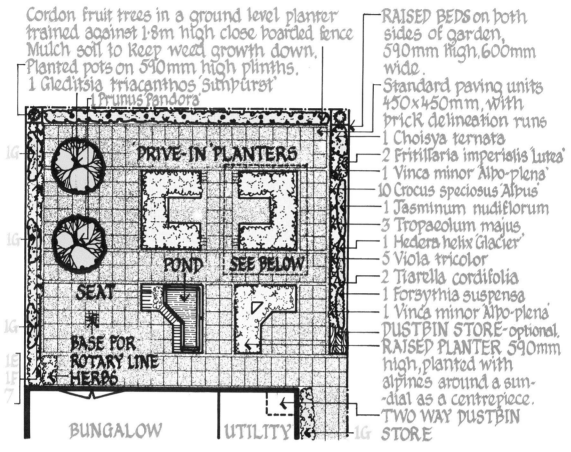

PRIVE-IN PLANTERS

POND

SEE BELOW

SEAT

BASE FOR ROTARY LINE

HERBS

BUNGALOW

UTILITY

1 Euonymus fortunei 'Emerald n' Gold'
1 Potentilla 'Longacre'
10 Narcissus 'Charity May'
1 Cytisus Kewensis
3 Viola tricolor

3 Viola tricolor
1 Ranunculus aconitifolius
1 Hedera helix 'Buttercup'
2 Hypericum x m. Tricolor
1 Mahonia a. 'Apollo'.
1 Vinca m. 'Albo-plena'
3 Ranunculus ficaria 'Plena'
1 Philadelphus 'Manteau d'Hermine'

Drive-in planters, 690mm high with central 'table top' for 'face-on' wheelchair access. NB. Dimensions should be adjusted to suit individual needs.
Pond/Seat, the pond has a hand rail for support. The seat adjacent is 450mm high, 450mm wide.

ABOVE - planting details of top right raised planter.

To design your own planting for the raised planters refer to the plant lists at the end of the book.

Disabled Garden

72

Dust bins

There is a space for the dust bin on the far right hand side of the garden easily accessible for the obliging dustman to come down the side of the house. But if a disabled person is living alone, a two-way dust bin cupboard which can be reached from within the house and without, with a good lock on the inside, is ideally situated for dust bin collection.

A barbecue is a troublesome piece of paraphernalia for the disabled person living alone but, should it be needed, there is plenty of space to store a portable barbecue, as indeed there is for a clothes line.

Paving and Brickwork

Slabs of *simulated* York stone or concrete paving slabs can sometimes be uninteresting and severe if not relieved by the introduction of another material such as brick. Obviously for wheelchairs the surface should be as smooth as possible, so avoid too much detail, but runs of brick round the edge of the path to soften and enhance its appearance are worthwhile and do not need to be more expensive than paving slabs. Laying the bricks lengthways, thus using only half the number of bricks, helps to bring down the cost. Non-slip paving is essential in all gardens and most certainly for the disabled.

Boundaries

The boundaries of the garden can be well used to make a good support for cordon fruit trees in ground level planters at the far end of the garden. These should not prove too much trouble, especially if the roots are covered with a good mulch, avoiding the impossible task of weeding at below waist level. The fruit, on the other hand, is at exactly the right height for picking, pruning and training, and very tempting and enjoyable it will be too. The blossom of apple or pear is lovely in spring and will attract bees; and the fruit should be good to eat.

The two side walls can enjoy the company of sweet-smelling trouble-free shrubs such as choisya, which does not need pruning or training, or 'Mermaid' climbing rose which is also trouble-free and undemanding.

This practical and attractive garden should be a pleasure for the wheelchair-bound who want to get out and around to enjoy their garden.

Hypericum 'St John's Wort', *a wonderful ground cover plant with beautiful flowers.*

DISABLED GARDEN
Cream, yellow and gold colour scheme.
See back of book for more details.
T = *Trouble free*

Trees
Gleditsia triacanthos 'Sunburst'. *Grows slowly to 18–25 ft (5.5–8 m). Spread 12–15 ft (3.5–4.5 m) but is easily pruned to keep it smaller. Small, very finely divided, light yellow/gold leaves in spring and summer, turning brighter yellow in the autumn. Delightful 'sunny' tree, which has an interesting, almost gnarled shape in winter when the leaves have fallen. Needs a sunny place but sheltered, as the wood is very brittle.*

Prunus 'Pandora'. *A slender flowering cherry that grows to 16 ft (5 m). The pale pink flowers come in early spring and the leaves turn orange in autumn.*

Shrubs
T Mahonia aquifolium. *Evergreen shrub. This mahonia is low-growing, reaching 3 ft or more (1 m) and spreads a little by suckers to form a clump. Glossy dark green leaves and scented yellow flowers in March/April followed by blue/black berries. The leaves sometimes go dull purple/red in winter, especially in dry soils.*

T Potentilla 'Longacre'. *A dense low-growing mat-forming deciduous shrub. It has pale sulphur yellow five-petalled flowers throughout the summer and mid-green foliage with five leaflets (hence its other name, Cinquefoil). Grows to 1 ft (30 cm). Spreads to 3 ft (90 cm). Other varieties are taller and not so spreading.*

T Cytisus kewensis *(Broom). Long slender weeping branches with small mid-green leaves and a profusion of pale yellow flowers in May. Ideal for flowing over the side of the raised planter. The green stems are also effective in winter. Height 12–14 in (30–35 cm). Spread 4 ft (1.2 m). Sun-loving.*

T Ivy. *Also to flow over the side of the planter and give year-round interest.*

T Vinca minor 'Albo-plena' *(Periwinkle). A good evergreen creeping weeping plant for shade. Double white flowers. March to July. Small dark shiny leaves. Height 2–4 in (5–10 cm). Spread 3–4 ft (90 cm–1.2 m). Other varieties have blue or dark red single or double flowers and some have variegated leaves.*

T Hypericum × moseranum 'Tricolor' *(St John's Wort). Semi-evergreen. Green and white variegated leaves with red margins. This shrub will grow in any soil but will not tolerate shade. It has dazzling shiny yellow star-like flowers with a mass of golden stamens with orange anthers from June to September. This variety grows to 1 ft–18 in (30–45 cm) with the same spread. This is a sun-loving hypericum.*

Climbers
T Rose Mermaid. *Wonderful low-maintenance climber (almost evergreen especially in walled garden). Not prone to any of the usual rose pests. Delightful creamy yellow, single, open-faced flowers all summer. Fierce thorns but lovely shiny foliage. Rather vigorous and does not like regular pruning. Tolerates shade.*

Herbaceous

T Ranunculus ficaria 'Plena' *(Celandine). Very low-growing herbaceous hardy perennial. Masses of small bright yellow gold flowers in February/March. The leaves die away by June so can be grown under deciduous shrubs.*

T Miniature Daffodils 'Charity May'. *Grows to a height of 10 in (25 cm) and has pure yellow flowers in March/April.*

T White Pansies.
Crocus speciosus 'Albus'. *October flowering crocus.*

T Viola tricolor *(Heartsease). Sweet purple, yellow and violet flowers. Height 2–6 in (5–15 cm). Spread 8–12 in (20–30 cm). Flowers May to September.*

T Ranunculus aconitifolius. *Tuberous rooted perennial. Height 2 ft (60 cm). Spread 1 ft–18 in (30–45 cm). Mid-green leaves. Unusual border plant, likes half sun, half shade. A profusion of delicate small white flowers in May and June. Can be difficult to obtain.*

T Philadelphus 'Manteau d'Hermine' *(Dwarf mock orange blossom). Height 2–3 ft (60–90 cm). Spread 2–3 ft (60–90 cm). Tiny, double, heavily scented white flowers in June and July. Small, mid-green, prominently veined leaves cover this bushy shrub. Prefers sunny position.*

T Tiarella cordifolia *(Foam flower). Most useful evergreen perennial ground cover. Excellent in shade and beneath trees. Height 1 ft (30 cm). Slightly furry mid-green maple-shaped leaves which form clumps. Feathery white flowers on thin spikes from spring to summer. Shade-loving.*

One raised planter could be devoted to an alpine garden by adding rocks and pebbles (see *Alpines*) and small alpine plants can be planted in the joints of the brickwork providing the mortar has been omitted.

Plants for the **raised border**

T Convallaria majalis *(Lily of the valley). Hardy herbaceous perennial. Delightful sweet smelling small white flowers in May. Long slim mid-green leaf. Height 10 in (25 cm). Lily of the valley can be planted all along the low retaining wall beneath the Mermaid Rose. Lovely as cut flowers.*

Jasminum nudiflorum *(Winter Jasmine). Deciduous climber. Grows to 10 ft (3 m). Yellow flowers on naked green branches in winter to brighten up the dark months. Tiny oval green leaves.*

Forsythia suspensa. *Height 8–10 ft (2.5–3 m). Rambling shrub, excellent against a wall. Mid-green leaves. Yellow flowers March and April. Prune after flowering.*

Hedera helix 'Glacier' *(Variegated ivy) next to Forsythia. Vigorous grey leafed variegated ivy climber.*

Fritillaria imperialis 'Lutea' or 'Lutea Maxima' *(Crown Imperial). Impressive plant if you can stand the foxy smell of bulb when planting or when in flower each spring. Height 2–3 ft (60–90 cm). Long stout stems with terminal tufts of bright green slim leaves and yellow pendant bell-like flowers in early spring. For best results plant the bulbs on their side otherwise the water gets into the hollow crown and, if you are sensitive to smell, not too near the house!*

Other plants with white or yellow flowers for the disabled garden:
Nasturtium
Forsythia
Dogwood – *Cornus alba elegantissima*
Jasminum officinale
Cordon fruit trees
Camellias
Choisya
Bulbs *(cream and yellow tulips)*
Dwarf Azaleas *(white)*
Crown Imperial *(height 2 ft/60 cm) for under fruit trees*

12: *Georgian garden*

Whatever your dreams, it's good to have them and although everyone's dreams are different, if money were no object, children and pets did not need to be taken into consideration, and one lived in a world where afternoon tea was served on a silver tray, one might wish for a garden on the symmetrical and formal lines of this design. I drew this for a friend who sadly was gazumped on the house and the garden remained a drawing in a sketching pad. Not that I aspire or, I must hasten to add, wish to be a garden designer. Lynne Smith has beautifully designed nearly all the gardens in this book, and I remain in awe of her skill and craftsmanship. But it was nevertheless enjoyable creating this grandiose folly even if it was never constructed.

The garden, excluding the 30 ft by 70 ft (9 m by 21 m) terrace, was a walled garden 90 ft (27 m) deep and 70 ft (21 m) wide, a substantial amount of space for a Georgian town house garden.

The Garden

Standing on the terrace, the garden's formal shape with its blue and white planting scheme unfolds before you and your eye is immediately drawn to the fountain on the far side of the two large upright stone urns with yuccas or cordylines growing in them, with camellias planted on the right where they do not get morning sun and other flowering shrubs on the left. Built against the back wall which is covered with *Magnolia grandiflora*, wisteria and 'Bobbie James' climbing roses, a half pagoda in the centre dominates the far end of the garden. Three crescent-moon stone steps lead to the throne-like sitting area where table and chairs are set out under the green copper or lead canopy roof and look out over the bold stone fountain in the circular pond, edged by stone and surrounded by a low box hedge in the middle of the garden itself. The fountain makes a strong focal point and helps to screen the garden beyond.

On either side of the fountain, against the wall, are two huge mirrors framed by a classical trellis arch giving the impression the garden has more width than it actually has, and creating the illusion that one can leave the garden and walk beyond its four walls. The mirror also reflects the fountain and adds yet another dimension to the garden. The four busts, each placed on a 3 ft (90 cm) column entwined with ivy, stand elegantly on either side of the mirror, punctuating the arbour with architecture rather than horticulture. These statues or busts make an even stronger statement when lit at night.

The herring-bone brick path that weaves round the fountain marries the four areas together. The path starts at the top of the steps at the entrance to the garden proper and continues between the jardinières, round to the first sitting area on the left in front of the first mirror which enjoys the morning sun, then on to the pagoda to catch the majority of the sun from midday onwards, finally arriving at the third sitting area in front of the second mirror, where you can watch the sun set behind the trees. As dusk envelops the garden you can admire it being dramatically transformed by lighting when the busts or statues, pagoda, fountain and plants will all take on a new dimension.

The Terrace

The basket-weave brick terrace near the house has a traditional elegance all of its own, the detail on either side creating interest in areas which otherwise could be confining brick walls. Again a tall arch is created with a *trompe l'oeil* trellis and statue, or small bay tree, or half-standard rose, or flowering shrub planted in a stone jardinière in front. The small, raised, curved brick flower bed at the bottom of the trellis, is filled with variegated *Euonymus fortunei* periwinkle cascading over the edge of the brick work with sweet-smelling jasmine and *Felicité et perpétue* rambler rose growing on the wall round the arch, but leaving the *trompe l'oeil* trellis with the urn and shrub in front. A selection of stone jardinières are arranged around the terrace with sweet-smelling summer bedding plants and half-standard 'The Fairy' rose, introducing pink into this area of the garden. The quiet colour scheme of the rest of the garden is white and cream with a little blue introduced here and there to soften the edges.

GEORGIAN WALLED GARDEN
Walled Garden with Copper Roof Pagoda
White and blue colour scheme with a little pink introduced on the terrace near the house. See back of book for more details.
T = *Trouble free*

Trees
T Magnolia grandiflora 'Goliath'. *To grow up the back wall on either side of the pagoda. Magnificent slow growing evergreen shrub. Grows to 20 ft (6 m) or more but can grow much taller in the south of France or Italy. Best against a sheltered wall. Glossy dark green leaves with felty brown undersides. Very large waxy creamy white pungently scented flowers between July and September.*
or
T Betula pendula 'Tristis' *(Weeping birch). White bark. Tall and narrow with pendant branches. Yellowish green catkins in spring. Small light green leaves which flutter in the breeze and make this appear a very 'light' tree. Height 25 ft (8 m).*

or
T Eucalyptus niphophila. *Can grow to 30 ft (9 m). Soft grey evergreen leaves. This fast-growing tree looks good in all seasons and the leaves are excellent for cutting for flower arrangements. Develops an attractive white trunk with age. Needs sunny position.*

T Ginkgo biloba *(Maiden hair tree). Primitive slow-growing deciduous tree. Eventual height 50 ft (15 m plus). Spread 10 ft (3 m). Small leathery fan-shaped pale green leaves in spring, turning darker in the summer and golden in the autumn.*
or
Ficus carica, Moraceae *(Fig). A good tree to grow against a south-facing wall in a sheltered garden. They are not strictly low-maintenance as they need to be pruned and trained if growing against a wall. They add a period elegance to a garden, in the same way a* Ginkgo *or* Magnolia grandiflora *do.*

continued on p. 80

GEORGIAN WALLED GARDEN *(continued)*

Many trees and shrubs have a modern look, so in a Georgian garden 'old' trees help to give a garden atmosphere. If the fig is planted against a sheltered wall it can survive in the north. Height 8–10 ft (2.5–3 m). Spread 12–15 ft (3.5–4.5 m). But a free-growing bush will grow in the south to 12–15 ft (3.5–4.5 m) and spread 8–10 ft (2.5–3 m). Dark green glossy leaves. The fig tree will look interestingly gnarled after its leaves have fallen each autumn.

T *Syringa vulgaris 'Katherine Havemeyer' (Lilac). Hardy deciduous late-flowering shrub. Height 8–12 ft (2.5–3.5 m). Spread 5–8 ft (1.5–2.5 m). Strongly scented double purple/lavender flowers in May. Or, S.v. 'Vestale', which has single white flowers in late May. Prefers sunny position.*

Shrubs
Carpenteria californica. Quite hardy evergreen shrub. Can grow to 6 ft (1.8 m). Spread 5–8 ft (1.5–2.5 m). Glossy dark green leaves and pure white single open-faced poppy-like flowers in June and July. Most attractive plant when in bloom. Accepts hard pruning from time to time. Needs sunny position.

T *Viburnum plicatum tomentosum 'Mariesii'. Stunning white flowering deciduous shrub. Height 6 ft (1.8 m). Spread up to 10 ft (3 m). Horizontal tiered growth which becomes a mass of 2–3 in (5–7.5 cm) flat heads of white long-remaining flowers in May. One of the most handsome of the wonderful viburnum family! Tolerates sun or shade. The leaves often go reddish purple in October. Plant as a feature.*

Hydrangea macrophylla 'Blue Wave' (Lace cap hydrangea). Deciduous shrub. Height and spread 5 ft (1.5 m). Mid green leaves. Pretty delicate flat florets of blue sterile flowers 4 in (10 cm) across in June. (Needs acid soil to remain blue). Best in shade.

Hydrangea villosa (Lace cap). Deciduous shrub, up to 6 ft (1.8 m) tall and rather upright. Large, rough, mid-green leaves and lace-cap heads with blue florets even on alkaline soil. Needs good soil and half shade.

Skimmia japonica 'Fragrans' and 'Foremanii'. Excellent hardy evergreen dark leafed shade-loving shrub. Slow-growing. Height 3–4 ft (90 cm–1.2 m). Spread 4–5 ft (1.2–1.5 m). Cream white fragrant flowers in spring followed by red berries on female plants.

T *Itea ilicifolia. Evergreen shrub, holly-like leaves. Masses of long drooping racemes, rather catkin-like produced in late summer, pale green flowers. Height 6 ft (1.8 m).*

T *Garrya elliptica 'James Roof' (Silk tassel bush). Evergreen shrub. Can grow to 8–10 ft (2.5–3 m) and spread 6–12 ft (1.8–3.5 m). Male form is laden with 9–12 in (22.5–30 cm) long catkins in February/March. Thick leathery grey/green leaves. Ideal in walled garden as it is vulnerable to very cold winters. Shade-loving.*
   The two plants above will complement each other as one set of catkins will be followed by another.

T *Hebe andersonii 'Variegata'. Evergreen flowering shrub. Height 3 ft (90 cm). Spread 2–3 ft (60–90 cm). Lavender flowers 3–5 in (7.5–12.5 cm) long from June to October. Leathery cream and mid green leaves. Not very hardy but easy to root from cuttings in summer. Sunny position.*

T *Euonymus fortunei 'Silver Queen'. Evergreen shrub. Glossy, very white and very green leaves. Height 2 ft (60 cm). Spread 5 ft (1.5 m). Most useful and attractive creeping ground cover. Small greeny white flowers in May/June. (Will climb a wall or look really good growing through a dark conifer.)*

GEORGIAN WALLED GARDEN (*continued*)

T Lavandula spica (*Lavender*). *Hardy evergreen shrub. Height 1–2 ft (30–60 cm). Spread 2–3 ft (60–90 cm). Aromatic grey/green oblong leaves and blue/purple fragrant flowers July to September. Replace every 6 to 10 years. Cut back last year's growth only each year to keep it bushy.*

T Cordyline (*Cabbage palm*). *Striking plant for stone urn and surrounded by variegated* Vinca *or* Osteospermum ecklonis. *Evergreen palm-like shrub. (Needs to have its spiky long slim mid-green leaves tied up in winter to protect it from the frost.) Or Yucca which is a hardy evergreen and has a slightly less attractive spiky habit than Cordyline, but a Yucca does not need to be protected from the frost.*

Climbers
Wisteria floribunda 'Alba'. *To grow over the copper roof of the pagoda. (Not suitable over a slate roof as its vigorous growth soon works its way under the slates and causes expensive damage unless it is kept well under control.) Twining climber, not as vigorous as the blue variety. White flowers appear April/May before mid green foliage has unfurled. Can grow to 25–30 ft (8–9 m) against a wall.*

T Rosa 'Bobbie James' (*Rambler*). *For back wall. Vigorous rambler. Grows to 25 ft (8 m). Glossy pale green leaves. Large clusters of semi-double small white flowers with yellow stamens in June and July. Prefers sunny position. Beautiful fragrance. Or* 'Alberic Barbier', *another excellent rambler with some flowers in autumn. Tolerates shade or sun.*

T Hedera colchica 'Dentata Variegata' (*Persian Ivy*). *Handsome large-leafed variegated vigorous ivy to climb round the column of the statues and up the wall. Can climb up wall to 20–30 ft (6–9 m) if you let it. Vigorous and easy once established.*

T Jasminum officinale Affine. *Hardy deciduous twining climber. Can grow to 30 ft (9 m). Small mid-green leaves. Scented white flowers June to October. Most undemanding plant and will quickly clothe a wall. Prefers sun for more flowers.*

T Clematis macropetala. *Grows to 12 ft (3.5 m). Drooping, starry, blue flowers on old wood May/ June so doesn't need cutting back. Tolerates shade or sun.*

T Hydrangea petiolaris. *Near the house. Can grow to 30 ft (9 m) on a suitable wall. Excellent, undemanding, self-clinging climbing hydrangea on moist wall; otherwise it needs ties to keep it on target. White flowers all summer. Mid to dark green leaves with brown flaky stems. Prefers shade. Easy plant to prune.*

T Rosa 'Félicité et Perpétue' (*Climbing rose*). *Reliable rambler. Handsome rose in June and July. Clusters of small white flowers, each a perfect rosette, buds tinged with red before they open. Glossy dark green leaves. Splendid on a north wall. Therefore ideal to go over the trellis mixed with jasmine in the alcoves on either side of the terrace. Grows to 15 ft (4.5 m). This rose prefers little or no pruning. Hard pruning will result in less flowers. Cut out old stems to the ground when they do not flower well. Tolerates shade or sun.*

T Camellia × williamsii 'Francis Hanger', *with single white flowers which start in November and continue till April, shiny dark green leaves and upright growth to about 6 or 8 ft (1.8–2.5 m), are also excellent plants for this garden. This is a true low maintenance plant as its flowers fall when they fade, but camellias do not like to be planted where they get the early morning sun. They must have an acid soil that is not too heavy but retains moisture in summer. Top dress camellia roots each autumn with peat.*

continued over page

above: Another good value continuous flowering rose, 'The Fairy'.
left: Carpenteria californica *flourishes in this sunny protected corner.*

GEORGIAN WALLED GARDEN (*continued*)

Herbaceous

T Euphorbia characias wulfenii. *Magnificent sub-shrub. Hardy (in sheltered position). Height and spread 2–4 ft (60 cm–1.2 m). Masses of grey/green leaves on semi-woody stems. Tall spikes of greenish yellow bracts in winter and spring. This is more than just a plant. This decorative species is a statement and has a tremendous impact when in flower.*

T Stachys lanata *(Lambs' tongues). Hardy herbaceous perennial. Mat forming spreading habit. Height 1 ft to 18 in (30–45 cm). Soft grey/green hairy or woolly leaves. Woolly spikes of purple flowers in July. Good summer ground cover and ideal at front of border.*

T Alchemilla mollis *(Ladies' Mantle). Charming perennial which makes excellent summer ground cover. Vigorous plant once established. Light green flat leaves. Tiny star-shaped yellowish green flowers June to August. Height 1 ft–18 in (30–45 cm). Easily divided. Can seed itself and may become too big. Tolerates shade or sun.*

Zantedeschia aethiopica 'Crowborough' *(Arum lily). (Either side of the pagoda steps.) Hardy bulbous plant. Needs moist soil. Large white upward-facing trumpet flowers, height 2 ft (60 cm). Evergreen leaves (except in severe winter conditions). Handsome flowers from March to June. Prefers a sunny position.*

T Hosta sieboldiana 'Elegans' *and* Hosta fortunei 'Aureomarginata'. *Hardy herbaceous perennial. Excellent shade-loving, summer grown cover with attractive foliage.*
H.s. 'Elegans' – *height 2 ft (60 cm). Large blue/grey leaves. Pale lilac flowers from July to August.*
H.s. 'Aureomarginata' *(long stalked hosta). Grey/green leaf with narrow gold edge. Lilac flowers July. Tolerates sun or shade – always good value.*

T Campanula carpatica 'White Star'. *Low-growing hardy perennial. Mid-green leaves. Height 8–12 in (20–30 cm). Spread 12–15 in (30–40 cm). Ideal for the front of a border. Pure white flowers in June and July. Prefers sun.*

T Convallaria majalis *(Lily of the valley). Hardy herbaceous perennial. Delightful sweet smelling small white flowers in May. Slim darkish-green leaf. Height 10 in (25 cm). The lily of the valley is a joy and a surprise each year. The leaves are slow to die down. Prefers shady position.*

Tulipa turkestanica. *Wild species from central Asia. Grows to 8 in (20 cm). Narrow grey leaves. Small white flowers with yellow centre and green tinge (needs sunny position and good drainage), and* Tulipa Schnoord. *Lovely double white early flowering tulip. Height 12–15 in (30–40 cm). Grey/green leaves.*

T Nepeta faassenii (sometimes listed as mussinii) 'Six Hills Giant'. *This wonderful perennial is a must in any border. Its haze of blue/lilac flowers from May to September grows to 18–24 in (45–60 cm) and can spread as far or more in good soil. The grey/green leaves remain throughout mild winters.*

Anemone japonica or elegans 'Honorine Jobert' or 'White Queen' (Japanese anemone) *Herbaceous perennial. White flowers shoot up from nothing to 4 ft (1.2 m) to flower on long stalks in late summer.*

T Polygonatum multiflorum *(Solomon's Seal). Elegant herbaceous perennial. Excellent in the shade. Height 2–4 ft (60 cm–1.2 m). Oblong mid-green leaves on arching stems, with drooping white flowers along the stem in clusters in June. Shade loving.*

continued over page

GEORGIAN WALLED GARDEN (*continued*)

Iris sibirica 'Blue King' *(Beardless Iris). Grows to 3–4 ft (90 cm – 1.2 m). Mid-green evergreen leaves in solid clumps. Blue flowers mid-June. Also* Iris pallida dalmatica 'Argenteo Variegata' *(Tall bearded iris). Dark blue flowers June/July. Plant in sun. Grey/blue leaves with white stripes.*

T Geranium 'Johnson's Blue'. *Hardy herbaceous perennial. Grows to 8 in (20 cm). Excellent summer ground cover. Soft blue flowers May to October. Delicate mid-green leaves. Useful hardworking and pretty plant.*

T Pulmonaria saccharata *or* P.s. 'Argentea'. *Hardy herbaceous perennial. Dramatic plant. Shade tolerant. Large green leaves with white/silver blotches on it. White/sky blue flowers in March/ April. Grows to 1 ft (30 cm).*

T Helleborus niger *(Christmas Rose), appealing evergreen, shade-loving ground cover with white flowers from December to March.*

For the terrace:
T *Half standard rose* 'The Fairy' *in large container.* Ivy *and* Aubretia *planted round the base and under planted with spring bulbs.* 'The Fairy' *is a late flowering modern shrub rose with tiny dark green leaves. Flowering starts and finishes later than most roses. Sprays of small soft pink flowers.*

Underplant the beds with clumps of hardy miniature cyclamen 'atkinsii', snowdrops, grape hyacinths, narcissi and other white and blue bulbs.

13: *The garden mistake*

Mistakes can easily be made by taking the wrong decisions at planning stage, and I have been guilty of a few myself when aiming for a quick and inexpensive garden conversion on an addition to our cottage.

The result was that the economy was false and the low maintenance aspect of the garden totally unsuccessful; and if that wasn't bad enough, the garden looked very dull and it was an extremely hard area for which to find plants, as the beds were so tiny nothing would squeeze in them.

So I was left with no option but to cram into the 'cracks' (masquerading as beds) small plants like pansies or London Pride (*Saxifraga umbrosa*) as very little else would fit. It was even difficult to plant climbing plants as the space was so small. Had I planned the beds only 9 in (22.5 cm) wider, as advised, it would have made all the difference.

As it is, the lines are straight and unimaginative with pencil-slim beds. It was only due to my own stubbornness that the beds were so narrow; I imagined in the early days of my passion for low maintenance gardening that the smaller the beds, the easier they would be to manage.

But this was not the case. Firstly, the small beds were at the expense of decent trouble-free plants and, secondly, maintaining such narrow beds can be labour-intensive in itself, especially if you wish them to grow something more than London Pride, pansies and bulbs. Therefore to bring variety you are obliged to plant summer bedding plants each spring and then live with the garden being without interest or colour in the winter.

Pointing out the Faults

As you look into the garden from the house, the steps are too small, the run of bricks so close to the tiny beds it is lost, and the straight lines confining and uninteresting. The overall impression is unimaginative and claustrophobic.

But *if* the beds on either side had been irregular with two square inlets or a circle in the middle, the planting would have been much easier and the view from the kitchen window altogether better, as all the paving would not have been presented at once. It also would have been a more pleasant place to spend a sunny Sunday afternoon. Added to which the large variety of trouble-free and pleasing plants that could have been planted in the garden (had the beds been wider) would have made the garden a more attractive extension of the house.

In the end to 'cover over the cracks' and hide the 'desolate' square concrete look, I have planted and let run wild *Campanula portenschlagiana* between the concrete paving slabs, and bergenia to break up the straightness of the lines of the beds. The bergenia had to be planted when the leaves were one sixth of their full size in order to get them in and the camellia and hydrangea have to 'lean' out of the bed to get sunlight and air

The garden mistake: narrow beds and unimaginative straight lines, resulting in false economy; above: campanula has run wild, disguising the square concrete look (photo above by Susan Hampshire).

as they had to be planted so close to the wall. If it wasn't for the garden furniture and the climbers, the terracotta pots and the vigorous campanula now growing everywhere, the garden would be pretty desolate.

Unwisely, I ignored the constructing landscaper's advice and opted for economy at all costs. I am glad to say I have learnt by these mistakes.

So:

1. Don't rush plans.
2. Don't cut corners without considering the long term effects.
3. Do the garden in stages if you can't afford everything you want at the same time.

The importance of Latin names: either of these plants could be described as a shrubby cinquefoil. The one on the left is Potentilla fruticosa 'Red Ace' *(photo by Pamla Toler), the other is* Potentilla glabra.

Latin Names

Many of the plant names seem so long and complicated one wonders why we can't all use the plant's 'common name'. Unfortunately the only *certain* way to identify a plant accurately is by using its *Latin name*; the common name is too vague and unreliable. It's not just that expert gardeners and horticulturists use the Latin names to show off (although there are a fair number of them who do), they use them because the Latin name is *precise*.

I have always been terrified of Latin plant names myself, and I have put up much resistance to calling plants by them, although I appreciate that if I go into a garden centre and ask for a *shrubby cinquefoil*, not many of the assistants will know what it is. There are many varieties of potentilla, so if what I want is a *Potentilla fruticosa Longacre* and I only ask for potentilla, I could land up with *Potentilla Kathleen Dykes* which grows over 3 ft (1 m) high and is tall and slim – not at all like a *Potentilla fruticosa Longacre* that has a mat habit and spreads to over 3 ft (1 m) wide!

14: *Year-at-a-Glance Calendar*

JANUARY	FEBRUARY	MARCH
Make New Year's Resolutions Prune fruit trees	Prune roses Renew cat protection (*Renardine*) *See page 157*	Prune late summer flowering shrubs Mulch *see page 134* Plant container grown shrubs ■ (best time)

JULY	AUGUST	SEPTEMBER
Order bulbs Prune flowering cherries, roses (summer prune)	Keep watering! Cut lavender heads after flowering	Cut meadow grass of wild life garden Final weed

■ Important

★ not including paved garden

APRIL	MAY	JUNE
Feed *see page 135* Weed First grass cut★ Cut woody herbs and lavender. Do not cut into old wood of lavender	Plant up tubs, pots, urns and window boxes with summer bedding ■ *See page 119* (except Wild Life garden)	Prune spring flowering shrubs after flowering Water and feed to September especially tubs, pots, window boxes and newly planted trees and shrubs ■

OCTOBER	NOVEMBER	DECEMBER
Plant bulbs	Tidy garden (leaves) Plant trees, shrubs and roses Cut herbs	Top dress shallow rooted plants and tubs for winter protection, such as camellias and azaleas Plant trees

The rest of the book concentrates on the practicalities of making a trouble-free garden: the nitty gritty of how to plant, what plants to choose, selecting an object to create a feature, lighting, paving, fencing, planting on a slope, etc.

Plant association and the natural structure of the woodland, which is the basis of trouble-free gardening, shows the logic behind the choice of plants chosen for the garden designs and for the plant lists suitable for a 'little work' garden.

Not everyone will wish to design, plan and build a whole garden from scratch. But some of you may wish to rethink your planting scheme and include a higher percentage of trouble-free plants in your garden. Should this be the case, you will find a choice of suitable plants ranging from ground cover to shade-loving plants all listed in the plant section at the back of the book.

15: Plant association

If you mix trees, shrubs, herbaceous plants (perennials) and bulbs together you can cover up the ground in *layers* from the trees down, as with the natural structure of the woodland. This creates growing conditions for other plants and when you have plants of varying heights, you can have really attractive planting schemes. 'Ground cover' on its own tends to be all the same height and rather boring.

Plants naturally thrive at the different levels in the conditions created by the taller plants and this is the essence of the trouble-free garden. In a dense wood or on a tree-covered bank there may be only ivy on the ground as it is the only plant that thrives in the low light conditions. But in a more open wood there will be tall shrubs, brambles, herbaceous plants and bulbs. By choosing the right plants you can have them happily growing together, in the way that they have been selected for sections of each garden.

The main objective when choosing plants for a 'little work' garden is to have every inch of the soil surface covered by plants. That way there is no room for weeds. Plants and mixes of plants that need no more than an annual trim, prune or tidy up, mulch and feed are ideal. The plants that naturally keep the weeds down tend to be thick and bushy or to run underground with a dense network of roots and a mat display of foliage or spreading branches.

If the plants are not *carefully* chosen to mix well together (see plant guide for each garden design), they will grow into each other and the more vigorous ones will eventually take over. As illustrated in several of the garden layouts, one way to keep one plant from overtaking another is by laying paving stones or runs of bricks between them. This gives a formal effect dominated by the paving or bricks.

So each plant needs to be distinct in foliage, habit or flower in its own right. A large number of plants have quite a different pattern in winter: there are shrubs that are evergreen or deciduous; and some herbaceous plants die right down to the ground in autumn while others keep a cover of leaves just above the ground. These evergreen herbaceous plants are very useful to keep the earth covered in the winter months when many gardens tend to look bare.

Epimediums have nice leathery leaves while comfrey (*Symphytum*) and some cranesbills (geraniums) have soft, furry leaves. *Lamium* (deadnettles) have a white stripe down the centre of the leaf and the leaves of the variety Beacon Silver are silvery white. These are good spreaders as ground cover. Some plants which form a clump, such as hellebores, need to have several planted close together so that they join up when the clumps get bigger. Their leaves are large and fingered so they make an interesting contrast to the other plants.

Trees

One or two trees in a small garden give a feeling of height and space, but choose upright growing varieties. A spreading tree will dominate the garden and give much less chance to vary the planting beneath. (See *How to Plant a Tree.*)

In a large garden a clump of three or more trees will provide a shaded spot where shade-tolerant shrubs and perennials such as bergenia, hostas, sarcococcas and Solomon's seal can be planted.

THE NATURAL STRUCTURE OF WOODLAND

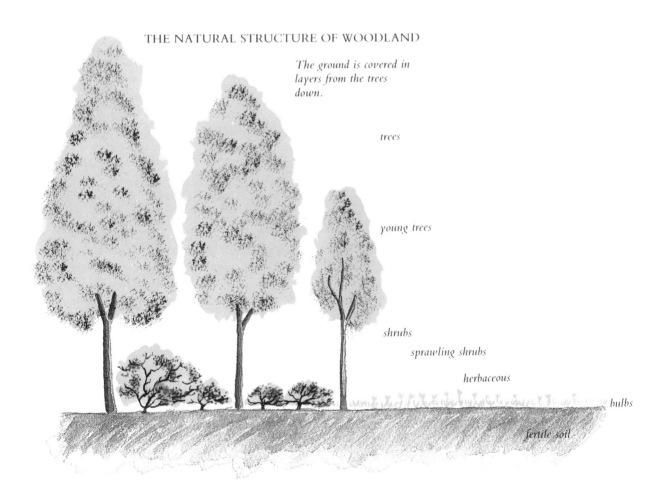

The ground is covered in layers from the trees down.

trees

young trees

shrubs

sprawling shrubs

herbaceous

bulbs

fertile soil

Shrubs

Really dense shrubs such as choisya (Mexican orange blossom), *Viburnum plicatum Mariesii*, hydrangeas, spreading junipers (*Juniperus pfitzerana* types), *Lonicera pileata* (shrubby honeysuckle) and *Cotoneaster salicifolius 'Repens'* do not really allow anything to grow under them except perhaps snowdrops under hydrangeas and viburnum, both of which are deciduous. Early flowering bulbs like snowdrops die down before the shrub comes into leaf and create a solid mass of foliage which makes the ground below too dark for the weeds to get a chance!

Then there are the more open shrubs that need herbaceous plants under them to keep the weeds down, as their open habit lets more light through and weeds can easily get established. Some are upright shrubs and can be used in contrast. Buddleias, for example, have upright growth that arches over later in the summer. Lilacs develop a bare stem as they get older, as do most varieties of Japanese maple. Really upright shrubs like Viburnum Dawn and Pereskia can have low shrubs around them as well as herbaceous plants.

Herbaceous Plants

The following herbaceous plants all tolerate some shade and can be found in the plant lists. Like most plants from woodland habitats, they are early flowering. The really easy plant to use (for a leafy cover) is the cranesbill *Geranium macrorrhizum*. It is about 8 in (20 cm) high and has pink, purplish or white flowers in May. You can select the flower colour by choosing the right varieties. The foam flower *Tiarella cordifolia* has a mat of leaves about 4 in (10 cm) high and masses of plumes of creamy white flowers that look light and frothy. *Symphytum grandiflorum* (comfrey), which flowers in spring and is good for compost, has a slightly taller spread of larger leaves and ivory bells in spikes that fall between the leaves. These plants really do look after themselves, once established. They do not even need the dead flower heads removing and the autumn leaves quickly rot down into the soil and leave a fair cover of fresh green leaves on them for the winter.

The herbaceous plants recommended in this book look after themselves and make attractive clumps with foliage down to the ground. Peonies, *Dictamnus* (burning bush), *Euphorbia polychroma* and *griffithii* are good, solid plants that are long-lived, and the tall grass *Miscanthus sinensis* and its colourful leaved varieties are also easy. Michaelmas daisies tend to wander a bit so unless you want them everywhere they should not be planted without thought.

The next layer, if you wished to imitate the natural structure of the woodland in plant association, would be bulbs, those undemanding darlings who require little and give so much.

16: *Bulbs*

One of the moments that gives me the greatest pleasure in our garden is in late spring, after the garden has rested for the winter and is suddenly awoken with a dazzling display of spring bulbs. The narcissi and daffodils are heralded by the earlier awakening of the snowdrops in February, and, in the sheltered tubs, hyacinths, grape hyacinths and tulips. Bulbs are the ultimate in low maintenance and a wonderful beginning to the flowering months to come.

Bulbs are so good-natured and undemanding: providing they have a yearly feed *after* they have flowered in spring, and their leaves are left to die down for six weeks before they are cut, they are absolutely no trouble.

In smaller gardens, the smaller daffodil is appropriate and it may be a good idea to choose shorter, early flowering varieties for planting in grass. February Gold is a wonderful one that spreads fairly rapidly, although I have only once or twice seen it in flower by the last day in February! Its cousin February Silver has pale yellow outer petals and does not spread rapidly (which means it is more expensive to buy). Jack Snipe and W. P. Milner also fill the bill.

The taller varieties are probably best in beds and borders, set back a bit so that the spring growth of the plants in front covers up the dying foliage. Plant them where they get *full sun* before the other plants come into leaf, and not in the shade of a dense evergreen or they won't flower more than once.

Large daffodils such as King Alfred (deep golden yellow), Magnet (creamy white) and Ice Follies (pure white with a large flat yellow crown) are all lovely planted in the grass in a large space. But in well-drained soil the shorter late-flowering Jonquilla, a 12 in (30 cm) narcissus and Minnow, a small 10 in (25 cm) daffodil with delicate pink and light yellow blooms, are delightful.

For the back of a border Crown Imperials (*Fritillaria imperialis*) grow to 3 ft (90 cm) and make a magnificent show each spring as their great clusters of yellow or orange flowers tower above the other plants. Crown Imperials are better planted individually about 12 in (30 cm) apart. (Their corms have a very strong and unusual, foxy smell.)

Snowdrops are very appealing in grass or under deciduous shrubs. They should be planted just after flowering while still in leaf. Dry bulbs are rarely successful, so if you cannot find a specialist nursery that sells them 'in the green', beg some from a friend's garden. It is quite safe to split them up into individual bulbs when planting, and they will multiply each year. You can go on and on dividing the clumps until you have a 'carpet' of snowdrops to herald the spring.

The sight of crocuses never fills me with anything more than faint admiration, although I appreciate that when little else is in flower and they appear in their hundreds in the park they do look wonderful. So providing you choose the colours the birds don't eat and plant them on a well-drained lawn or in the *front* of a border where their narrow leaves are not too obtrusive when they die down, they are worth

Cyclamen hederifolium, *an excellent plant for underplanting, giving autumn and winter colour (photo by Pamla Toler).*

the little effort needed to plant them. The early flowering winter crocuses are more elegant than the spring flowering hybrids.

One of the loveliest of bulbs is the lily of the valley (*Convallaria*). In France on the first of May they give bunches of 'muguet' (lily of the valley) or muguet plants in the same way here we give camellia plants or bunches of flowers on Mother's Day. The sweet smell and delicate white flowers of the lily of the valley are a delightful asset to any garden when they flower in late April or early May. They benefit from a good covering of peat, mulch, leaf mould or organic matter in the autumn and their leaves take a long time to die down. But they are lovely in the garden and delightful if picked to have in the house. *And*, like snowdrops, they multiply and multiply all on their own.

For the undiscerning, the root system of the lily of the valley is not dissimilar to that of ground elder, and I made the mistake of asking a novice gardener to weed a bed in which there was ground elder and where the lily of the valley had died down. I regret to say he managed to pull up hundreds of yards of lily of the valley roots and leave the ground elder intact. 'Cleared that for you,' he said happily as he pushed the wheelbarrow full of the roots of one of my favourite spring bulbs towards me. So I had to weed the bed and replant the lily of the valley roots myself.

But bulbs don't begin and end with daffodils, hyacinths, tulips, bluebells (*Scilla*) and other bulbs that flower in the spring. There are the wonderful lilies such as the hardy *Lilium macklinae* and the sweet-smelling *Lilium regale*, both of which flower in June and July.

Crinium powellii is a majestic bulb and bears beautiful autumn flowers if planted in a sheltered spot at the base of a wall where it is well protected.

The cyclamen, which flowers from October to March, is yet another splendid bulb, and the ever-useful bergenia flowers twice a year, is evergreen, trouble-free, shade-loving, wonderful ground cover beneath shrubs and attractive when planted to overlap on to paving stones or bricks. Bulbs that are ideal for planting under shrubs include the spring flowering aconite (*Eranthis*), *Anemone blanda* which has blue flowers and *Chionodoxa gigantea*, bright blue flowers. All die back until they reappear to glorify the ground without a grumble the following year.

Bulbs are a large and wonderful family and not to be overlooked.

17: *Alpines*

Whether you plant alpines in a terracotta dish or old sink, or make a special feature of them in a rockery, they will be the source of great pleasure with a unique and irresistible charm, as long as you choose the right combination and plant them in *well-drained* soil.

Alpines will not do well in dark, damp areas of the garden: that is one reason why old sinks or troughs placed on the terrace are so popular. This way you can position the trough where it can get the most sun. Should you plant up the sink from scratch, you can guarantee it is well drained by putting a good 2–3 in (6–7.5 cm) layer of broken crocks and shingle at the bottom of the trough before adding sandy, well-drained earth.

If you already have a rockery in the garden, before planting any alpines, make sure the soil between the stones is deep enough, otherwise these small plants will not be able to send out shoots, which sometimes go several feet (a metre or more) deep if the soil allows.

To create interest among your alpine plants, select one or two taller plants to give height amount the low-growing ones. *Juniperus communis compressa* is a splendid choice as it is very slow-growing and does not reach more than 1 ft (30 cm) high. Another good plant for adding height and interest is the spiky-leaved *sisyrynchium* which grows between 6–12 in (15–30 cm) and has a charming white summer flower.

It is important in a small space not to mix fast-growing alpines such as *alyssum*, *aubrietia* and *helianthemums* with slow-growing ones, otherwise they will completely take over and the slow-growing plants will be smothered, but the above fast-growing alpines are ideal planted beneath the taller alpines mentioned earlier. While a rockery is establishing itself there are many places for the weeds to get a hold, so put in a few *vigorous* plants to cover the soil.

If you want to admire a variety of alpines it is wise to grow them in a sink or trough near the house. A well-planted trough or sink can last for ten years or more provided it has sandy soil, proper drainage and the plants are well selected with all slow-growing ones together.

How to Plant up a Trough

1. Make sure there are good drainage holes at the bottom of your sink or trough before planting.
2. Fill the bottom of the trough with 1–2 in (2.5–5 cm) of old crocks and small stones.
3. Add sandy, well-drained soil up to the level of the top of the trough.
4. Make a mound of soil in the middle or at the side of the trough (so when the plants have grown the mound creates interest and the planting isn't flat).
5. Plant a selection of slow-growing alpines with one or two taller alpines for focal points in between.

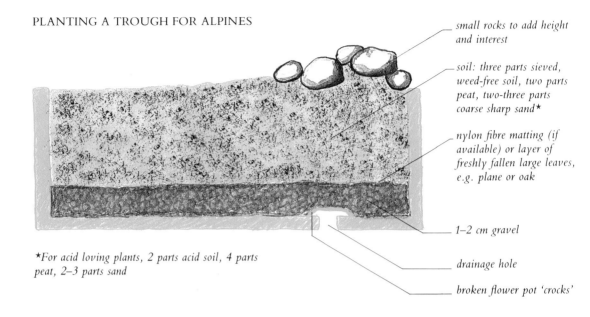

small rocks to add height and interest

soil: three parts sieved, weed-free soil, two parts peat, two-three parts coarse sharp sand★

nylon fibre matting (if available) or layer of freshly fallen large leaves, e.g. plane or oak

1–2 cm gravel

drainage hole

broken flower pot 'crocks'

★For acid loving plants, 2 parts acid soil, 4 parts peat, 2–3 parts sand

6. Add a few largish stones or small rocks in the soil to make the whole arrangement look part of a landscape.
7. Fill the areas round the plants with grit, pea shingle or stone chippings to prevent weeds and give the trough a stylish finish until the plants have grown enough to cover the whole surface.

Terracotta Dishes

The same instructions in smaller proportions go for shallow terracotta dishes. For best results choose a dish that is at least 12–18 in (30–45 cms) across and 5–6 in (12.5–15 cm) deep. The wider the better. When planted up, a dish that is 2 ft (60 cm) across looks stunning if placed on the ground or table in the conservatory or on top of a waist-level shed. You'll have years of pleasure for very little trouble. Good luck!

ALPINES
Some of the easier Alpines worth consideration are:

Sempervivum tectorum *(house leek) slow-growing*
Dryas octopetala *(mountain avens)*
Geranium Ballerina

Campanula carpatica *varieties*
Saponaria ocymoides *(alpine soap wort)*
Polygonum affine *'Dimity'*
Phlox subulata *(moss phlox) – lots of varieties*
Dianthus *'Little Jock' (pink alpine) and other varieties*
Thymus *(Thyme) – lots of varieties*

18: Ground cover

To better understand the nature and function of ground cover plants, you have only to walk in the Alps of Austria or Switzerland. It was on such a walk in the Austrian Tyrol that I first saw many of our cultivated varieties growing wild.

In their natural habitat not an inch of ground is left uncovered and there are stunning carpets of potentilla and late flowering azalea (stone rose), which are much smaller than when cultivated. These grow cheek by jowl beneath the trees with shade-loving hellebores whose delicate flowers appear before the snow has melted and *Hypericum* (St John's wort), whose flowers and leaves are also much smaller and prettier than the many cultivated varieties, all proving that Nature herself is an inspired gardener.

Reliable and undemanding spring and summer ground cover plants such as *Alchemilla mollis*, campanulas and geraniums have their delicate leaves and blue flowers fluttering in the breeze, together with violets, anemones, *Sedum* and evergreen *Ajuga reptans*.

Nature doesn't plan unimaginatively; she arranges luscious sweeps of colour and variety in the shape of the leaf. The balance between the vigorous, such as oxeye daisies and marjoram, and more delicate plants like pansies, violets, cornflowers, wild strawberries, forget-me-nots, cats paw, cowslips, auriculas and lilies of the valley, is controlled naturally. In the summer the cows are taken up into the high meadow to graze where they keep down the more vigorous plants and grass, allowing the smaller and more beautiful to continue growing.

But now that milk is so plentiful the danger is that only horses will be put out to pasture in the high alpine meadows and that many wild varieties will become extinct. The horses' teeth will rip up the more delicate plants and leave only the tougher grasses, *Erica* (heather) and saxifrages.

One of the keys to keeping the work in the garden down to a minimum is having a good selection of hardy ground cover plants. Ground cover is usually fairly vigorous (sometimes too vigorous!) and will quickly cover the earth under trees and shrubs and save you a lot of weeding. Ground cover plants are either evergreen or perennials which die down in winter. But you need to choose the correct plant for the spot as some ground cover plants do better in the sun and others in the shade.

Hardy ground cover such as *Geranium endressii 'Wargrave Pink'* and *Diascia rigescens* and *Diascia vigilis* which are not quite so hardy, is particularly pretty; these plants have charming flowers, bright pink and dark pink respectively. They flower all through the summer then die down each winter.

The flowers of some of the other ground cover plants are insignificant but they have leaves that are colourful and interesting the year round, which certainly makes up for it. Whether it's a dry sunny bank or dark shady corner, there's usually a suitable ground cover plant. (Check the plant list at the back of the book when choosing for your garden.)

But should you have a bed of shrubs which are not likely to be moved, graded bark flakes or bark nuggets are ideal to cover the ground. They are very smart, give an elegant finish and certainly keep the weeds down if 3 in (7.5 cm) or so deep. (Suppliers' addresses at the back of the book.)

GROUND COVER
(See also list of ground cover plants at the back of the book.)

The following plants are trouble free, vigorous, spread easily, divide and most are evergreen – not a bad recommendation!

Sun-loving ground cover
Arabis *(Rock Cress), grey/green foliage, small white flower. Excellent for sunny, well-drained soil.* Lamium maculatum 'Silver Beacon', *green/silver leaves, pink/purple flowers in May.* Sedum 'Ruby Glow', *pink flowers July/August, and* Thymus 'Silver Posie' *will do well in sunny, well-drained soil.*

Campanula carpatica 'Blue Chip' *is a vigorous grower with lovely blue flowers in July and August.* Campanula garganica *and* Convolvulus mauritanicus *are splendid for rockeries, dry stone walls and planted between the cracks on terraces and patios. Once it gets going campanula seeds itself.*

Campanula portenschlagiana *is a very 'useful' dwarf perennial with blue flowers from June to November. It is an invasive plant which will make its home happily between cracks in paving or brick walls. Prefers lightly shaded position. Once planted it will spread and seed itself everywhere.*

Heuchera sanguinea 'Bressingham Blaze'. *Deep coral flowers in summer. Hardy herbaceous perennial.*

Shade-loving or not fussy plants
Saxifraga umbrosa *(London Pride) is not fussy. It is good in all soils and the shade. It has small rosettes of fleshy leaves and tiny pink flowers in May/June and spreads slowly.* Ajuga reptans 'Atropurpurea' *is very good in shade. It likes a moist shady position. It has dark purple/green leaves and blue flowers in June and July.*

Alchemilla mollis *(Ladies Mantle). Delightful mid-green leafed herbaceous perennial.*

Bergenia *(Elephants' ears). Pink flowers in spring. Large, round, flat, evergreen leaf.*

Hellebores. *Hardy winter flowering plant. Single open-faced flowers from white to plum purple.*

Hostas. *Summer-flowering herbaceous perennial with broad plain green and variegated leaved plants.*

Pachysandra terminalis 'Variegata'. *Pale evergreen leaf edged with cream. Nice bushy shrub, grows to 6 in (15 cm), spread 18 in (45 cm) or more.*

Primula vulgaris *(Primrose) and* Primula veris *(Cowslip) will grow in any soil. Flowers in spring and a few flowers in autumn.*

Skimmia japonica 'Rubella'. *Dark evergreen leaves, crimson buds all winter, turning to white flowers in the spring. (Can be used to pollinate a female variety and get lots of shiny red berries.)*

Tolmiea menziesii 'Taffs Gold'. *Flat maple-like lime green evergreen leaves. Red flowers on spikes in June. Wonderful undemanding ground cover plant.*

above: Alchemilla mollis *(Ladies' Mantle), one of the most useful summer ground cover plants.*
left: A difficult west-facing border in my country garden. All except the climbing rose was planted four years ago. The tall spiky-leaved plant at the back is a tree peony, Paeonia lutea ludlowii, *with* Choisya *in front of it; the red flowers in front of me are* Pieris, *with* Viburnum bodnantense *on the left; along the border (top to bottom) are* Senecio, *hebes and* Phlomis fruticosa; *and the splash of yellow at the bottom left is broom,* Cytisus spachianus.

19: *Weeds*

What is a weed?
A plant growing in the wrong place (*Anon*).
A plant whose virtues have not yet been discovered (*Ralph Waldo Emerson*).

Weeding can be very time-consuming, and to reduce this, especially in the early stages while the shrubs are getting established, it's important to have a good variety of ground cover plants (see plant list at the back of the book). If you are sure you won't want to move the plants, or add more, bark chippings are excellent for keeping down weeds and they also give the garden an elegant finish when planting is complete. But bark flakes are *not* advisable if you are still undecided about the placing of plants, and are best for beds containing flowering shrubs. They can be obtained from Melcourt Industries Ltd, Three Cups House, Tetbury, Gloucestershire, Tel: 0666 52711/53919 and quite a few other suppliers.

Large round cobblestones placed together between the shrubs also make excellent ground cover and weed deterrent. They keep the weeds out, the moisture in and look very attractive between small plants. They are best on very sandy soil as they could sink into mud. Should weeds come up between the cobbles, they are very easily pulled out.

Couch grass

There are times when chemicals are necessary and we have to rely on them to do the work for which hands may not have time. A case in point is getting rid of couch grass, every gardener's nightmare.

If used as directed, Weedout is a safe and effective chemical and, amazing though this may seem, does not harm the neighbouring plants. One sachet in a watering can full of water as directed, will soon see the couch grass withering away. This saves hours of intensive weeding, and, unless it is done meticulously with every underground root or rhizome of couch grass teased out of the soil (and then burnt), this persistant weed will soon reappear and spoil the bed again.

For those who enjoy weeding, couch grass and ground elder (which does not respond to Weedout), the two most resilient of weeds, are extremely satisfying to 'manhandle'! I have to confess that if I have time on my hands (which is rare) after a good rainfall, there are few jobs I find more rewarding.

Ground Elder

The other garden enemy, ground elder, can also be disposed of with chemicals if weeding by hand does not appeal. Spray the ground elder leaves in early autumn, three times (once a week for three weeks) with Tumbleweed. Do not pull out or touch after spraying, just let the chemical work its way into the root system and slowly destroy the plant. It will die away and should not reappear the following spring.

20: *The interest created by foliage*

A garden can be made more interesting not only by having features such as statues or fountains, but by the deliberate use of different shaped and coloured foliage. It is easy to make the mistake of planting six similar dark evergreen leafed shrubs together. No matter how beautiful they are individually, they will appear unimaginative and 'samey' and make it hard to distinguish one plant from the other.

I have been guilty of putting too many similar leafed grey plants together such as *Ballota, Senecio* 'Sunshine', *Phlomis fruticosa,* sage and *Stachys lanata* (Lambs' Ears) when choosing plants for a silver and white theme in the garden. But whatever the theme the plants must be of different heights, with as much variety in the leaf and habit as possible.

It is not necessary to have a large number of dramatic and unusual plants in any one bed. But one or two such plants certainly do draw the eye and make an otherwise unexciting area visually vibrant and interesting.

INTERESTING FOLIAGE

Here are some of the plants that can be relied on to add drama to a bed.

Fatsia japonica *has huge fan-shaped shiny dark evergreen leaves, is a bold and dramatic plant to dominate the back of the bed. Large heads of tiny pale green flowers light it up in the autumn. It is a most undemanding, trouble-free plant which is better in shade and can survive under a tree.*

Phormium Tenax purpureum *is a spiky plant like a huge iris and is splendid punctuation in any border of a town garden. There are many new varieties with colourfully striped leaves.* Yucca gloriosa *will have the same striking effect.*

Acer palmatum 'Dissectum Atropurpureum' *has feathery copper red leaves;* Senkaki *is taller and not so rounded, with pale green leaves and coral twigs.*

Medium height plants such as *royal ferns, clumps of* hellebores *or the tall upright and thin leaf of the* iris *make a good contrast against softer plants for the middle of the bed.*

Bamboos *are most striking plants and can be used to great effect, but many bamboos are extremely robust so it is best to choose* Arundinaria viridistriata *which has a good gold and green striped leaf and needs full sun or the leaves will go shades of pale green. It grows to 3 ft (90 cm) and is an exciting plant if you have the space.*

The broad mid-green or grey leafed hostas and bergenia *are excellent for use at the front of the bed as they break up hard lines when spilling over on to the terrace or path and the grey leaves of* Senecio *or* Stachys lanata *add another colour and texture.*

Other excellent possibilities are:
Rheum palmatum Atropurpureum *(ornamental rhubarb),* Acanthus *(bears' breeches),* Polygonatum multiflorum *(Solomon's seal),* Fritillaries *(Crown Imperial),* Rhus typhina *(sumach),* Euphorbia wulfenii, Iris, Miscanthus sinensis 'Silver Feather' or 'Zebrinus', Lilies, Mahonia, Paeonia lutea Ludlowii *(tree peony),* Prunus laurocerasus Zabeliana *(spreading laurel),* Magnolia grandiflora

above: Euphorbia characias *in a border of different greens. An old corn stoop 'mushroom' adds a little extra detail (photo by Susan Hampshire).*

left: An example of interest created by foliage on a west-facing border, with differently shaped leaves and different shades of green; bottom to top, Viburnum davidii, Vinca major elegantissima, Helleborus *and* Senecio 'Sunshine' *(photo by Susan Hampshire).*

21: *Dividing plants*

It is very expensive to keep buying plants to fill every space but ground cover does keep the weeding down and improve low maintenance. Happily in the autumn and spring there are plenty of plants, including ground cover plants, that can be divided and anything which helps garden economy is definitely worth the trouble.

Anemone japonica, primulas, hellebores, *Alchemilla mollis* (Lady's Mantle), *Tolmiea menziesii* (pig-a-back), bergenia (elephant ears), gladioli, bulbs, bearded iris, Michaelmas daisies, phlox, heleniums, lupins, delphiniums, chives, *Stachys lanata* and even shrubs like heather, *Kerria japonica* and Scotch rose all divide splendidly.

The majority of these plants should be divided between October and April, except bearded iris which should be divided after flowering in July, and hellebores in early September or in early spring (I have divided them in the summer with good results but they were watered well for three weeks before dividing), and snowdrops should be divided when they have just flowered and are still 'green' (in leaf).

The method of dividing varies, depending on the type of root system – fibrous, tuber, rhizome or those with a woody crown.

The easiest plants to divide are those with fibrous roots such as primulas, and small

left: Anemone japonica, *an easy plant to divide. This one came originally from my mother's garden in Kent over twenty years ago (photo by Susan Hampshire).*

above: Tolmiea menziesii, *the pig-a-back plant, is another excellent ground cover and dividing plant. It derives its name from the unusual way one leaf grows out of another (photo by Susan Hampshire).*

herbaceous plants like *Tolmiea menziesii* and *Alchemilla mollis*. In a low maintenance garden *Tolmiea menziesii*, pleasing yellow/green leafed evergreen ground cover, is well worth dividing to be used elsewhere and save the weeding. *Alchemilla mollis* dies back in the winter but it is decorative ground cover also worth dividing although it will seed itself.

First dig up the fibrous rooted plants and gently tease away a section by hand and then replant in a vacant space allowing room for growth, for both these plants spread fairly vigorously.

Larger clumps of Michaelmas daisies or delphiniums need two garden forks, placed back to back down the centre of the plant's roots and then prised apart. A sharp knife is best for the fleshy root system of say the peony, which should be divided in October.

Rhizomes like bergenia and bearded iris which have long, thick, horizontal roots like old gnarled tree roots should be cut off in 2–3 in (5–7.5 cm) sections each with the new growth of young leaves on them. These sections should then be planted horizontally just below the soil or on the soil, at whichever depth they were growing.

Tubers, such as Jerusalem artichokes and potatoes, only need to be cut into pieces; providing each piece has a bud or an eye on it, it can then be put back into the soil and should grow.

Anemone japonica needs careful dividing and replanting in spring.

DIVIDING A PLANT

One of the easiest ways of dividing larger plants: place two garden forks back to back down the centre of the roots and prise apart.

22: *Herbs*

The majority of herbs originally came from the Mediterranean and have been used for their medicinal purposes as well as culinary flavours and aromatic odours for thousands of years. They are trouble-free, attractive, easy to manage and ideal for low maintenance gardens. A large number of herbs prefer full sun and on the whole they like poor soil, so they should be planted in a sunny south facing position with plenty of protection. They like still, warm air and are happiest if sheltered by a hedge of lavender or box, or protected from the breeze by other plants. They will not do well if planted in an exposed position.

Soft herbs such as mint, chives, chervil, basil, dill, parsley, tarragon, angelica, sorrel, lemon mint, yellow-leaved feverfew, double-flowered feverfew and the regular feverfew grow happily in raised planters, troughs, window boxes, tubs and terracotta pots where they can dry out quickly between watering, but feverfew needs to be watched as it seeds itself and can quickly land up growing everywhere.

If the soil is too heavy, peat and compost can be added to lighten it. I have even found mixing in a couple of handfuls of sand and shingle or grit makes the soil more porous and helps recreate Mediterranean soil conditions for such herbs as rosemary, rue, hyssop, thyme, lavender and savory.

But the most effective way of improving heavy soil conditions for herbs is to build up the height of the bed at least 6 in (15 cm) by adding soil plus a mixure of *sharp* sand and/or grit to the top of the bed. This mound will help the bed to drain more easily.

Herbs like rosemary, bay, sage, thyme and marjoram also prefer full sun and indifferent soil, but as they need more space they should be planted in the beds. Most herbs *do not need feeding*: the exceptions are chives, parsley, basil and comfrey. Use only organic fertiliser, otherwise you'll be eating chemicals.

Herb Calendar

In *March* chives can be separated. Dig the clumps out of the soil with a trowel and tease them in half by hand, then replant. It is useful to have the second clump growing on the kitchen window sill, particularly in the winter.

April is the best time to sow dill and fennel and layer the thyme by pinning down the sprawling growth with a stone. Once it has grown shoots, the stem can be cut off and transplanted in shallow soil.

In *May* basil seedlings should be planted and in September you should sow parsley for the spring. Parsley takes six weeks to germinate, so be patient. Your own fresh seed sown in early autumn will germinate quickly and overwinter safely.

But all of these herbs need not be grown from seed as the plants are readily available in health shops, greengrocers and garden centres, and it goes without saying that buying them in pots is far less trouble even though it is more expensive.

Before September herbs should be pruned. Try to time the cutting back to as soon after the plant has flowered as possible, so as to preserve the plant's energy from trying to make seeds. The advantage of cutting back is that it prevents the plant from becoming too woody. Straggly lengths of hard herbs can be cut back in the spring. Try not to cut old wood as it is on this wood the new growth is produced, and never cut old wood of lavender.

Keeping Herbs under Control

Many herbs (like mint) grow pretty vigorously and need a little controlling otherwise they tend to run wild. But herbs can be planted in such a way as to create a very attractive feature while still keeping them in check.

A popular method of managing herbs in a small garden is planting them between the segments of an old cartwheel. If you can't get hold of a cartwheel you can set out a cartwheel design with bricks. Another alternative is to put down runs of bricks or large stones between the plants to stop them getting out of hand. In a large garden a chess board pattern with paving slab squares is very decorative. The vigorous nature of soft herbs is one of the reasons why they are such a success in terracotta pots. This confines their roots and keeps maintenance down to a minimum.

Basil

If you want an excellent basil crop, it needs to be given rather different attention than the other herbs. Half an hour of your time is all that is needed to have a splendid basil plant flourishing from late May right through to December. But bring basil inside in October and put it on a sunny window sill. Basil is said to be very calming, as is mint.

To plant, empty one basil plant, which is usually made up of six or eight small basil shoots growing together, on to a newspaper and tease the individual plants apart. Once separated, plant each plant in a large pot filled with compost – preferably terracotta (not plastic as it doesn't dry out or retain moisture in the same way as terracotta does). Make holes for the roots by pushing a pencil or small stick into the soil, then lower the plant's roots into the hole and firm it round with your fingers. You should have about six or eight separate plants spaced round the 10 in or 12 in (25 or 30 cm) pot. This individual planting enables the plants to fill out into a bushy plant and give much better value. Place in a sunny sheltered spot, or warm window sill. Water freely *only* when the soil has dried out.

When picking basil nip off the *leaf only* with your nails or scissors. Do not remove whole head of the plant as you would with parsley or mint as it will not grow again.

Some herbs should be replaced every four to five years but mostly they just need to be divided and replanted every three or four years. Even if you only buy them in pots and keep them on a warm window sill, they are a healthy and worthwhile addition to any household, not to be overlooked.

23: *Trees*

The striking red foliage of a Cotinus coggygria *is set off by the weeping pear in the background (photo by Susan Hampshire).*

Planting a tree is the joyous responsibility of anyone who has the opportunity to do so. Human and animal life depend on trees for oxygen, trees are our life line, our life support system. Yet trees are being cut down all over the world at an alarming rate – an area the size of a football pitch disappears every minute – and an enormous amount of the wildlife that is dependent on them faces extinction. This tragic and unnecessary destruction of the forests is upsetting the balance of nature, so it is all the more important that those of us who can plant a tree do so. If you haven't any space yourself and would like to contribute to the tree population of the world, you can always contact The Conservation Foundation, Lowther Lodge, 1 Kensington Gore, London SW7. Or if you would prefer to use wood from sustainable forests, consult *The Good Wood Guide*, available from Friends of the Earth.

ORNAMENTAL TREES AND SHRUBS FOR SMALL GARDENS

If your garden is very small do not choose a tree that grows to more than 15 ft (4.5 m).

If your garden is about 60 ft (18 m) long, don't choose a tree that grows to more than 20 ft (6 m).

If your garden is more than 100 ft (30 m) long you can easily grow a tree that grows to more than 35 ft (10 m).

When choosing a tree, check the size of the *spread* of the tree as well as its height as it can sometimes be as wide as it is high.

Acer japonicum 'Vitifolium' (Maple). *Grows slowly to 20 ft (6 m), spread 10 ft (3 m). Soft green leaves which turn a wonderful crimson in the autumn.*

Acer palmatum Atropurpureum (Japanese Maple). *This shrub has feathery purple leaves. Only grows to 3 ft (90 cm). Ideal for planting in a large container in a sheltered corner.*

Acer palmatum Aureum (Maple). *Slow growing. Grows to 15 ft (4.5 m). Spread 8 ft (2.5 m). Yellow/ green leaves turning rich crimson in the autumn.*

Amelanchier lamarckii. *Grows to 10 ft (3 m). Spread 10 ft (3 m). White spring flowers, black berries and bright red autumn leaves.*

Arbutus unedo (Strawberry tree). *Large shrub or small tree growing to 15–20 ft (4.5–6 m). Spread 10 ft (3 m). An evergreen with dark green leaves, white flowers in October/November and strawberry-like fruits at the same time.*

Buddleia alternifolia (Butterfly Bush). *Amazing sweet aroma from soft pendulous lavender blue flowers in the summer. Height 15 ft (4.5 m). Spread 15 ft (4.5 m) – 20 ft (4.5–6 m). Narrow pale green leaves. A wonderful aromatic bush.*

Catalpa bignoniodes (Indian Bean Tree). *Grows 20–30 ft (6–9 m). Spread 15–20 ft (4.5–6 m). Bright green flat heart shaped leaves. Yellow and white flowers in July followed by long slim seed pods. A difficult tree to get established. Best in South East.*

Corylus avellana (Hazel cob-nut). *Grows to 20 ft (6 m). Spread 15 ft (4.5 m). Mid green leaves. Yellow male catkins 2 in (5 cm) long in February.*

Cotinus coggyria (Smoke bush). *A large shrub. Mid green leaves with dull pink wispy flower heads which give an attractive diffused smoke effect in the summer. Grows to 10 ft (3 m).*

Cotinus coggyria 'Royal Purple'. *This shrub has dark wine coloured leaves which go red in autumn. Also grows to about 10 ft (3 m) and is another lovely shrub. They look most attractive side by side.*

Eucalyptus niphophila (Alpine snowgum). *Not for a small space. Extremely hardy. (Beware, some Eucalyptus can grow to 50 ft (15 m)). Cut back constantly once or twice a year if you do not want a 30–40 ft (9–12 m) tree in 10 years! Delightful grey/green evergreen leaves. Trouble free, extremely hardy, easy to grow, prefers sunny position. Lovely leaves for cutting for flower arrangements.*

Fraxinus excelsior 'Jaspidea' (Ash). *Grows to 25 ft (15 m) or more. Golden yellow leaves in spring turning to yellow green leaves in summer then yellow autumn colour.*

Gleditsia triacanthos 'Sunburst' (Honey Locust). *Light golden leaves, turning clear yellow in autumn. Height 18–30 ft (5.5–9 m). Spread 12–15 ft (3.5–4.5 m). Wonderful 'glowing' tree.*

ORNAMENTAL TREES AND SHRUBS FOR SMALL GARDENS (*continued*)

Ginkgo biloba (Maidenhair tree). *Primitive slow growing deciduous tree. Height 30 ft (9 m). Spread 10 ft (3 m). Small leathery fan shaped pale green leaves in spring, turning darker green in summer, then golden in autumn. Most interesting tree, seldom seen in the average garden perhaps for fear it will get too big.*

Koelreuteria paniculata (Pride of India). *Grows to 10–18 ft (3–5.5 m). Spread 8–10 ft (2.5–3 m). Mid green leaves up to 14 in (35 cm) long. Yellow flowers 6–12 in (15–30 cm) long in July which give a wonderful yellow haze, like mimosa in full bloom.*

Laburnum Watereri Vossii (Golden Rain). *Grows to 15–20 ft (4.5–6 m). Spread 10–15 ft (3–4.5 m). Yellow flowers tapering from 10–20 in (25–50 cm) long in May. The leaves, twigs and particularly the seeds are poisonous, but this variety produces few seeds. Most attractive when in flower.*

Liriodendron tulipifera Aureomarginatum (Tulip tree). *Grows to 18–25 ft (5.5–7.5 m). Spread 10–15 ft (3–4.5 m). Delightful tree with yellow tulip type flowers in the autumn which do not appear before the tree is 10 years old. My tulip trees have been fairly slow growing, but these trees are not for a small garden.*

Magnolia. *This is one of the most attractive groups of trees and shrubs for a small sheltered garden, and personally I would give it priority above most other trees along with Gleditsia Sunburst, rowan and some of the ashes.*

Magnolia soulangeana. *A delightful spreading bush. Grows to 15 ft (4.5 m). Spread 10–15 ft (3–4.5 m). Large waxy white flowers with pinkish base when in bud. Flowers open in April before the mid green leaves have unfurled.*

Magnolia grandiflora. *Owing to their beautiful flower, all magnolias are impressive. The evergreen Magnolia grandiflora with shiny dark green leaves and waxy cream flowers in July/September is splendid and imposing in a small or large garden, preferably against a wall. None of the magnolias grow very tall although I have seen this species in Provence standing 50 ft (15 m) tall.*

Malus floribunda (Flowering Crab Apple). *Grows to 12–15 ft (3.5–4.5 m). Spread 10–15 ft (3–4.5 m). Rounded compact branches with mid green leaves. Carmine red buds open into pale pink blossoms in May. Yellow fruits.*

Malus 'Golden Hornet'. *Grows to 15–18 ft (4.5–5.5 m). Spread 10–15 ft (3–4.5 m). Pale green leaves. White blossoms May, and lots of striking yellow crab apples in autumn.*

Prunus lusitanica (Portugal Laurel). *Grows 15–20 ft (4.5–6 m) by 15–20 ft (4.5–6 m). Glossy dark green leaves with red stalks. Cream scented flowers in June. Fruit which turn black. Can be trained up into a small tree.*

Pyrus salicifolia 'Pendula' (Pear Tree). *Lovely shaped small weeping tree. Grows to 8–10 ft (2.5–3 m). Spread 6–8 ft (1.8–2.5 m). Silver grey willow-like leaves. Pretty white flowers in April. Makes a good feature in the garden and is easily pruned into a compact shape.*

Salix elaeagnos (Hoary willow). *Large shrub. Grows to 10 ft (3 m). Spread 8 ft (2.5 m). Narrow green leaves. Yellow male catkins 1½ in (4 cm) long in April.*

Sorbus aria 'Lutescens' (Whitebeam). *Height 15–20 ft (4.5–6 m). Spread 10–15 ft (3–4.5 m). Lovely downy grey/green white leaves which when they flutter in the wind look silver.*

continued over page

ORNAMENTAL TREES AND SHRUBS
FOR SMALL GARDENS (*continued*)

Sorbus aucuparia (Mountain Ash). *Grows to 15–25 ft (4.5–7.5 m). Spread 8–12 ft (2.5–3.5 m). Mid green leaves with grey undersides. White flowers in May and June. Orange to red berries in July which ripen in August. Not suitable for shallow alkaline soils.*

Sorbus sargentiana (Mountain Ash). *Grows to 10–18 ft (3–5.5 m). Spread 8–12 ft (2.5–3.5 m). Mid green leaves turning to dazzling red in autumn. White flowers in May. Orange-red berries in September. Exciting tree.*

Prunus cerasifera nigra (Ornamental Plum). *Height 25 ft (7.5 m). Spread 25 ft (7.5 m). Purple leaves, white flowers in the spring. In a garden where there is room for several ornamental trees any of the purple leafed trees make a good and interesting contrast. Many people do not like their almost black leaves, but if there is room for several trees this tree certainly adds variety to the space. Easily pruned to form a compact head.*

Planting Trees

Apart from correct planning and construction, one of the most important ingredients of a successful garden is careful planting. Good planting makes all the difference between a tree thriving or dying. A tree dying is an expensive and disappointing loss.

But if a tree or shrub is planted correctly, it should flourish, live up to expectations and reward you with the pleasure and sense of achievement that goes with watching something you have planted grow. If a tree or shrub is badly planted, it will never catch up in size with one that is planted properly.

Choosing the Correct Tree for the Site

Once you have decided upon a spot (where there is enough space and light for a tree), it is important that you choose a tree that is suitable for the site. Time and thought should also be given to the effect you wish the tree to create: countrified, elegant, severe, dramatic and so on.

Many big trees like sycamore and lime are totally unsuitable for small gardens: their leaves do not make good leaf mould and they have bad habits such as a sticky aphid excretion in summer and greedy roots. Also the fully grown canopy of these trees can be overpowering in a small space, throwing the garden into shade and taking all the moisture from the ground.

Trees in containers in the garden centre look so small and insignificant, it is difficult to imagine that some of them may grow to 60–100 ft (18–30 m). Do check before buying a tree how big it will grow and if it is suitable for your space. I have been growing some oak trees in pots from acorns, and they are still no more than 6 in (15 cm) high. If you plant them in a small space not knowing what size an oak tree can grow to, your grandchildren might be left with a tree that would completely overpower the area and they would have no option but to cut it down.

The same goes for willows. Some willows grow very big indeed and drink gallons and gallons of water a day. If there isn't sufficient rainfall a willow tree will draw its moisture from under the brickwork of a house. There have been cases, especially on clay sub-soil, of thirsty willow roots near houses cracking the foundation of the brickwork in their efforts to draw out all available moisture.

The crown of a tree is as important as the height. *Malus floribunda*, the crab-apple tree, the popular spring flowering kind, has a very broad bushy crown, but does not grow very tall, yet it casts a wide shade. Another crab-apple, *Malus tschonoskii*, has an upright crown and can get very tall (35 ft/over 10 m) but casts very little shade. The same applies to flowering cherries: *Prunus Tai Haku* grows very wide and *Prunus hillieri Spire* grows very tall, so both spread and height should be taken into consideration.

So obviously choosing the right tree for the space is important. There are a great many lovely trouble-free ornamental trees ideal for small gardens. But give time and thought to the effect you wish the tree to create. Hawthorn will look countrified, magnolia is appropriate to a smart town garden and *Paulownia* is spectacular when in flower, but grows to 25 – 30 ft (7.5 – 9 m) and is not for a tiny garden.

If you wish to restrict the size of a tree, plant it in a large tub at least 3 ft 6 in (just over a metre) deep and 2 ft 6 in (75 cm) wide in the same way as they do in many of the château gardens of France. As long as the tree is *fed* and *watered* regularly it will survive quite happily, and not grow too large because of the confined root space.

Another manner of restricting the size of a tree is to follow the Japanese method and prune the tree continually, keeping a small manicured shape. But this is very time-consuming and expensive and certainly *not* low maintenance.

The legal position regarding trees is as follows. If the tree is on your property you are responsible for it and any damage caused by its roots and branches. Tree roots are often mentioned as causing damage to buildings but the case against them is rarely proved. But there is a real chance of damage from subsidence *on shrinkable clay soils by trees that take a lot of water out of the soil*. You need to check if you are on shrinkable clay. Some soils called clay are not shrinkable when water is drawn out of them. All this refers to the sub-soil and not the top soil.

If your house is a new one the developers will be able to tell you the type of sub-soil you are on. Otherwise look at the local geology map in a library. They are not always easy to understand, so you could try asking for help at your local council.

Really vigorous trees like poplars and willows have very strong roots that seek out water, and they can get into drains and sewers and under foundations. But other physical damage by tree roots is very uncommon.

Important Rules for Planting

(Especially for bare-rooted trees)

There are several important rules that you should abide by especially when you buy *bare-rooted* trees as opposed to those that are container grown.

1. *Do not* expose the roots of bare-rooted trees to wind, sun or air for more than two or three minutes. If you have to leave the tree for a time once you have started planting, immediately cover the roots with damp sacking or earth.

    Trees can die when their roots are exposed to the elements, be it hot sun or cold wind, for as little as five minutes, so it is vitally important to keep the roots covered at all times (including transportation), leave them wrapped in damp sacking, in their package, or heel in (cover roots with earth).
2. *Do not* soak trees in a bucket of water overnight, as the roots cannot breathe in water. Roots need oxygen, so leave them in damp sacking and just plunge the tree into tepid water for five minutes before planting.
3. If the weather is icy or there is night frost, do not water the tree after planting as ice will form round the roots and distress and perhaps even kill the tree.

These rules apply to trees bought at any size ranging from 2 ft (60 cm) to 12 ft (3.5 m). Larger trees will usually come with a root ball.

Planting in Autumn and Winter

Dig a hole *1 ft (30 cm) in diameter wider* than the tree roots and *6 in (15 cm) deeper* than the root depth. Place the soil from the hole on to a plastic sheet ready to be mixed with *moist* peat and/or *well-rotted* organic matter (such as leaf mould or *well-rotted* kitchen or grass compost if available).

Next use a fork to break up 1 ft (30 cm) of the soil at the bottom of the hole (*vitally important* to encourage the roots to *grow down*) and mix in moist peat and a trowelful of calcified seaweed (to help improve the structure of the soil), bone meal, and a little dried blood, in the bottom of the hole. (It is essential that a tree has nourishment at its roots when planting, so buy at least dried blood and bone meal, even if you don't have calcified seaweed.)

Add to the soil from the hole (on the plastic sheet) a bucket of *moist* peat (dry peat will absorb all the moisture from the tree roots) and add a trowelful of bone meal, calcified seaweed and dried blood. Next try the tree in the hole to calculate a good position for the tree stake (at the side of the hole). The stake need only be 2–3 ft (60–90 cm) out of the ground. This helps the tree to root better and develop a strong stem. The tree should then be well enough rooted so that the stake can be removed after a year. Hammer the stake into the ground a good 10 in (25 cm) below the bottom of the pit and then place the tree into the hole and half cover with the earth and peat mixture. Gently shake the tree up and down to ensure the soil has filled in all round the roots and repeat the process. Then fill the hole with more soil and push in with the *heel* of your boot – *not* with a flat foot – firmly on sandy soil and lightly on clay soil. Then fill in the rest of the soil and firm in again. Tie the tree to the stake and put rabbit guard round the base of the trunk if you have rabbits in the garden.

Then water with two large watering cans full, if the weather is mild after planting but, I repeat, not in icy weather. If it snows *after* you have planted the tree, the snow will keep the warmth in the soil, so don't worry that the tree will die of cold!

PLANTING A TREE

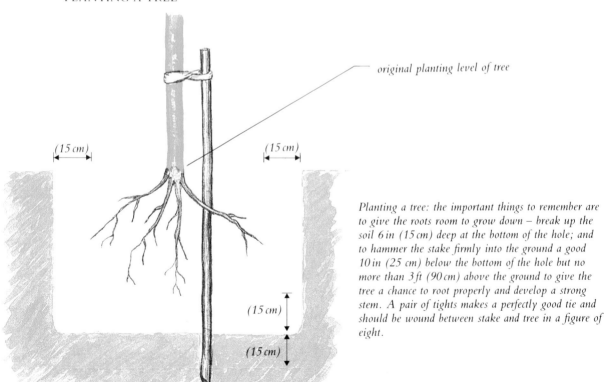

original planting level of tree

(15 cm)

(15 cm)

(15 cm)

(15 cm)

Planting a tree: the important things to remember are to give the roots room to grow down – break up the soil 6 in (15 cm) deep at the bottom of the hole; and to hammer the stake firmly into the ground a good 10 in (25 cm) below the bottom of the hole but no more than 3 ft (90 cm) above the ground to give the tree a chance to root properly and develop a strong stem. A pair of tights makes a perfectly good tie and should be wound between stake and tree in a figure of eight.

After Care

Water in spring and summer. In dry weather water at least three times a week with two large watering cans full of water for each tree the first year.

Feed in the second spring with an all purpose organic or chemical fertiliser. The fertiliser in the hole will feed the tree the first year. Top dress *after watering* round the root of the tree each spring with mulch (a 3–4 in/7.5–10 cm layer of well-rotted grass cuttings, leaf mould, peat or organic matter) at least until the tree is well established (two or three years). Keep the base of the newly planted tree *weed free* in at least a 3 ft (90 cm) wide circle.

Container-grown Trees and Root Ball Trees

For container-grown trees and root-ball trees (which have their roots surrounded by earth and are then tied up with sacking), follow the same procedure as planting a bare-rooted tree. But with a container-grown tree, remove the plastic or pot, and with root-ball remove the sacking carefully when you have placed the tree in its hole. (If you wish, you can leave the sackng as this will rot away in time and leave the tree's roots free to spread. But it is preferable to remove it.)

24: *Roses and shrubs*

For those who love roses and are faced with the same airless problem as I have in my town garden, patio roses on their own roots in tubs put into an open area of the garden to avoid the still air syndrome should do well. (See *Planting Roses in Tubs*.)

Low maintenance roses are not totally out of the question. *Phylis Bide* (rambler) and *Rose virginiana* (shrub) are two delightful roses which need little or no attention.

Phylis Bide flowers throughout the summer. The slightly ragged flowers are small in a wonderful colour mixture ranging from gentle orange and pink to cream.

Rose virginiana is good in most soils, even light sandy soil, and flowers in summer. It has pretty, deep pink flowers, rich green leaves, nice autumn foliage and fat orange hips in the autumn.

If you don't want a rose shrub or rambler to get too big, just cut hard back in the autumn. But even if they are left for years they will not be a problem.

Two ground cover roses that really live up to the name are *Grouse* and *Partridge*. Both are sprawling shrubs with glossy mid-green leaves. *Grouse* has lovely pale pink flowers and *Partridge* clusters of white flowers.

Mermaid, a semi-evergreen climber, is another splendid rose and requires very little attention. In fact it benefits from being pruned *sparingly*. I have two Mermaids that have not been touched for years, except to cut off the dead heads (and then only occasionally) and they still look terrific. I have never seen them without their lovely shiny dark green leaves, even in the depths of winter, nor have I ever seen them attacked by any of the usual rose pests. Both my Mermaids are planted on a north wall, flower throughout the summer and do not complain about the shade. Roses that like shade are worth their weight in gold, added to which the Mermaid's flower is lovely, a single pale yellow-gold.

New Dawn is a lovely rambling rose which flowers all summer with blush pink scented flowers. It is very popular, but similar to and not to be confused with *Dr Van Fleet* which only flowers *once* a year. Make sure you have *New Dawn* if you want continuous flowering.

Felicia is another lovely pink rose. This hybrid musk is a real charmer, so if you have the space (it grows to 4 ft (1.2 m) by 4 ft (1.2 m)) and don't mind using the secateurs and doing a bit of judicious pruning once a year, it is not to be missed. It has certainly been a big plus in my garden. Its sprays of scented deep to pale pink flowers last from summer to autumn, it is an excellent shrub, and the cut flowers look good in a vase too.

If you want a splash of splendid neon pink colour, terrific light coppery green healthy foliage, *Bonica* is a good bet. It was grown by Mielland (the same rose grower who introduced the deep pink *H.T. Susan Hampshire Rose* all those years ago) and is relatively new (1984). This modern disease-resistant shrub has abundant flowers and adds pep to any border.

Félicité et Perpétue is another lovely old (1827) white rambler that needs little or no pruning. It grows happily up a north wall (to 15 ft / 4.5 m). It has abundant clusters of small white flowers, the buds being pink/red before they open. It is long and late flowering and absolutely beautiful. This climber, like the majority of roses mentioned here, requires virtually no work and is wonderful value.

Should your newly planted climbing roses not produce many flowers (or no flowers at all) in the first few years, do not despair. While a rose is getting established, it does not flower abundantly, but as long as it is well planted and fed, it should take off after a few years. Ramblers seldom produce continuous flowers, but most climbers will give you a splendid display of flowers throughout the summer.

Roses in Tubs: Disease and Soil

The new patio roses on their own roots are ideal for growing in tubs because roses need fresh soil and the great advantage of a tub is that you can start off with virgin potting compost.

Nematodes tend to thrive in the soil in which a rose has grown, and these will affect any new rose planted in the same soil. So a tub with fresh compost could not be a better place for planting a rose. But make sure you have good drainage (about 3 in/ 7.5 cm of small stones), then add John Innes Potting Compost No 3. If you water, liquid feed and give bone meal, the roses should live happily in a tub for a couple of decades.

It is best to ask for roses 'on their own roots' for tubs rather than budded ones which have fang-like roots and prefer to be in soil. 'Own root roses' have much more fibrous roots and grow much better than budded roses. You can tell a budded rose as it has a 'swelling' before the roots and all the shoots tend to come from one place on it. 'Own root roses' have a root system more like a normal shrub and you don't get any troublesome suckers. Ground cover roses and patio roses are often available on 'own root', especially if you order direct from rose growers. (See list of addresses at the back.)

How to Plant a Rose

Many people say roses are labour-intensive, but even if they do need a prune and feed once a year, the rewards far outweigh the little attention they demand.

A rose once planted will continue to flower without complaining for fifteen years or more while *lavender* which is thought of as a relatively low maintenance plant needs cutting back once a year and will need replacing after six or eight years. The planting of a rose is less work than that of a tree mainly because the hole only needs to be a little bigger than the width and depth of the rose's roots, roughly 2 ft (60 cm) wide and 10 in (25 cm) deep.

PLANTING A ROSE

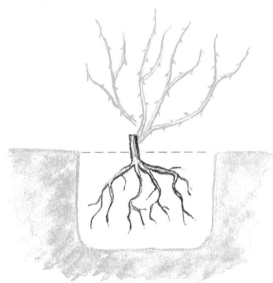

If the rose has a budding union as shown, plant it so that the union is 2 in (5 cm) below the surface, to encourage the rose you want to grow out on to its own roots. If there is no budding union, the rose has been grown from a cutting: any suckers will be true to type and you can leave them to grow.

But whether the rose is bare-rooted (and to be planted in the autumn or early spring); or in a container ready for year-round planting, the method of planting is much the same. There are important rules which should be followed, as there are for trees. The same rules also apply to shrubs. (See instructions for planting trees, p. 110).

Important Rules for Bare Rooted Roses

Do not expose the roots of bare-rooted roses to wind, sun or air for more than two or three minutes. If you have to leave the rose for a time once you have started planting, protect the roots by covering them with damp sacking or soil.

Like trees, bare-rooted roses die if their roots are exposed to the elements for as little as five minutes, or if the roots are dry. Dip the roots into a bucket of lukewarm water for a few minutes before planting. But *do not* soak rose roots in a bucket of water overnight, as plants cannot breathe if left more than five or ten minutes in water. Roots need oxygen. Just plunge the rose into water for five minutes before planting.

Do not plant or water roses if the weather is icy or there is night frost.

Prepare the tools and things you are going to need *before* starting to plant. You will need a spade (for ladies light weight makes it much easier), black plastic dust bin sheet (to mix the soil from the hole with peat), watering can, bucket of tepid water, gloves (if you don't like working with bare hands although bare hands are easier for mixing the soil, peat and bone meal), 1 large bucket full of moist peat, bone meal, organic fertiliser (calcified seaweed is optional), damp sacking to cover bare root, secateurs and knife or scissors to cut the over-long roots.

Planting Instructions

Dig a hole slightly larger than the rose's roots (the average hole needs to be 2 ft (60 cm) wide and 8–10 in (20–25 cm) deep) and put the soil on to a polythene sheet. Mix this soil with *moist* peat or compost, add a trowelful of bone meal and one of calcified seaweed (optional), and mix together.

Place the bare-rooted rose in the hole, making sure that the roots are 'comfortable' with room to lie in their natural shape. Never cramp roots into an 'uncomfortable' position. If the bare roots are excessively long, it is wise to snip them back to about 1 ft (30 cm). Place rose in hole and then start filling the hole with trowelfuls of the soil mixture, occasionally lifting the rose slightly and shaking it gently, so the soil falls between the roots. Some say you should not cover the bud union at the base of the rose's stem with soil unless you want the rose to root out. This should remain exposed and be 2 in (5 cm) above the *level* of the soil. (But several exceptional rose growers have said that they *cover* the union and this helps to strengthen the rose and protect the plant in a hard winter.) When all the soil is in the hole, firm round the outside of the rose hole with your heel so that the roots have a nice, firm surround, but do not stamp down the soil or use a flat foot. Then water and spread a layer of moist compost or peat over the roots.

Container Roses

First of all, *water container thoroughly before* planting. Dig hole about 6 in (15 cm) wider and deeper than the container. Break up the soil at the base of the hole, then fill in about 6 in (15 cm) of soil and compost mix which you have prepared with the soil from the hole: one third peat, one third compost, one third soil, plus a trowelful of bonemeal and one of calcified seaweed (optional) and some organic fertiliser.

Next carefully place the rose in its container into the hole. Remove the container very carefully by cutting down the side of the plastic cover. Try not to disturb the soil and rose's roots when taking away the cover. Next fill round the rose with your peat/compost and soil, bone meal and calcified seaweed mixture. Then firm with your heel (not flat foot), water and cover round the root with moist compost or peat.

If you are planting a container rose when it *is not in leaf*, it is best to remove all the compost in the container and plant as if it were a bare-rooted rose. (See above.)

Planting Shrubs

One of the most important things to remember when planting shrubs is to *water* the shrub in its pot or container *before* planting. Watering afterwards is not good enough, because if the soil in the container is dry and you water afterwards, all that happens is the water runs down between the dry soil surrounding the plant and the new soil, still leaving the plant in the middle longing for a drink! Plant as for roses in containers.

25: *Tubs*

The Advantage of Tubs

In a garden where you wish work to be cut down to the minimum, tubs are ideal. If low-maintenance planting is successful there will be no room in the beds between the permanent ground cover, plants and shrubs to plant annuals. Summer colour can be provided with summer bedding in the tubs which will be far less trouble.

A handsome mixed urn: fuchsia, polyanthus,
campanula, nicotiana, aubrietia and variegated ivy.

Pots and tubs also help vary the height of interest and colour in the garden, added to which it is easy to replace the soil, feed, water and plant tubs. Tubs give so much value for comparatively little work, but they do need *watering* regularly in the summer, even more so if they are in positions where they will not get the rain such as under the eaves of the roof or the canopies of large trees. Even in *winter* tubs in this situation should be watered once a week, although tubs that get the rain may only need watering every so often.

One frequently notices dead bay trees in tubs outside town house front doors; this is not usually due to a cold winter or even a too-small tub, but mainly to lack of water.

How to Plant up Tubs

If you want to plant a tub, urn or pot up from scratch, the most important ingredients are good potting compost with good drainage (or the soil will become waterlogged) and healthy plants. Once you have chosen your container, if it is more than 2 ft (60 cm) in diameter, put in a 2–3 in (5–7.5 cm) layer of gravel, stones or crocks at the bottom of the tub for drainage, and then add John Innes Potting Compost No. 3 except for rhododendrons and camellias. They need lime-free compost and should be planted in *Ericaceous compost* (from garden centres).

The containers, whether they are tubs or pots, look more attractive if you choose a large plant as a focal point for the middle. Evergreens such as dwarf conifer, *Yucca filamentosa*, cordyline, camellia or small bay trees are all perfect choices. Cordyline needs a warm sheltered spot and should be tied up in November to protect its 'heart' from frost during the winter months.

REQUIREMENTS

Container – *all containers must have drainage holes at the bottom of the tubs so the roots don't get waterlogged.*
Gravel *or* broken crocks
Trowel
John Innes Potting Compost No. 3 *or* Ericaceous compost *for camellias and rhododendrons*

John Innes Potting Compost No. 2 *for small plants in small pots*
Secateurs (*to cut back damaged or withered growth*)
Gloves
Watering Can

Plants

The average tub will need a focal plant for the middle, any of the plants mentioned earlier, which should be at least 1–3 ft (30–90 cm) taller than the other plants. Then four variegated ivy plants for round the edge, and four grey-leafed plants such as *Senecio bicolor* 'Silver Dust', to make up an elegant year-round container which will need no more than feeding in spring and watering during the summer. A small pot of say 18 in (45 cm) will need a plant in the middle that is about 10 in (25 cm) higher than the others. But in a 3 ft (90 cm) container, the central plant can be anything from 2 ft to 4 ft (60–120 cm) higher than the surrounding plants.

Evergreens such as rhododendrons, camellias, bay and ivy need water during the winter, so remember to water them all year round. If you wish to add seasonal colour, plants such as geraniums and petunias can be added in May and pulled out in December, and you can underplant with grape hyacinths, miniature tulips and miniature daffodils for colour in the early spring.

Pansies will go on flowering throughout the seasons; they are an excellent, reliable, if familiar, stand by, and will continue from one year to the next. They are particularly attractive if you select all one colour.

Once you have the basis of the container (a tall plant in the centre and ivy trailing over the edge) you can add as many geraniums, hostas (half-hardy for semi-shade), nasturtiums, oxeye daisy, *Senecio cineraria* (full sun), *chlorophytum* (spider plants), petunias, fuchsias, *Lobelia erinus*, Michaelmas daisies, *Tolmiea menziesii* (pig-a-back), white alyssum, *Lobularia mantina*, Busy Lizzie, miniature roses, feverfew, asparagus ferns, tobacco plants, campanula, *Alchemilla mollis* (ladies' mantle) and *Helichrysum petiolatum* as your heart desires or you have room for. *But* a few plants carefully selected for their colour are sometimes more impressive.

Ivy

The hard edges of the containers are best broken up by trailing plants such as variegated ivy, which is also a good camouflage for the sides of an ugly tub. Ivy can be rather expensive, but it is easily propagated and if you buy one or two plants these will soon put out new shoots, and this new growth plus the new root tentacles should be cut off and put into a glass of water. After a few weeks, plant the cutting in moist peat. You should soon produce enough ivy to trail over the sides of half a dozen containers! But you have to be patient as it takes time to get *established*. Ivy sold as house plants is much cheaper and perfectly suitable for using in the garden.

Mature ivy roots can be a bit 'pushy' so you need to cut down through the ivy root system with your trowel every year or two to break the root system so that other plants' roots have a chance.

above: King of the Balkans.

left: Fuchsia, petunia and lobelia.

opposite: The silvery grey foliage of Helichrysum and a pink geranium are ideal in a small container.

122

Colour

Colour is a question of taste. I prefer variegated ivy, grey foliage such as *Helichrysum* and a pink trailing ivy leaf geranium called 'King of the Balkans' which has a continuous show of masses of delicate bright pink flowers. Coupled with white campanula, this makes a quiet pleasant display. An all grey and white arrangement of *Senecio bicolor* 'Silver Dust', white petunias (which need plenty of water), *Helichrysum* and white campanulas is very smart.

But I have seen many dazzling patios, small gardens or balconies filled with every colour under the sun. As I said, it is just a question of your own preference. There are no rules and some of the most unlikely combinations take on a new charm when put together. Even plants I don't really like, such as marigolds, can look pretty in the right setting. But the rule tends to be, in the country colourful displays are more in keeping and in towns the quieter more select choice is preferable.

Important

Remember once your tub is planted up to *water* daily during the summer, and feed the plants a liquid manure such as Bio plant food in the watering can *once a week*, or you can use a good feed in spring with a slow release fertiliser. But most important, water well *at least* three times a week, as containers dry out quickly, especially in full sun. Rain tends not to soak into the earth; usually it just moistens the surface as it splashes off the leaves. So a good *soaking* with a hose is vital.

Holiday Watering

If you go away, take the containers out of the sun and leave them grouped together near a few buckets of water, so there is moisture in the air around them. Before leaving, drench the containers thoroughly, then pack moist peat, moss or bark chips over the soil to retain the moisture. Otherwise ask your neighbour to water them with the hose over the garden fence.

You could buy a timer cap. The simplest ones are *Hozelock ASL Aquameter Water Controller* and *Garden Watertimer*. Both turn the water off after a fixed time. They do need to be reset each day, but nevertheless they will save your neighbour a lot of time and hard work.

26: Planting on a slope

Should your garden be on a slope it does not necessarily mean you will be planting on a slope, as the garden may be terraced and have retaining walls. But planting on a slope is slightly more difficult and requires a different technique from planting on the flat.

The main rule is to cut into the *back* of the hill and make the part of the hole which is furthest uphill *twice* as deep. Try not to disturb the soil more than you have to, otherwise when it rains the loose earth will slip away. So make your hole so that when you place the plant in it both the front and back of the plant fit snugly in the space. Then firm down the earth around the plant on all sides. If only the back of the plant is in the hole, the roots in the front will not be properly covered and will dry out; it will be very hard for the plant to get established, and it may never succeed.

Another big problem with plants growing on a slope is the difficulty in watering them properly. Water tends to run off a slope very quickly, so when it rains plants don't have the nice soaking they would normally have. Adding 3–4 in (7.5–10 cm) of mulch helps to retain the moisture.

The soil on some banks is very well drained. If you have a well-drained, sunny slope, choose plants that like well-drained soil, such as many hard herbs (rosemary, sage, thyme). Most alpines which grow well in a rock-garden like well-drained soil. On banks of this kind you already have the conditions of a rock garden for alpines without having to go to the trouble and expense of making one. By strategically placing the odd stone in a niche dug out for it between the plants, you will create the impression of a rock garden. Try to pack stone chipping between the plants until they get established, to keep out the weeds.

I had a number of difficult banks to cope with in my two-acre field conversion and

PLANTING ON A SLOPE

When planting on a slope, make sure you dig the hole larger at the back so that the plant can grow upright. Fill the hole so that the soil is not quite level with the original slope. This depression will make watering easier and prevent erosion.

I eventually resorted to variegated periwinkle and ivy. This I was advised was fine for a small bank but rather dull on a large bank. As the soil was very acid, the bank was ideal for a feature such as dwarf evergreen azaleas, top-dressed with a good mulch to keep in the moisture which azaleas badly need. I only saw the bank after the azaleas were planted for one spring, but for those few weeks in late spring it was sensational. Many of the good ground cover plants (see *Ground Cover*) have exciting leaves and make excellent planting for slopes, with their dense root system and rapidly growng suckers. *Hypericum calycinum*, which has bright yellow star flowers in summer, is excellent for the job. It spreads well, holds the soil together and keeps the weeds out. *Sedum spurium* 'Ruby Glow' and *Saxifraga umbrosa* are also among the many plants suitable for slopes.

If you have to cope with a damp shady bank and you don't want ivy or periwinkle, try bergenias. Plant them at the top of the slope – they will soon cover the surface as their rhizome roots creep down the slope. Banks and slopes are not easy but can look very effective; if you plant correctly, the plants will live as happily there as anywhere else.

27: *Pruning*

In the same way that human life needs water, food and a short back and sides, plants too need food and water, and some need regular pruning, especially roses and lavender. Pruning increases a plant's strength, growth, form and beauty. Although a proportion of low-maintenance plants will never need to be pruned, those plants that do need annual attention, such as roses, buddleias and lavender, will not grow so well unless they are pruned.

Personally I enjoy pruning. In the country I seldom go into the garden without a pair of secateurs in my hand. There is invariably the odd dead stem, spindly growth or diseased shoot to be removed, not to mention the joy of cutting the odd bloom to take inside, and once a year clipping the yew and beech hedge.

There are many types of pruning, such as *heading back* of fruit trees, which means cutting back to just above a well-developed dormant bud, two thirds of the way down last year's shoots; *thinning out*, cutting off alternate branches to make a tree or shrub less dense; *top cutting*, cutting the top of any stem or branch; *tip cutting*, cutting the uppermost growth of a non-flowering plant shoot so that it will bush out, and so on.

But don't let all the different names for the types of pruning put you off. Basically, it is all just cutting back. The most an average low-maintenance gardener will be required to do, if the planning is right, is *light pruning*. But it is worth doing correctly and at the right time of the year, so it's best to start with the right tools.

Pruning Tools

Anvil secateurs and *parrot bill secateurs* are a must for roses, twiggy shrubs and evergreen hedges. *Long handled secateurs* are ideal for high level thick twigs and small branches, and *shears* are needed for hedge cutting. (N.B. Keep these tools cleaned and oiled and out of the reach of children.) But in a small garden you probably won't need more than anvil secateurs or kitchen scissors.

Pruning Roses

If you are planting roses in the autumn, you should prune them hard back (see diagram) when planting them or, as most people prefer, the following March/April. But ramblers, climbers and shrub roses should be pruned less hard. Cut only one third to a half of the shoot. To establish a good framework while the roses root system is still 'vulnerable' and not yet established, cut back any shoot that has flowered the previous year and cut back from the tip to the hard wood of the main growth.

A young standard needs to be cut back to help it strengthen but an established standard needs to be cut less. The weeping standard should be pruned according to the type of climber budded on to the standard. Basic pruning for the weeping standard is to cut off any dead tips or shoots and remove old flowers. Do not cut hard back, but leave the weeping branches still flowing down so the fall increases each year. Take out whole shoots when they have stopped flowering well.

Climbers are more complicated, mainly because you need a ladder and it takes longer! But climbers should be pruned in spring, cutting back all last year's strong shoots as necessary and cutting very old wood to the ground. Short lateral shoots which will bear the current year's flowers must also be cut back in spring, just leaving two or three buds.

Most ramblers are later flowering and less fussy than many roses. *Rubrifolia*, for example, needs almost no pruning. But for the average rambler, cut off flowered shoots as soon as they finish flowering, providing there is enough new growth. Cut out old shoots to the ground when they don't flower well any longer.

PRUNING ROSES

ramblers   climbers

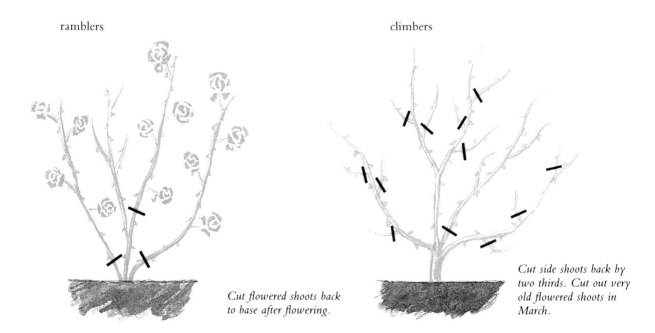

Cut flowered shoots back
to base after flowering.

Cut side shoots back by
two thirds. Cut out very
old flowered shoots in
March.

PRUNING CLIMBERS

Climbers such as spring-flowering clematis, wisteria, jasmine and passion flowers need little or no pruning and can survive quite happily if they are neglected for a year or two without any cutting back.

Cutting out the dead wood, thinning of overcrowded shoots or trimming when the climber becomes too heavy for its support are the main reasons for pruning. But these plants do not *have* to be cut back in order to produce a healthy growth.

The Clematis montana flowers on last year's growth so, after flowering this year, old flower heads should be removed.

Clematis × jackmanii *flowers on the current year's growth. Cut it hard back.*

Passiflora *(passion flower): thin out in February/ March and take out any frost damaged shoots. Cut overgrown shoots back to main stem.*

Jasminum officinale, *which is hardy, will only need thinning out, but do not shorten shoots.*

Jasminum nudiflorum *should be cut hard back when winter flowering has finished in April. Cut all dead wood and for good new growth clip back the shoots to within 2–3 in (5–7.5 cm) of main stem. Only a little pruning is needed when J. nudiflorum grows as a shrub.*

PRUNING HYDRANGEAS

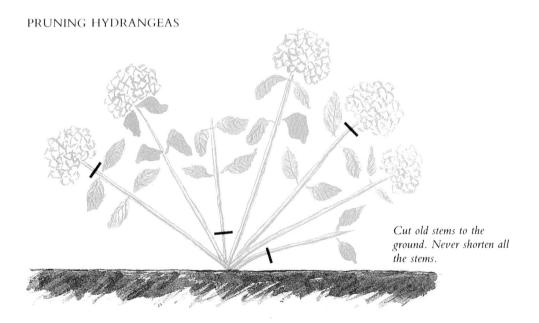

Cut old stems to the ground. Never shorten all the stems.

Shrubs

The sort of evergreen shrub required in a low-maintenance garden will need very little pruning, if any, and rhododendrons and camellias need no pruning at all. Only deciduous shrubs (which lose their leaves each winter) will need regular pruning. There are two types of deciduous shrubs, those that flower on last year's wood, like forsythia, and those that flower on new wood which has grown this season, such as buddleia. It is important to establish in which category the plants fall before pruning. Forsythia will need pruning in spring, as will buddleia which flowers in summer. If you are not sure when to prune, it is best to leave it until either spring or autumn!

PRUNING SHRUBS

It would be impossible to list here when to prune each and every plant. But be comforted with the thought that with sensible low-maintenance planting not too much pruning will be needed.

Lavender, *for example, should have the dead flowers removed in late summer plus a light trim. To encourage bushy growth, cut off all straggly growth and cut the plant back to the base of last year's shoots between March and April. Do not cut old wood.*

Hydrangeas: *the dead heads from the previous year's growth should be removed in March. Also remove 10 in (25 cm) of dead or weak shoots. The heads can be cut back after they have flowered but if you leave the flowers their 'cobwebby' beauty will enhance the garden in winter. Never trim hydrangeas all over or they will not flower. Cut back shoots that are too long right to the ground.*

Rosemary *should have its dead growth removed in March as well as the unsightly and straying shoots trimmed after flowering to retain its compact shape, but rosemary may go several years without needing any 'trim' at all. It can grow quite tall, 5–6 ft (1.5–2 m) if left unpruned.*

Rhododendrons: *remove seed pods as soon as possible after flowering by nipping with finger and thumb just beneath the cluster, without removing any of the new young shoots just below. If you do not do this you will not have flowers the following year.*

Tall herbaceous plants: *the low-maintenance gardener has a special trick to keep these bushy and to avoid staking. Cut the whole clump back to 6 in (15 cm) when about 1 ft (30 cm) high. This will only delay flowering for a week or so and the dense clump will keep the weeds down better and will not need staking. (Don't do this to peonies).*

28: *Low-maintenance vegetables*

Vegetables on the whole are *not* trouble-free, but they are so rewarding and enjoyable that if you can spare the time for them, I too should devote a little space to them – just to whet your appetite!

Two of the most important factors to be considered when planning a low-maintenance vegetable garden are layout and choosing the correct position. Choose one that has full sun and is not too difficult to get to from the house. Vegetables should run in rows from north to south. This is of primary importance. Laying paving slabs or paths between the vegetables will cut down the weeds and make access to the vegetables and weeding easier.

The paths should be 3 ft (90 cm) apart so that you can reach the vegetables in the middle of the bed from either side. With a solid path you can then weed, harvest or thin, whatever the weather, without sinking into the mud if the ground is wet.

When laying the path, take the soil from *under* the slabs and place it on the bed so as to raise up the bed for greater soil depth and better drainage. Vegetables need at least 12–18 in (30–45 cm) of good top soil for best results. If you do not have this depth, add organic matter and raise the level of the bed. This may mean having low retaining brick walls round the bed. Old railway sleepers make an excellent soil support.

To keep weeds under control in a vegetable garden, the vegetables can be planted through a slit in a black polythene sheet. This also conserves moisture. The sheet needs to be secured down at the side with bricks or soil put along the edge, before planting.

You must select a *low-maintenance crop* (not low-yielding). When starting to grow vegetables it is wise to start with a *small area* and keep it tidy, weeded and under control, rather than a big area which easily gets out of hand.

And finally *good soil*. If you have poor soil you have to improve it (see *Organic Fertilisers*) by adding organic matter such as mushroom compost, peat, shredded newspaper and compost. Preferably start your own compost pen. (See *Compost*).

In a 25 sq. yd (20 sq. m) area you will not need to spend more than twenty hours a year, less than half an hour a week. Most of this time will be used in preparing the ground, sowing and planting in March, April and May. June will be concentrated on weeding (cut down to the minimum by the paving slabs) and watering (which also can be cut down by using a Hozelock Aquameter or sprinkler to water the crop). The joyous and rewarding job of harvesting will be in July, August and September, when you'll have the enormous satisfaction of eating your own vegetables.

The following vegetables are to be avoided as they are prone to disease and pests or are labour-intensive: asparagus (needs hand weeding), carrots (prone to carrot root fly), cauliflower (needs accurate watering), celery, chicory, hot pepper, soft fruit (all labour-intensive).

VEGETABLES

There is a large choice of easily grown and trouble-free vegetables such as:

broad beans   – *sow in November for easy crop and fewer pests.*

runner beans★   – *sow seeds end of May or plant out from pots at the end of May for an early crop, they will need 7 ft (just over 2 m) canes.*

beetroot   – *sow April/May. Eat July onwards.*

calabrese   – *sow seed in March, then transplant when big enough. Eat July.*

courgettes★   – *sow May outdoors, or in pots on the window sill in March for planting out in May. Eat June to December.*

★ = *very easy*

marrow★   – *sow May. Eat July to December.*

lettuce   – *sow March to August in succession. Eat summer and autumn.*

potatoes★   – *plant March/April. Eat June onwards.*

red salad bowl *(birds don't eat it)*   – *same as lettuce.*

shallots   – *plant January/March. Eat July onwards.*

spinach *(leaf beet)*★   – *sow June/July. Eat August onwards. Swiss Chard has green leaf and white mid rib that can be cooked separately. Keep pulling off leaves and it will keep growing.*

There are comprehensive instructions on most seed packets and if you are seriously interested in growing vegetables there is a small but wonderful book called *The Vegetable Grower's Directory* by Susan Conder (Macdonald).

Although onions are cheap in the shops, when you grow your own you can be sure that they have been grown without chemicals. Also they store well. Starting with onion sets is *much* easier than seed.

If you only have space for one vegetable, I would recommend runner beans. They're really easy to grow (though they do need rain), delicious to eat freshly picked from the garden, and they freeze well. Added to which they're expensive to buy in the shops so it's economical to grow your own.

Growing Runner Beans

1. Prepare soil by digging over in December.
2. If the ground is not prepared, dig in compost about 18 in (45 cm) across and 12 in (30 cm) deep in spring.
3. In *May* sow seeds 3 in (7.5 cm) deep and between 9–12 in (22.5–30 cm) apart, in *two* parallel rows 12–15 in (30–37.5 cm) apart.
4. Push 6–7 ft (about 2 m) bamboo bean poles into the ground at the side of each seed and tie to the top of *opposite* poles with a strengthening strut across the top.
5. Plant four seeds one in each corner of an 'imaginary' 18 in (45 cm) square and place 6–7 ft (about 2 m) bamboo bean poles next to the seed and tie at the top like a wigwam. A single row can also be grown up poles against a brick wall or wooden fence. 'Butler', 'Megoles' and 'Streamline' are all good to eat.

Pests and Vegetables

There are effective and natural ways of keeping undesirable insects away from vegetables in the vegetable garden without using pesticides.

French marigolds in the greenhouse keep whitefly *out* of the greenhouse, and if planted outside between vegetables they will attract the hoverfly, which in turn eats the larva of blackfly and greenfly. Also *marigolds* keep pests at bay if planted near tomatoes.

Summer savoy planted amongst broad beans deters blackfly and *chervil* planted amongst the radishes deters borers and weevils. *Sage* and *thyme* planted between carrots and cabbage deter the cabbage moth and the cabbage white butterfly. *Celery* and *celeriac* also help keep the cabbage white butterfly away. Potato chunks left in the ground attract *wire worms* and tomatoes planted between brassicas (i.e. sprouts, broccoli and cauliflower) stimulate the growth of the brassicas as well as warding off pests. Thyme, marigolds, sage, celery and onions are all being used to great effect in our own organic vegetable garden.

Organic Pesticides: Pyrethrum and Derris, both of which come in spray form, can control aphids, caterpillars, thrips, flea beetles and the grubs of raspberry beetles. But they are harmful to ladybirds, so don't spray if there are ladybirds around. Pyrethrum and Derris should be sprayed *after sunset* when the wasps and bees are no longer on the wing. Neither has a long lasting toxic residue to harm humans or wildlife.

29: *Compost*

I am a compost fanatic, pride myself on my compost and derive tremendous pleasure when I see the positive results of my own compost. So it is understandable that I want to encourage others to do likewise, so if there's an opportunity to have a compost bin, it seems madness not to take it and put back into the soil what has been taken out of it. Root vegetable peelings, outside leaves of cabbage and lettuce, dead flowers, grass cuttings, leaves, weeds, shredded newspapers and even citrus fruit skins which are slow to decompose, are all perfect for compost. But not meat or fish scraps as they smell and also they encourage rats and mice.

Compost-making is not time-consuming yet it is very rewarding, and is a natural way of improving the structure of the soil, with the nitrogen, potash, phosphorus and trace elements that are slowly released into the earth. Compost is also an excellent mulch to top-dress the beds, keep in the moisture and keep down the weeds.

There are several kinds of compost containers, everything from chicken wire cages, wooden slatted pens, upside down plastic dust bins, manufactured compost tumblers to compost heaps covered by black plastic and held down with bricks, and holes in the ground covered with old carpet to keep the heat in. Not forgetting the good old dust bin bag, excellent for making leaf mould. But it is important that your compost container is aerated from the sides or below, so that the air can circulate through the matter. For this reason earthworms are invaluable as they help to aerate and break down the waste.

Be sure that each layer of grass cuttings, kitchen waste or leaves for your compost is damp and only about 6 in (15 cm) deep before spreading a thin layer of newspaper, preferably shredded or torn up (not the *FT* or colour supplements as they contain chemical dyes) and also a compost activator such as Garotto. But comfrey and nettles are an extremely effective activator so Garotto compost activator is not essential.

A sprinkling of nitrogen fertiliser also helps to break down compost. On clay and compacted soils use the compost before it has fully rotted down, as it helps to open and aerate the soil. Otherwise wait until the compost is fully rotted (dark and crumbly) before using. This generally takes about ten months, so be patient.

Should your garden have weeds such as ground elder or couch grass, these should be burnt and *not* put into the compost, otherwise they will seed themselves. Avoid putting holly, ivy, large twigs, bits of wood, conifers into the compost, as these will not compost easily, and man-made materials such as plastic will not compost at all.

If you can spare the time to make compost, I'm sure you will find it extremely satisfying, and be gratified to see the good it does your plants.

Organic Feed and Compost: Wet Seaweed

A friend who lives in Devon and has a smallish walled garden containing the usual selection of low-maintenance plants (London pride, camellias, azaleas, climbing roses, heathers, potentillas, bergenias, jasmine, clematis, and so on) tells me that twice a year he collects large quantities of seaweed from the rocks along the coast and places it round the plants roughly 4 in (10 cm) deep.

When the seaweed is put on to the beds it is still wet and has not been rotted down. The result is (1) he never has any weeds, (2) the plants appear to flourish on the seaweed, (3) the salt does not seem to have an adverse effect on any of his plants, (4) after several months the seaweed has completely rotted down into the soil, and (5) the garden tends to be *pest free*.

Rabbit Droppings

Rabbit droppings come higher in nutrient content than the droppings of sheep, pig, poultry, horse and cow! Not much consolation, I know, if they are eating their way through your shrub garden or herbaceous border. But if you have them as pets, do keep their droppings for the garden.

Fertilisers

As humans and animals need to be nourished and fed regularly, so do plants. It is *essential* that plants in small cultivated gardens which do not have the benefit of nature's own feeding, such as fallen leaves forming humus/compost and improving the top soil (as happens in woodland areas) have regular feeding.

The following list of fertilisers and what they do, and for which type of plant they are best, will give you some guide as to how to feed your garden each year. Instructions on the quantities to feed the plants will invariably be on the package. You are not likely to overfeed anyway with organic fertilisers, as they are natural products.

FERTILISERS

Nitrogen [N] *is for leaf and shoot growth*

Potassium [K] (Kalium *in Latin) is for flowers and fruit*

Phosphorus [P] *is for roots*

Sterilised bone meal *(roses, trees, shrubs)* [P] [K]

Seagold calcified seaweed *to improve the quality and break down the soil (good for everything)*

(J Arthur Bowers) Hoof and Horn *(flowers and vegetables)* [N] *slow-acting*

continued over page

FERTILISERS *(continued)*

(J Arthur Bowers) Dried Blood *(all growing crops)* [N] *quick-acting*

(J Arthur Bowers) Blood Fish and Bone *(salad crops)* [N] [P] [K] *balanced*

Growmore (chemical all purpose fertiliser – use with care: it can easily burn plants if you are too generous) [N] [P] [K]

Chase Organic Fertiliser *(flowers, fruit, vegetables)* [N] [P] [K]

Top Rose *(roses)* [high in P]

Phostrogen *(flowering plants)* [P]

Fresh seaweed

30: *Fencing*

In a small garden the structure surrounding the property can be as important and as enhancing to the area as the garden itself. In the early stages of a garden's life, when much of the boundary is still exposed to the eye, choosing the ideal surround is vital.

The choice of fencing is vast, and the difference in price is as great as is the variety available. Apart from the hard rustic boundaries like dry stone walls in local stone or flint stone walls, there's the choice of cottage style rose, hawthorn and holly mix hedge, formal yew, beech or box hedge, tapestry hedges, brick walls, post and rail fences, basket-weave and slatted fences to name just a few. From this wide selection, both aesthetically and for durability the *mature beech hedges* and *dry stone walls* have remained firm favourites over the years and are still the best, should money be no object. Although I appreciate that picket fences, wattle hurdle fence, conifer hedges, all have their place, especially when economy is a priority.

The romantic image of a walled garden has persisted through history books and literature. A walled garden conjures up the splendour of scenes set in the grounds of great historic castles and country homes. But the majority of us will own no more than a cottage with a walled surround or terraced house with a walled garden if we are lucky. But these walls too have their beauty.

Properties that already have their boundary defined by walls, be they brick or stone, start off at an advantage as it is the texture of stone or brick or flint that is so wonderful. The natural beauty of a surface that with a little encouragement can grow in the cracks (on a sunny wall) *Sempervivum montanum* and *Alyssum saxatile* or (on a shady wall) *Arenaria balearica* and *Campanula portenschlagiana* is magical.

A beech or yew hedge has great charm too, but they both need to be clipped each year, and therefore no matter how lovely, cannot come high on the list for a trouble-free garden.

Building a stone wall is extremely expensive, unless you are able to do it yourself. So it is vital that you choose an expert for your dry stone walling or brick laying. Make sure you have seen a sample of his work *beforehand*. A botched up job is not only a waste of money, it is also an eyesore. As you are the one who is going to have to live with your choice, think carefully at planning stage and choose a brick or stone that is in keeping with the house, although you may not want exactly the same stone or brick. And even if you wish to whitewash the wall or grow plants in front of it, the original work must be good.

Making a Fence less Obtrusive

No matter what kind of fence you have defining your property boundary, it is important that you do not have the edge of the lawn running parallel to it, as this only draws attention to the fence, and its height, as indeed does a straight narrow border running down the side of the fence. A curved border with flowers at varying

Two handsome, traditional style enclosures.
Stonecrop (Sedum) grows over a dry stone wall
(above); and a wattle fence maintains the natural
look.

opposite: A very ordinary post and rail fence is
disguised by a pretty climbing rose (photo by Susan
Hampshire).

heights draws the eye away from the boundary and makes the fence seem less overpowering. Alternatively, introduce an attractive feature half way down the fence – say an urn or statue placed in front of an arch of climbing roses growing over a simple structure behind the statue. This relief makes the fence seem less important as the eye is naturally drawn to the feature in front.

All wood fencing should be 'pressure impregnated' – a treatment that will ensure that the wood lasts for fifty years, even in the ground. Pressure impregnated wood posts not only look better than concrete posts but also last longer.

Painting Fences

A wooden fence doesn't have to be white. In Florida, Bermuda and the Caribbean fences are painted and stippled to great effect. For example, if you have a white picket fence or ranch style fence, it can be painted pale grey, green or white with a hint of pink! It is also very effective, and painting the fence green and then stippling it with black makes the fence blend beautifully with the vegetation. The same goes for concrete walls which can be fairly stark on their own: painted a subtle green they become part of the landscape.

FENCING

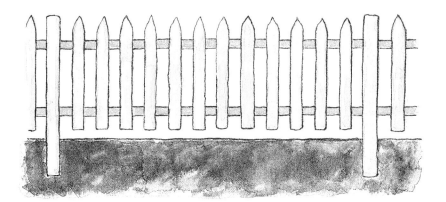

picket style fence

close boarded fence

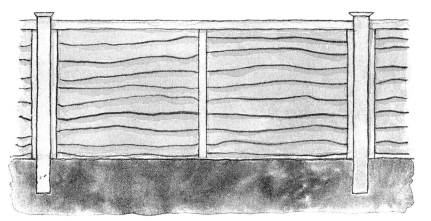

horizontal boarded fence

Three possible forms of wooden fencing. Always use pressure impregnated timber: it lasts longer, even for the posts, which look better than concrete ones.

The Legal Position

You can usually fence your boundaries up to just over 3 ft (1 m) high at the front and 6 ft 6 in (2 m) high at the back. (Check with your local planning authority if in doubt, especially if you have a corner plot.) You do not *have* to fence or protect your boundary unless there is a covenant in your deeds to this effect. If you do have to put up a fence then you will probably have to keep it maintained too.

Planting a Beech Hedge

Planting a hedge is an enjoyable labour but given that many hedges need pruning once a year and the hedge site has to be kept weed free until the hedge is established, it is not low-maintenance, and you could well say has no place here! But the final effect of, say, a laurel or beech hedge is so handsome that I am envious of anyone who has the space and opportunity to plant one.

A beech hedge well planted *now* could go on enhancing (with its light green leaves in spring, turning darker in summer and its lovely burnt brown/rust leaves in winter) and protecting the property until well after we are 'gone'.

If you wish to plant a beech hedge, do not attempt to do so if you have heavy wet soil, when you can plant hornbeam instead. Unless you are able to improve the soil conditions sufficiently by adding a considerable amount of organic matter and calcified seaweed and then raising the height of the bed by 1 ft (30 cm) deep and 2 ft (60 cm) across to improve the drainage, it is not worth it. Beeches will do well on all other soils.

Weed the hedge line thoroughly, removing all weeds and *keeping weed free* for six months from the spring ready for autumn planting in October. *Well-prepared soil is essential.* Then in the autumn fork in 1 ft (30 cm) deep a good organic fertiliser and well rotted compost.

Plant the young beeches (*Fagus sylvatica*) when they are 18 in (45 cm) high. The plants should be spaced about 18–24 in (45–60 cm) apart. Use a string line to keep the planting straight. Alternatively the plants can be staggered forward and back in a zigzag to make a thicker hedge. I prefer this latter method, but I have televised with expert gardeners who tell me a single straight line is better. Take your choice.

Each plant needs a hole roughly 1 ft (30 cm) deep. Plant each beech with fine soil already well mixed with bone meal and calcified seaweed or dried blood, put round its roots. If you can get some beech leaf litter to mix in, this helps rapid establishment, as a cosy relationship with a particular fungus helps the plants take up water and nutrients. Firm well with the weight of your body gently weighing on your fists, so that the root is secure. After planting press your *heel* firmly round the base of each plant. If the plant is not well firmed in, it cannot survive as its roots will be flapping about in the gaps in the earth. So firming in well is very important.

PLANTING A HEDGE

Beech hedge (or other hedge)

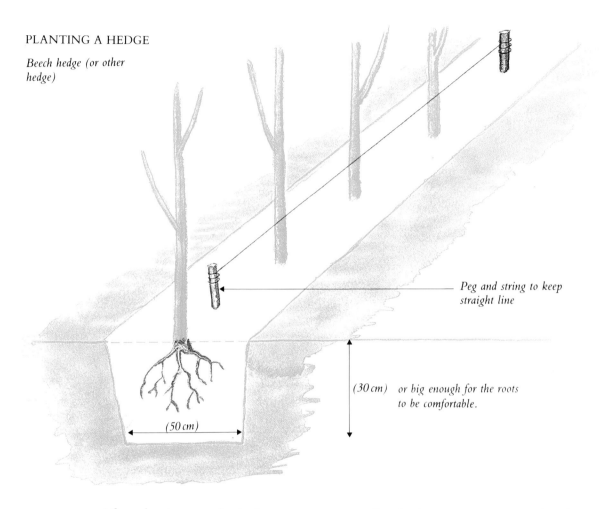

Peg and string to keep straight line

(30 cm) *or big enough for the roots to be comfortable.*

(50 cm)

   After planting, cut back the upper quarter of each shoot to encourage the plant to bush out. Repeat this 'tipping' process the following July. By the third summer the hedge should be established and from then on cut into the shape required each July or August.

Watering

Apart from preparing the soil correctly, and making sure the plant is well firmed into the earth, *watering* is the next great must. The young beech, or box or privet, will need at least two gallons (9 litres or two watering cans full) a week for *each* plant in dry spells. If it does not get this water in the dry weather during the first few years the plant will die. If you haven't time to water, it is easy enough to set up a sprinkler on a timer meter. A good soaking is needed, not 'little and often'. But the watering in the early stages while the roots are getting established is *essential*. We cannot live without water, neither can a young hedge.

Young plants of this size (18 in/45 cm) will not need staking or training as they are too small.

Beeches do not grow very quickly whereas privet (*Ligustrum ovalifolium*) and cypress (*Chamaecyparis leylandii*) do, but then they are not so pleasing. Feed regularly once a year in spring and enjoy your hedge. If you want to plant close up to your hedge, lay heavy duty polythene in a 2 ft (60 cm) deep trench 2 or 3 ft (60 or 90 cm) from it, to restrain the root growth.

31: *Paving and hard surfaces*

The easy alternative to grass for small gardens

Brick

Before buying the cement or levelling the ground, the most important decision to be made for paving is the choice of material, and there is a huge variety from which to choose.

As I have mentioned, to my mind brick is one of the most beautiful. There is nothing so pleasing as mellow brick. It adds a special quality to any garden. Brickwork in Victorian and Edwardian gardens achieved the high level of craftsmanship for which England was noted, and such work can still be seen and admired today.

But when choosing brick, select one that is *frost-resistant* and has a *non-slip surface*, otherwise once brick is wet and a little slime or algae has accumulated on it, it can be very slippery. It's important not to buy smooth engineering brick for the garden paths, steps or terrace.

Another advantage of brick is that it is very adaptable and can be worked easily into any space or design. There are a variety of brick patterns such as herring-bone or basket-weave, both which look most attractive when laid. Brick is expensive but it is long-lasting and it improves with time.

Choose a shade that will blend well with your house or boundary walls. If your house is a yellow brick, try to find a brick in a similar shade that will tone, rather than a contrasting colour such as dark reddy-black or bright red brick. Redland Bricks have a wide selection as do some building merchants. The Brick Advisory Centre can help match bricks and comment on their quality and stability (addresses at the back of the book).

Synthetic Material

Smooth and riven concrete slabs come in many shades, shapes and sizes, and there is also a great variety in smaller coloured concrete slabs. A good many are non-slip, frost-resistant and inexpensive in comparison to brick and York stone. If carefully selected, they look very pleasing, especially if they are broken up with small areas of brick, cobbles or have sections omitted for the planting of low growing-plants. A selection of terracotta pots or containers can also help to break up the monotony of concrete slabs.

If you like synthetic materials, there is a huge selection to choose from including concrete blocks in brick size or smaller. More than a dozen different types, shapes and shades can be found at Reed Harris Tiles in London and other tile specialists and large garden centres (addresses at the back of the book).

PAVING

brick in a herring bone pattern

brick in a basket weave pattern

York stone

Three of the many choices of paving. All expensive, but they mellow and look better with age, and last a lifetime.

Tiles

Quarry tiles are very attractive for a small patio or conservatory. Terracotta tiles also (check they are frost resistant) have great style and lend a Continental flavour. There are also precast textured slabs, cobbles, stable tiles, and simulated granite setts.

Pea Shingle

Pea shingle is another material for which I have a weakness. (Suppliers: Mid Essex Gravel Pits (Chelmsford) Ltd, Broomfield, Chelmsford, Essex, CM3 3PZ, tel: 0245 440621, if you can't find it locally.) If you pick up a handful of pea shingle after it has rained you will observe the wonderful variety of subtle colours, colours which most gravel does not possess. Much of the crushed shingle or gravel tends to be uniformly beige, rust, rusty beige, beigey pink, pinky grey, grey-y brown and so on. But among the tiny pebbles of pea shingle there is a whole range of exquisitely gentle natural colours. Most suppliers of crushed shingle or gravel will send samples in the post, so you can see it before deciding which one looks best with your house.

LAYING PAVING

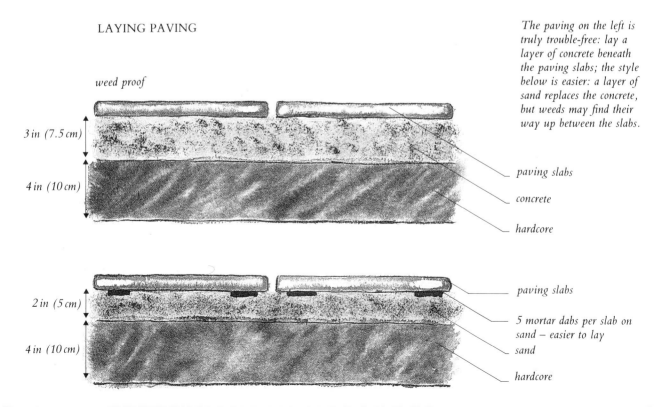

weed proof

3 in (7.5 cm)

4 in (10 cm)

2 in (5 cm)

4 in (10 cm)

The paving on the left is truly trouble-free: lay a layer of concrete beneath the paving slabs; the style below is easier: a layer of sand replaces the concrete, but weeds may find their way up between the slabs.

paving slabs

concrete

hardcore

paving slabs

5 mortar dabs per slab on sand – easier to lay

sand

hardcore

But whether you choose gravel or pea shingle, in time they both attract weeds. These weeds are easily removed by raking or a solution of a weed killer such as Path Clear, but if the area is driven or walked on regularly, the weeds will be crushed and not have the opportunity to come through. It is unfortunate that one is obliged to use chemicals to kill weeds, as so many small creatures' lives depend on our using natural methods and organic materials. If you feel strongly about it a good rake is extremely effective.

If you have 2 in (5 cm) or more of pea shingle, cars and walking on the surface will usually keep down the weeds. But remember that 2 in (5 cm) of pea shingle under foot is less comfortable to walk on and certainly *not* suitable for the elderly. Crushed pea shingle is not suitable for wheelchairs. These gravels produce an uneven surface, so prams and wheelchairs get stuck and cannot run smoothly, and the older generation will find shingle and gravel very unsteady under foot.

N.B. 6 in (15 cm) deep shingle is thought very good under children's swings and play equipment. Not quite as good as shredded bark, but surprisingly effective.

Cobblestones

To conclude, another absolutely beautiful surface is flint stone cobbles. They are not comfortable to walk on but they do make a very attractive paving surface.

If used in 2 ft (60 cm) widths as edging round a terrace, or for adding detail down the edge of a path or to a paved focal point such as a statue or fountain, they are unsurpassed. Even whole areas paved with cobbles look stunning, especially if 'olde worlde' ornaments such as old farmyard implements are placed on them.

Cobbles should be set into mortar, otherwise in no time the weeds will completely cover this beautiful surface. Again these are not suitable for wheelchairs or older people.

Laying Paving

Unless you are a good 'do-it-yourself' enthusiast, laying paving, bricks and cobbles is a professional's job and is best left to the skilled, as paving has to be graded so the rainwater can fall away. But if you have an adventurous spirit, strong back and plenty of energy, you can do it yourself.

The laying of paving slabs as described in the front garden (page 38) is quite simple if laid on sand but this is not good for low maintenance as weeds grow between the slabs. Lay standard paving units of 18 × 18 in (45 × 45 cm), 9 × 9 in (22.5 × 22.5 cm) or 18 × 9 in (45 × 22.5 cm) on to a flat bed of sand, though for true low maintenance it is more satisfactory to lay them on a bed of concrete. With sand, the paving after heavy rains can often become uneven and slippery because the slabs retain the moisture that seeps up from the sand below, and weeds will grow between the slabs. It's important to remember when putting sand beneath the slabs that it should be under the whole slab and not just under the corners, otherwise when the temperature beneath the slab changes it will crack. First, level the space, then all you need to do is:

1. Check the surface is even with string and a spirit level.
2. Spread sand or concrete over the whole area and again check the level.
3. Lay the standard paving slabs, but if the paving is for a patio by the house, it *must* be *graded* so the paving slopes gradually to one side into a proper drain or soak-away, and not towards and into the house.
4. Finally point between the slabs with cement mortar.

Drainage

If your garden drains to a pipe, ditch or a stream you probably have a right to it and no one may interrupt it. You can check with your local Water Authority or Internal Drainage Board. But you cannot drain your paving on to somebody else's land without their consent and similarly they may not do this to you.

This section is only a guide to give some ideas for choice of material. But if you really want to have a go at building walls and patios yourself, the following booklets are worth buying: *Bricks, Concrete and Stones* (Reader's Digest £1.95); and *Concrete Around Your Home and Garden*, £1.00 available direct from Cement and Concrete Association, Wexham Springs, Slough SL3 6PL.

32: *Ornaments*

Punctuation or Features

In a trouble-free, low maintenance garden that does not rely on vast displays of carpet bedding, grand herbaceous borders, imposing vistas or specimen plants, well-chosen garden ornaments can enhance a garden in the same way as interesting foliage can. So special features such as a large mirror against a wall framed by an arch of roses, a jardinière filled with spring-flowering bulbs and trailing plants, a fountain or sundial, will punctuate a garden, create interest and make the fact that the majority of plants are evergreen shrubs less important.

'Punctuation' or garden features can range from stone ornaments to ornamental trees. Groups of tubs or terracotta pots, sundials, sculpture, fountains, stone lions, dogs, cats, hedgehogs or baskets, bird baths, statues, groupings of large stones, farm implements (such as old cart wheels), garden gnomes, a painted wooden wheelbarrow filled with flowers, and a strategically placed standard weeping rose tree are all excellent features to punctuate the garden.

Garden ornaments and statues do not necessarily need to be of exceptional beauty or of great value. Just right for their setting. Years ago I agreed to a television I didn't really want to do so that I could buy a pair of genuine Queen Anne stone baskets of fruit for the terrace. It was sad to discover having bought them that no matter where they were placed they have never looked as remarkable as I had anticipated. The only remark that has ever been made on them is, 'Oh, you've got those nice reconstituted stone reproductions.' I'm glad they didn't see the bill!! So much for buying things at an exorbitant price!

So broken statues or pots, fibre glass or plaster animals, or busts made by teenagers at school can all look intriguing if given the right background and a single spotlight at night. Even discarded props from a play look interesting (while they last), especially with ivy growing over them.

Finding the correct sized object for the space is an art in itself. The smaller the garden, the more careful you need to be in your choice.

If, for the sake of economy, you buy plastic containers, avoid using them too near the house and make sure ivy is planted to hang over the side to camouflage the plastic material. Natural textures are more in keeping in the garden and tend to look better than man-made ones. But there are places where you can economise. At the end of the garden you can always get away with less expensive tubs or ornaments, especially if they are under overhanging trees which will help weather them.

Larger features such as wells or fountains are interesting in small gardens as well as in large. Their impressive size gives importance to the space and they lend a romantic rustic quality, as do stone corn 'stoops' or mushrooms, stone troughs and benches.

In a large garden, should the well not be a genuine one for drawing water, it can be placed where it is of most ornamental use, away from the house to draw one's eye

opposite and left: Ornaments: a small mirror (with Morning glory (Ipomoea) growing over the surrounding trellis) gives a feeling of space in a small garden; the tiny wheelbarrow containing New Guinea busy lizzie adds a splash of colour to a paved area; the elegant urn adds interest to a large garden; and newly planted variegated ivy flows over the sides of a Victorian iron urn.

below: A now purely ornamental 16th century Venetian well and a functional one in a cottage garden. Both have different decorative uses.

into the distance like this simple 16th-century Venetian well. But a functional cottage well needs to be near the house so that the water can easily be drawn if there is a drought. Both wells make attractive features and even the well that is only ornamental could look quite spectacular filled with flowers or placed in the middle of a courtyard or small paved area in a pint-sized garden.

Suppliers

Haddonstone and Chilstone (addresses at the back) produce splendid architectural ornaments and these can be mellowed and made to look as if they have been in the garden for years with a special paint from Haddonstone called Stone Age Paint. Do not be alarmed if the stonework looks very dark immediately it is painted. The intense colour will fade within a few weeks, but one coat should be enough, otherwise as reconstituted stone is very absorbent, it will look very dark.

Better still let nature do its work and time will make reconstituted stonework look old, especially if it is washed over with a mild solution of cow manure or Bio plant food to attract lichen and moss.

33: *Lighting*

If you have created something beautiful, it is a great sadness not to be able to appreciate its beauty after sunset. If you think of the garden as another room, is it not odd to have a room you *cannot* use after dark? So it is well worth the trouble of installing garden lighting or just one light, if only to make a large-leafed plant at the far end of the garden look more interesting, or so that you can admire the magic of the garden on the rare occasions it is covered in snow. More importantly, a garden's shortcomings are disguised in artificial light.

The drama and contrast achieved by lighting is mainly due to the fact that artificial light tends to come from the side or below the plant, whereas nature throws her daylight from above. The different angle of light contributes to the dramatic effect.

Lighting is also an excellent deterrent against intruders, recommended by Crime Watch as one of the best ways to keep down the instances of breaking and entering over garden walls and through back yards or tiny back gardens.

I must stress that installing a simple garden light is not expensive. The light can cost as little as £5–£10 plus installation, around the £35–£40 mark. Try to have the switch *inside* so that if you hear a noise – even if it is only the cat – you can switch on the light from inside. A small price to pay towards personal and property safety.

Locks and lights make good sense. It is false security and foolish economy to imagine that if you have nothing to steal no one will bother you. 'No one' doesn't know that you have nothing until 'no one' is in there looking and if you disturb that 'no one' you'll wish you hadn't.

Illuminate side passages, patios, small terraces, back yards, back gardens, even front gardens if they are dark, with a simple utility garden light. It's worth it.

A high-powered mains system lighting the whole garden is an expensive luxury and needs to be carefully considered at the planning stage, with electric points strategically placed round the garden, plus the main switch to turn the lights off and on installed conveniently inside the kitchen door. If you have to crawl on your hands and knees to the back of the dust bin shed to turn it off and on, it will never be used.

Should you not wish to splash out and have lights placed round the whole garden, it is worth considering lighting a special feature, especially in a town garden. Whether it is a fountain or statue or tree, the rules are the same: the switch must be easily accessible inside the house and the light should be considered at planning stage and professionally installed. Even an ordinary ornament or pot lit at night by a low power light will suddenly take on a fresh dimension.

If you don't want to install a high-powered mains system, there are plenty of low-voltage garden lights that are less expensive and which will do the job quite satisfactorily in a small garden.

Garden candles, hurricane lamps and fairy lights are very pretty and ideal for a party, but for day to day use a simple electric garden light fixed to the back of the house is invaluable and more practical. *N.B.* Always extinguish garden candles after use, do not leave them to start a fire and preferably place them on stone paving or a hard non-inflammable surface.

When your lighting is in place, try focusing the light at different angles so as to achieve the most interesting and exciting effect. If the light doesn't look right, try out a new angle to improve the result.

Important

Children and lights: it is not advisable to have a complicated lighting system where there are children. One or two security lights fixed to the house will be safe and adequate.

Both ponds and electricity should always be avoided when there are young children.

Preparation

If you are redesigning your whole garden and you can't afford lighting at construction stage, lay the cables or pipes (called ducts) *under paving or underground*. If these are laid when constructing the garden, it will save money and a great deal of inconvenience later on when the lighting is installed.

It's important not to forget to put a piece of nylon string through the duct so as to draw the cable through at a later date. Remember to secure the end of the string in a place where you can find it again, otherwise all this preparation is wasted.

34: *Pests*

Fast-moving insects are friends. Slow-moving insects are foes.

There are a large number of garden pests. Despite the fact that the list of plants, trees and shrubs chosen for this book have been recommended as they are in the main trouble-free, there are, nevertheless, a great many roses that are vulnerable to greenfly and blackspot. An attack by either is unsightly and a cause for concern. But both can easily be kept under control.

To deter greenfly, fill an old squeezy bottle with soapy water made with soft soap, not detergent, and spray it over the offending insects – the liquid will not harm the roses.

Blackspot, yellowing leaves, mildew or other fungi on roses are best dealt with by Benlate, a reliable chemical and one of the few remedies to do the trick. If used as directed, it is quite safe. Make sure any diseased leaves are burnt or put into a plastic bag or thrown away. Do not throw the leaves back on to the soil or into the compost heap; if you do the trouble will persist.

Slugs

Slugs tend to be more of a pest in vegetable gardens than anywhere else, because they get to your food before you do. But slugs are partial to all young leaves and shoots. You may not wish to use slug pellets as they are harmful, so glass jars sunk into the ground to the level of the earth and filled to the brim with half beer, half water and a little sugar usually do the trick. The slugs, attracted by the smell, are overcome by the fumes and fall into the beer and drown. Should you choose this method, prepare yourself to see the odd inebriated bird, intoxicated by beer-marinated slugs, mistaking the cherries on your sun hat for real! To say nothing of the drunken hedgehogs who love slugs. Thrushes luckily eat snails so won't be affected, unless you are fortunate enough to trap the snails this way as well.

Another way to deter slugs is carefully to lay soot round your most treasured plants. Do not let the soot touch the leaves as it will burn them. Small stones, ashes and egg shells can also be used, as slugs do not like anything rough under their belly. A collar of perforated zinc about 3 in (7.5 cm) high around a stem is another way of deterring slugs from eating a special plant.

In order not to encourage slugs, try not to leave logs or rubbish lying around: slugs are attracted by the dark damp underside of the wood, pots or debris.

Snails

It is not uncommon to see keen garden lovers of a certain age walking round their garden crushing snails with the butt of their walking stick to stop them eating tender young shoots.

If nature was doing its stuff, the birds would eat and keep down the snail population, but unfortunately the snails outwit the birds by hiding under large leaves such as bergenia where the birds can't get at them. So if your garden has a lot of snails (they love moist leafy spots and feed on the young shoots and leaves of any plant), I'm afraid you have to get rid of them, especially in the vegetable garden where they can do so much damage.

Other than picking them out of their hidey holes by hand and crushing them, the best methods are either the same technique recommended for slugs (see above) i.e.: use beer in a yoghurt pot sunk into the ground; or protecting your young plants in glass cloches; or put gravel, ashes or soot round the plants you wish to protect. Snails do not like to travel over surfaces that are not smooth.

Slug pellets are harmful to pets, slow worms, hedgehogs, beetles and birds, so if you can deter slugs and snails other than by using chemicals, you should do so.

Animal Pests

Gardens can easily be ruined by domestic animals. Dogs weeing on the grass leave unsightly yellow patches and cats constantly scratching in the soil disturb and burn the roots of young plants, to say nothing of rabbits and tortoises who can, in an afternoon, if given the chance, indiscriminately eat their way through your flower bed and leave an alarming trail of plants nipped off at the root never to flower again. Three years' growth of a fair sized border can be severed in half an hour. That's why many people favour the animals Medusa has already cast her eye upon as stone cats and rabbits are much less trouble. (See *Ornaments*.)

The legal position regarding animals is that it is the responsibility of the owner to keep his or her animal in his or her garden. Cats are an exception to this rule and they can wander where they will and no one can do a damn thing about it. Even if the cat sits in the pram on your baby's toes, you are the one who should have had a cat net.

Dogs

On the whole dogs are easier to control than cats, as you can have some say over their movements. Provided they are taken for a walk twice a day they should not need to foul the garden.

If you have no option but to let the dog use the garden, then 'Doggie loos' bins set in the ground filled with chemicals and covered with a lid are one solution. The mess can be scooped up and dropped into the bin.

If you have a dog and a newly planted garden, it's important to protect the trunks of young trees by surrounding the base with chicken wire at least 18 in (45 cm) from the trunk of the tree so the dog's acid excrement is not constantly eating its way into the young roots.

Cats

A newly planted garden is extremely tempting to cats: they love the soft earth of freshly prepared beds. Unfortunately their excrement burns the leaves and their scratching disturbs the roots of young plants. Until a plant is well-established this disturbance can be very damaging.

It may not be your own cat that will cause the problem: she or he will usually use someone else's garden. So it is more likely to be your neighbour's cat that will be tempted by the soft soil and bird life in your garden. The solution is simple and needs about one hour of your time.

1. Buy some Renardine in a garden centre, or direct from Gilbertson and Page Ltd, Corrys, Roestock Lane, Colney Heath, St Albans, Herts HL40QW.
2. Wear rubber gloves when doing this job.
3. Saturate chopped firewood in Renardine, then push the sticks into the earth around the newly planted shrubs and plants. Do not let the Renardine sticks touch the leaves of the plants as it is a rather strong substance and will burn them.

The smell of Renardine will remind you of a fox or skunk rather than lily of the valley, and it is this strong smell that deters the cats. It is not harmful to pets but do remember to wear gloves when handling the saturated sticks, otherwise the smell on the hands lingers and lingers and lingers!

There is an alternative solution, other than standing guard on your plants for two years until they are well-established. An old lady whose neighbour had 17 cats advised that if you leave a small area of soft soil without plants in one of the flower beds in the corner of the garden for the cats to foul, they will not disturb the rest of the garden. Worth a try, and not so smelly as Renardine. But credit where credit is due, cats do catch rabbits, one of the garden's worst enemies.

Rabbits

Fortunately moles and rabbits are unlikely to invade town gardens but whatever gardens they do invade, they are persistent intruders. Rabbits are particularly destructive and should be deterred as quickly as possible, before they have done too much damage.

There are many methods of trying to keep rabbits out, but few are completely successful. Special rabbit fencing which goes down beneath and along the soil can keep rabbits *out* but it can also keep them *in*. If their run goes deep under the fence and the rabbits are inside as well as out, your rabbit kingdom will rapidly increase and experts will have to be called to gas all the warrens. Also rabbit fencing is useless if gates are left open for any length of time, as they will soon find the alternative route.

Renardine is very effective in deterring rabbits (see above.) Renardine used as a 'smell fence' around your favourite plants can certainly help to keep this destructive animal away. One sniff of this fox-like smell and the rabbit will turn tail.

To protect a large group of shrubs and plants, a boundary can be created by saturating string and sticks in Renardine and then attaching the string from stick to stick, thus cordoning off the plants.

If you have rabbits *all* young trees should be protected by plastic tree guards. (If rabbits eat round the bark the tree will die.) You could always get a cat. They deter rabbits, although they do have a few destructive habits of their own (see above).

Moles

Moles are pretty elusive creatures. They have confounded better folk than me. There are many devices that can be used to deter moles: Murphy Mole Smokes or steel traps (from garden centres), thorny rose branches laid in the hole, milk bottles, moth balls put in the ground and garlic or Jeyes fluid poured into their run. All these are moderately effective.

If your house is situated on the edge of a common, park or village green and the moles there are abundant, the primary task is to track down the *main* run from the 'outside world' to your garden.

Moles usually only have one 'entrance' run, so once you have located it, place your chosen device in their run and once that 'entrance run' has proved fatal, they should not invade your garden again. But moles can easily turn one to drink and one man was reportedly in such a state that he mistakenly took the Jeyes fluid himself instead of giving it to the moles.

Gardeners have resorted to recruiting masses of children to jump up and down on the grass singing at the top of their voices for hours on end to frighten the moles away with the noise of their feet and larynxes. I have myself resorted to this method and no one has complained, not even the moles. Hardly surprising as they live happily beside motorways.

Other people have taken the view that more drastic steps are called for, and dug a hole in the ground near the main mole run. They have then placed a loud speaker wrapped in a black dust bin bag in the hole, then connected the speaker to a tape recorder and played heavy rock music at full volume to frighten the moles away. 'Rock and mole' as it's known in the underground world.

But moles are not all bad; they eat many unwanted grubs and bugs in the soil and, more important, where there are moles there are worms. Lovely worms which do so much to improve our soil. But remember if a mole has been on the rampage beneath your flower bed, heel in plants again after moles have disturbed them.

If all else fails and the moles persist as a last resort you can always call in the local council's Pest Department. They may deal with the problem free of charge. In some areas the local council are unable to help, but the Ministry of Agriculture will give you the name of a mole catcher who will put strychnine-coated worms into the run. Moles eat dead moles so, provided one mole has eaten a strychnine-coated worm and has died, the chain reaction results in the rest of the moles dying too. Nasty but effective. Otherwise there is Baron Pest Control, Chase Centre, Rugeley Road, Hednesford, Staffs, WS12 5TB, Tel: 078321 4946/46731, one of the pest control companies who have had success deterring moles.

Starlings

Starlings are deceptive. One imagines that those dear little birds that make such a racket roosting in the tree at dusk are perfectly harmless. But if they are roosting in your tree you should deter them as quickly as possible as their acid droppings prevent anything growing beneath the tree, and the tree itself will eventually die if they do not move away. Indeed, whole copses have been ruined by roosting starlings.

Frightening them with fire-arms is inadvisable unless you are a game-keeper, and banging wooden spoons on saucepans and singing loudly as they start to settle is not always satisfactory, especially if the neighbours don't like your voice! Added to which I know from experience that they come back to roost the moment the noise stops and it's impossible to plan one's life to be available each evening to deter starlings. But the Royal Society for the Protection of Birds (telephone 0767 80551) are very helpful and can advise you on starling alarm tapes used by the Forestry Commission.

If you want to know more about starlings, get *The Starling* by Christopher Feare, The Shire Natural History Series.

For deterring pests in the vegetable garden see last section of *Vegetables*.

35: *Insurance*

Statistics have shown that the contents of a garden shed in the average household is around the £1000 mark and, should a thief break in and walk off with the lot, i.e. mower, tools, bike, garden chairs, hose, pram, garden umbrella and so on, it is an expensive loss. So it's wise to think about insurance. If you prefer not to insure, put a good strong padlock on the garden shed and keep it locked. It is expensive and tiresome to have to replace things and no one likes losing a favourite spade or bicycle.

There is also another form of insurance worth considering: Public Liability protects you should someone trip over your front step, or slip and twist their ankle on your path, or should your window box or flower pot fall on their head. Public Liability can be built into household contents policy. If you feel you are vulnerable in either case, contact a broker and ask for advice. Both insurances are moderately inexpensive.

Gardening from Which? is a most reliable gardening monthly and receives many letters each year regarding legal problems, mostly relating to landscapes, faulty machinery and tools as well as the problems between neighbours relating to boundaries and overgrown trees.

All landscaping work such as turfing, paving, or planting is covered by the Supply of Goods and Services Act (in England and Wales). The landscaper has an obligation to supply goods or materials which are of merchantable quality and to carry out the work with reasonable care and skill. If either the materials or the way the job is done are not up to scratch, you are entitled to compensation which will allow you to get the job done to a reasonable standard. This Act doesn't apply in Scotland but common law, which would treat the deal as two contracts – one of sale, the other of service – gives much the same protection to the consumer.

Which? Personal Service gives advice and help to individual members when something goes wrong and they find themselves unable to get redress following a complaint about faulty goods, poor service, shoddy workmanship or such like. There are now over 29,000 subscribers to *Which?* Personal Service and their Personal Service lawyers deal with over 3,000 cases a year. For details of how to subscribe to *Which?* Personal Service, write to Dept BJJ/G, Consumers' Association, 2 Marylebone Road, London NW1 4DX.

Trees and the Law

A tree on the boundary of two properties is owned by both parties. The only way to deal with problems is by agreement, as if any unilateral action made the tree unsafe it would prove a legal minefield. As the owner of a tree, you are responsible for damage caused by the overhang of branches or growth of the tree's roots.

The usually accepted idea is that the amount of light you are entitled to is for 'comfortable use and enjoyment'. So if your *house* is very shaded by a neighbour's tree, you could ask to have its crown thinned, or removed (lopping only causes denser growth in later years) to let more light in. This does not apply to gardens, so unfortunately you cannot force a neighbour to prune or remove trees to get more light into your garden.

This is also true of your view. You don't generally have a right of a view over another person's land. Similarly there is no right to shelter from a neighbour's trees if he chooses to cut them down.

Trees are the property of the landowner and are subject to the usual rights and liabilities. If you are in doubt about the safety of a tree, consult an expert, preferably an independent Arboricultural Consultant, and not a tree contractor. A very old tree should be inspected at regular intervals.

DO'S

Garden

Feed bulbs just after they have flowered in the spring.

N.B. Remember not to cut daffodils down until *six weeks* after flowering.

Go to reliable garden centres for plants. The ones in the centre of towns tend to be more expensive, but ask around to find out the best in the area.

Cut lavender back in spring but never cut into old wood.

Cut nepeta in autumn or spring and it will flourish again in the summer. If you wish, cut after flowering to keep them busy. Water and feed to help regrowth.

When planting under established trees the ground will be poor due to the tree's greedy roots. So double-digging for each individual plant (twice the width and depth of the normal size) is essential to improve the soil and give the plant a chance. Replace the old soil with well-rotted organic compost (with organic fertiliser) before planting, so each hole has mostly new soil. Suitable plants for these conditions under trees are *Aucuba* (spotted laurel), *Skimmia* (male and female), *Viburnum tinus (laurustinus)*, *Euphorbia robbiaie, Fatsia japonica, Garrya elliptica* and *hostas*. Once all the new plants have been planted liberally sprinkle slow-release fertiliser round the base of each plant. Use calcified seaweed, bone meal, blood fish and bone.

Watering. Remember to water *regularly* during the first summer until shrubs and trees are established.

Protect new plants against cats with sticks saturated in Renardine (see *Pests*).

DO'S *(continued)*

Mulching. When the garden is completely planted lay a thick layer of mulch, preferably in April when the ground is still wet, so that it will retain the moisture in the drier weather and help the new plants to get their roots down. This can regularly be topped up with grass clippings put directly on the bed so long as the clippings are *no more than 2 in (5 cm)* deep and they are kept well away from the stems of any plants as they (the stems) may rot away. Also if the cuttings are too dense over the roots of a plant, the heat created by the new grass rotting down will burn the roots.

Make a plan of the planting areas and write down what has been planted and where – especially the plants that die down each winter like *Alchemia mollis*, geraniums and *hostas*.

Remember the most innocuous little tree could grow to 60 ft (18 m). So check the size of tree before buying or planting.

Before each winter clean, oil and put away all garden tools.

Get lawn mower overhauled *before* the grass starts growing in the spring when everyone else is needing the mower checked.

Label and put into screw-top jars screws and nails so they are not lying about to give rusty cuts and grazes.

If a branch, twig, stalk, stem or flower is diseased or has died, remove it with secateurs to give the rest of the plant a better chance.

Transplanting. Water well for at least a week (*three* weeks if it's in the summer when you shouldn't transplant!) before transplanting.

DO'S *(continued)*

Construction

Before planting the garden contact the local council to see if you need permission to reduce the canopies of trees so as to get more light. Do not cut down trees without checking with the council, as the trees might be protected by a tree preservation order. You will also need permission if your house is in a conservation area.

Reducing the canopy of trees is a skilled job and if it is done by someone who does not know the subject and just lops off branches, this can produce an ugly mess of regrowth. So contact a tree surgeon and ask to see examples of his work, as some tree surgeons are better than others. It takes minutes to cut a tree but it may never regrow into an attractive shape again if it has been brutally cut back.

When starting a garden from scratch, build the hard landscape features such as paths, terraces, raised planters, fountains and ponds first.

When using wood for the garden only use *pressure impregnated* wood which will not rot and can be stained to the colour of your choice; ordinary soft wood will not last. There are many new paint-on wood treatments but nothing is as good as pressure impregnation.

Health

Wear leather gloves if you use a bow saw as the blade is very sharp and can cause a severe cut if it jumps on to your hand.

Wash cuts and grazes thoroughly and use a disinfectant cream. Use sterilised needles to remove thorns and splinters. Clean the wound afterwards and use disinfectant cream.

Wear gloves when picking up branches, twigs and rose cuttings.

Keep knees bent and back straight when lifting heavy gardening gear to avoid back strain.

DON'TS

Garden

Don't prune camellias. Cut back the odd branch if you wish to reshape them. *N.B.* Both camellias and azaleas benefit from a top dressing of peat round the roots before the winter to protect their roots.

Don't cut hydrangeas uniformly hard back, just about 8 in (20 cm) in the spring plus any dead wood down to the ground.

Don't cut daffodil foliage down for at least six weeks after flowering.

Don't buy a lot of 'pretty looking' flowers and trees without knowing what conditions they like, how big they grow and so on. Aim for flowering evergreens, shrubs and perennials, otherwise you will have to be planting continually season after season.

Don't pull out potentillas that 'look dead' in the winter. They are not and they will flower again next spring.

Don't *transplant* deciduous shrubs when they are still in leaf.

Don't listen to well-meaning advice (regarding the garden) if you don't like it. People tend to give more unasked for advice in the garden than anywhere else. Firstly their advice may be incorrect and secondly it may not be suitable for your *low* maintenance garden. So ignore 'Oh wouldn't lots of annuals give the beds colour?' (Yes, they would, but you would be forever gardening!)

Don't accept plants for the garden and feel you have to plant them if they are not suitable for your planting scheme. Encourage people to give you the trouble-free plants you *need*, such as perennials or evergreen flowering shrubs.

DON'TS *(continued)*

Don't plant too many dark-leaved plants such as laurel, azalea and camellia together. Try to vary the planting with plants with differently shaped and coloured foliage, grey and variegated. It is easy to make the mistake of planting a lot of dark greens together as many of the trouble-free evergreen flowering shrubs have dark green leaves.

Don't plant wistaria to grow up the side of the house if there is any danger of it growing near the roof and under the slates. Once wistaria is mature, it can cause thousands of pounds worth of damage to guttering, slates and tiles. So watch it!

Don't plant vigorous climbers such as Russian vine, honeysuckle and *Clematis montana* on a flimsy structure. These climbers can get very heavy and need strong support. So make sure you have a solid wall, trellis or frame before planting such robust climbers.

Don't start planting up a bed unless it is *completely cleared of weeds*, especially such persistent ones as ground elder and couch grass, otherwise you will *never* get rid of the weeds and they will take over the plants. (See *Weeds*.)

Don't assume a plant is dead just because the twigs look dry and there are no leaves. Before removing the plant check to see if there is still sap in the shoots or stem by scratching the surface with your thumb nail. If it is green beneath the bark then the plant is still alive. If it is brown or beige beneath the surface when scratched or cut back, the plant is probably dead. If you are not sure, just cut the plant hard back and wait to see if new growth appears.

Avoid digging soggy clay. Dig this type of soil when it is almost dry.

DON'TS *(continued)*

Construction

Don't overload your car with more bricks or paving stones than it can safely carry.

Don't start work on the garden construction without first getting several estimates, preferably from landscape contractors who have been recommended *and* you have seen *examples* of their work.

Water and Drainage. Water has to go somewhere, so don't direct the water off your paving without a drain or soak-away, otherwise the water will go into your house!

Health

Ladies, don't try and work with men's heavy tools. Buy a light weight spade and fork, they make garden work so much easier.

Don't try and prune trees without wearing glasses. Protect your eyes with sun-glasses or goggles. Many accidents involving eyes happen in the garden each year.

To avoid back problems when digging: Don't use tools that are too heavy or dig over wet soil.

Don't dig *non stop* without standing up straight and stretching and having a break. Keep stretching.

Don't twist when digging, lifting or loading into a wheel barrow. *Turn the whole body* the same way as the feet and the object to be lifted.

Don't wear flipflops in the garden; wear practical shoes and comfortable clothes. Flipflops are dangerous as you can not only cut your feet but also trip over paving or roots of trees.

DON'TS *(continued)*
Don't wear flowing or flapping clothes; they can be dangerous when working in the garden. They can catch in machinery such as hedge trimmers and chain saws and also catch on branches, twigs or garden gates and can throw you off balance.

Don't use bare hands when working in soil in a new garden where there may be broken china and glassware left by the previous owner. Wear gloves. (The tetanus bacteria lives in the soil and if you have a cut or graze and are not immunized against it take care as there have been cases where it has been fatal.)

Don't get your fingers trapped in the deck chair or folding chair. 2500 gardeners each year find themselves in the casualty unit. Check the chair is in good condition before sitting down as you don't want to fall through rotted material and hurt your back by landing sharply on the ground.

Security
Don't leave obvious signs of being away such as milk bottles outside, drawn curtains and six house plants sitting in the kitchen sink. An empty house is easily spotted by potential intruders. Leave easy, long-suffering plants like grape ivy and spider plants on window sills at the front and back of the house.

Don't leave the garden looking a mess (when away) if it is normally tidy. A tidy garden makes a house look occupied. A low-maintenance garden will not go wild while you are away, but if you have grass try to persuade your neighbour to cut it.

Don't leave tools, especially ladders and hammers, outside the house at night *or* when you are away. Lock them up as they are just the thing to help intruders into your house.

DON'TS *(continued)*
Don't forget to turn on the security light at the back of your house at night or when away for the weekend.

Don't leave unlabelled jars with poisonous substances in the shed or greenhouse. Always label materials clearly.

Do's and Don'ts for children and their safety are at the end of the Children's Garden.

The plants in these lists are grouped to suit the differing ways they are used in the gardens. Firstly they are divided into plants that tolerate either sun or shade, or plants that prefer one or the other: if a sunny or shady border is to be planted, you will need to choose plants to suit these conditions. Under each heading the plants are divided into evergreen or deciduous, so that you can achieve a balance between spring and summer colour and the substance of evergreen shrubs in winter; then they are subdivided by 'habit'. This is vital in a low maintenance garden as it will tell you if it will keep the weeds down itself or if it needs underplanting.

Accent plants get a separate listing as they are so necessary to stop any planting being dull. If your border has few flowers, bold foliage or form is the answer.

Trees, bulbs, alpines and herbs have their own separate needs, so they get their own sections.

The plants are arranged to make it as easy as possible to design your own borders *a)* where there are no planting plans or *b)* if your garden has a different orientation to the plan. Most of the plants on the plans are included, with a few others for you to try out. Planting should be fun. Be adventurous. If you don't like the results make notes during the summer and re-arrange the plants in the autumn.

THE PLANT GROUPINGS
The plants are arranged by height in each group
1. **Sun or shade tolerant** (but not deep shade)
1A. Shrubs – Evergreen – Dense and weed suppressing
1B. Shrubs – Evergreen – Need underplanting
1C. Shrubs – Deciduous – Dense and weed suppressing
1D. Shrubs – Deciduous – Need underplanting
1E. Herbaceous perennials – Ground cover
1F. Herbaceous perennials – Clumpy
1G. Climbers
2. **Plants for sun**
2A. Shrubs – Evergreen – Dense and weed suppressing
2B. Shrubs – Evergreen – Need underplanting
2C. Shrubs – Deciduous – Dense and weed suppressing
2D. Shrubs – Deciduous – Need underplanting
2E. Herbaceous perennials – Ground cover
2F. Herbaceous perennials – Clumpy
2G. Climbers

3. **Plants for shade**
3A. Shrubs – Evergreen – Dense and weed suppressing
3B. Shrubs – Evergreen – Need underplanting
3C. Shrubs – Deciduous – Dense and weed suppressing
3D. Shrubs – Deciduous – Need underplanting
3E. Herbaceous perennials – Ground cover
3F. Herbaceous perennials – Clumpy
3G. Climbers
4. **Accent Plants** – Shrubs
5. **Accent Plants** – Herbaceous perennials
6. **Small trees**
6A. Trees – Evergreen
6B. Trees – Deciduous
7. **Bulbs**
8. **Alpines**
9. **Herbs**

1. SUN OR SHADE TOLERANT

1A. Shrubs – evergreen – dense weed-suppressing

Euonymus fortunei 'Silver Queen' *Sprawling evergreen shrub with really striking variegated leaves with a broad creamy margin and a dark green centre splashed with pale green. Good against dark foliage or growing through a dark evergreen, it can be used as foreground planting to hang over a wall or for underplanting. Given a wall it can climb to 10 ft (3 m). Usually up to 2 ft (60 cm) high with a 5 ft (1.5 m) spread.*

Cotoneaster 'Autumn Fire' *This is a big spreader or it can climb up a trellis. Dark green narrow leaves, small white flowers in June and plenty of red berries in autumn. Wayward shoots need shortening to keep the growth dense and the weeds out. It reaches 3 ft (90 cm) high and can spread to 10 ft (3 m) if you let it. Cotoneaster salicifolius 'Repens' is neater and grows up to 18 in (45 cm) with just about the same spread.*

Senecio 'Sunshine' (often called greyii) *Does well in shade despite its name which refers to the yellow daisy flowers in summer. The rather rounded leaves are olive greeny-grey on the top and silvery grey underneath. It is more compact in sun and needs a trim in spring to keep it bushy. If you don't like the yellow flowers with other plants around, then prune it hard in spring and only a few flowers will form. Usually below 3 ft (90 cm) with a spread of 4–6 ft (1.2–1.8 m) or so. Very easy to grow and easy from cuttings.*

Pyracantha 'Soleil d'Or' *There are a lot of Pyracanthas or firethorns to choose from but this one has a good spreading habit. The usual glossy green leaves and off-white flowers in June are followed by an impressive display of orange-yellow berries. It is thorny but worth the risk of a scratch. 4 ft (1.2 m) high with a 5–6 ft (1.5–1.8 m) spread. Most other varieties are taller with open growth, so insist on this one if you want a firethorn this size.*

Euphorbia wulfenii (Shrubby spurge) *The long narrow dark green leaves arranged all round the upright stems make the plant very striking. Last year's shoots flower in the spring with long candelabras of green-yellow bracts often as early as February. These can be attractive into the summer and should be cut out when you tire of them. New shoots are always springing from the base of the plant. It is a very handsome 'filler' for a niche or corner. All euphorbias have a white, gummy juice that can irritate your skin, so wear gloves when you prune. About a 4 ft (1.2 m) height and spread.*

Olearia haastii (Daisy bush) *A neat dome of matt olive green leaves is lit up in summer with slightly off white daisy flowers which are pleasantly fragrant. Very easy and reliable; grows about 4 ft by 4 ft (1.2 m by 1.2 m).*

Choisya ternata (Mexican orange blossom) *Choisya really is Mexican and is related to oranges! The handsome, shiny, trifoliate (like a clover) leaves have the same spicy fragrance as orange trees when crushed. The sweetly fragrant lemon blossom comes in clusters at the ends of the shoots in spring with a smaller repeat in autumn. A good dome-shaped habit up to 5–6 ft (1.5–1.8 m) and a little wider. The flexible shoots can be trained up a trellis to 12 ft (3.5 m) or so as in my garden.*

Mahonia *These are easy to grow in sun or shade so it is worth knowing about the different kinds and their different effects.*

The shortest is aquifolium with glossy pinnate (like an ash) leaves and clusters of yellow scented flowers in spring followed by blue berries. It spreads slowly by suckers to reach about 4 ft (1.2 m) high by 5 ft (1.5 m) wide.

There are two slightly taller types that can be used in larger plantings. Both have more flowers all the way up the stem than aquifolium. Undulata has very glossy leaves with wavy margins and is an exceptional foliage plant, while pinnata has quite greyish leaves.

The biggest is japonica, which has stout stems and big spiny pinnate leaves that are bold and glossy. In early spring each shoot is topped with drooping strands of yellow flowers with a lily of the valley scent. These are followed by bloomy blue berries but if the shrub is growing too big be ruthless and cut the shoots back before the berries form and it will stay bushy. Grows 6–8 ft (1.8–2.5 m) by 6–8 ft (1.8–2.5 m).

1B. Shrubs – evergreen – need underplanting

Cotoneaster franchettii *This gracefully arching shrub has sage green leaves which are grey underneath. The small white flowers in June are followed by orange berries which are very attractive against the* foliage. Grows to 5 ft by 5 ft (1.5 m by 1.5 m).

Pyracantha watereri *This firethorn and most of its relatives are rather tall and open but easily pruned. The usual glossy leaves and off white flowers are followed by brilliant red berries which make this a very desirable variety. Also good on a wall where it grows taller than the usual 6 ft (1.8 m) by 5 ft (1.5 m) spread.*

Viburnum burkwoodii *A tall, open-growing shrub with rounded dark green leaves, buff underneath. From January to May the clusters of pink budded flowers open white, with a sweet scent of cloves. Can reach 8 ft (2.5 m) but not much wider than 4 ft (1.2 m) unless trained on a wall or fence.*

1C. Shrubs – deciduous – dense, weed suppressing

Potentilla 'Longacre' *Dense, low-growing and mat-forming, making a good ground cover. The pale yellow five-petalled flowers are produced throughout the summer. It has small leaves with five leaflets. Grows to 1 ft (30 cm) with a 3 ft (90 cm) spread.*

Potentilla × 'Elizabeth' *This is a more dome-shaped variety with bright yellow flowers over a very long period from early summer. Reaches about 3 ft (90 cm) high with a slightly wider spread. Very dead and twiggy-looking in winter but quite acceptable against evergreens.*

Salix lanata *This willow is very unlike the usual streamside or weeping willow. The round leaves are covered with a grey felt and make this a valuable foliage shrub. The pussy willow catkins come in April. 3 ft (90 cm) by 4 ft (1.2 m) of good dense growth.*

Viburnum plicatum tomentosum
'Mariesii' *Stunning white flowered shrub with wide-spreading horizontal branches in tiers. The heads of white fertile flowers are surrounded by white sterile flowers and are placed elegantly along the branches in May. In a dry autumn the long leaves turn reddish purple. It can grow up to 5 ft (1.5 m) and spread 18 ft (5.5 m) or so. 'Lanarth' is similar but a little more vigorous. They can both be trained up a wall or trellis to provide a very striking cover.*

1D. Shrubs – deciduous – need underplanting

Daphne mezereum (Mezereon) *A neat growing shrub with the special attraction of deliciously scented purple-pink flowers from February to April. The red berries that follow these are poisonous. The light green leaves are quite a good summer foil for underplantings of dark green leaves. It grows to 3 ft (90 cm) by 2–3 ft (60–90 cm). There is a beautiful white variety 'Alba' with pale orange berries, also poisonous.*

Fuchsia magellanica gracilis (Hardy Fuchsia) *Leafy and arching with long narrow leaves, this fuchsia has plentiful slim purple flowers with red sepals in late summer and autumn. The variety 'Versicolor' is very distinctive, as the leaves have a narrow creamy-white variegation and are a soft grey, rose-tinted when young. With the flowers this produces a lovely soft colouring that goes with almost anything. Both attain 3–4 ft (90 cm–1.2 m) with a 3 ft (90 cm) spread. If they are damaged by frost after a cold winter, cut them back hard and they will continue to grow vigorously.*

Weigela florida 'Variegata' *Another good variegated foliage shrub and very easy to grow. The leaves have creamy-white margins and pale green centres. The pale pink funnel-shaped flowers in May and June add a gentle touch of colour. Up to 5 ft (1.5 m) high and wide but easily pruned.*

Rosa rubrifolia (glauca) *This graceful wild rose from Central Europe is an open-growing shrub with beautiful leaves of purplish red, overlaced with grey more muted when in shade. The young shoots are reddish tinted and the mature ones are purplish red, so it gives a warm glow even in winter. The rather small pink and white flowers are followed by round, shining hips from August onwards. Rubrifolia mixes well with many colour schemes and has very few thorns. 7 ft (2 m) high by 5 ft (1.2 m) wide, but easily kept smaller.*

Magnolia liliiflora nigra *A handsome, bushy magnolia that will tolerate quite a bit of shade. The dark purple flowers have a paler inside to the petals which shows as the flowers open up when they mature. The special attraction is that the first flowers come just before the leaves open in March and they carry on well into summer when they contrast with the big deep green leaves. If your soil is alkaline the leaves will be a disappointing pale green. Can reach 7 ft (2 m) and spread 6 ft (1.8 m), but is often more compact and can be pruned in spring.*

1E. Herbaceous perennials for ground cover

Heuchera sanguinea (Coral bells) *The low cover of jagged leaves is a fine background for the light plumes* of little red bells about a foot (30 cm) high. 'Bressingham Blaze' and other varieties are very bright coloured and they all flower longer, in early summer, with good soil.

Saxifraga umbrosa *(London's Pride) The deep green rosettes of scalloped leaves cover the ground and are topped by little spires of white and pink flowers about a foot (30 cm) high. Very dainty in spring.*

Tolmeia menziesii 'Taffs Gold' (Pig-a-back plant) *The hairy leaves with pointed lobes form a good ground cover lavishly splashed with yellow. In shade there is rather more green but still a strong contrast of colour. Little plantlets form at the junction of leaf and stalk and can be potted up very easily. The foot (30 cm) high spikes of brownish flowers are more curious than attractive. Easy to propagate.*

Centaurea montana (Mountain knapweed) *The leaves are a bit weedy, long, pointed and rough but are a good cover in a sunny or not too shady spot. The real attraction is the blue cornflowers really early in summer. There are also pink and white varieties. An easy going plant about 18 in (45 cm) high.*

Hostas (Plantain lily) *Very fine big-leaved perennials that spread slowly from a tight clump and the leaves, 1–2 ft (30–60 cm) high for those listed below, give a good weed-proof cover. Spires of white, mauve or purple flowers overtop the leaves in summer but the leaves die away completely in winter. They can be moved or divided when in full leaf if well watered in.* Hosta sieboldiana 'Elegans' *has big, rather crinkly, intense grey-blue leaves a foot (30 cm) or so across. The pale lilac flowers in July and August are on rather a dumpy spike.* Hosta crispula *has broad dark green leaves with a conspicuous white margin. The pale lilac spires of flowers come in early summer.* Hosta fortunei 'Aureomarginata' ('Marginata') *has a greyish overtone to the leaves and a thinner yellow margin. Handsome lilac mauve flowers.* Hosta ventricosa 'Variegata' *has broad green leaves with a wide and irregular cream margin. The violet purple flowers come in late summer on striking spikes and are more dumpy than the usual funnel-shaped flowers. One of the latest flowering is* Hosta lancifolia, *with narrower, lance-shaped leaves which overlap and arch over a little to build up a handsome clump. The flower spikes carry on into September. They do not set seed so it is less pressing to cut off*

the old flower stalks.

Geraniums (Hardy cranesbills) *These are all the leafy ground cover kinds that have rather round, deeply divided leaves, over spreading clumps, overtopped by flowers of blue, mauve, pink or white.* Geranium endressii 'Wargrave Pink' *is very reliable and has a long flowering period from early summer of silvery pink flowers over fresh green leaves.*

Geranium 'Johnson's Blue' *is closely related to the blue cranesbill of country lanes. This one has slightly darker flowers, again over a long period from early summer. A taller one is* Geranium magnificum *(also* ibericum *or* platypetalum*) with soft furry leaves and taller stalks of violet blue flowers. It is a hybrid and does not set seed, so it is less important to cut off the old flower heads.*

The lightest of all is Geranium 'Kashmir White', *with deeply divided leaves and white flowers with a thin pencilling of purple to liven them up.*

The totally reliable ground cover on its own or under anything is Geranium macrorrhizum. *The leaf cover is under a foot (30 cm) high and the flowers just overtop them. The crushed leaves smell rather like pot plant pelargoniums (geraniums).* Ingwersen's Variety *is a good pale pink and* album *is white with a faint pink tinge.*

Bergenias (Elephants' Ears) *The big round leaves are evergreen and these are accompanied by broad spikes of magenta pink, pink or white flowers all through the spring.*

Bergenia cordifolia *has big foot-and-a-half (45 cm) leaves and flowers of magenta pink. These are darker in 'Purpurea' and its leaves also go purple in winter if it is growing in sun in a dryish soil (or next to a low wall). There are a lot of named varieties and the pink flowers of 'Schmidtii' and the white, faintly pink tinted flowers of 'Silberlicht' show up well in the dull days of spring. In Ballawley the flowers are almost crimson.*

Alchemilla mollis *A symphony in green. Rounded leaves up to 9 in (22.5 cm) across which are lobed and then lobed again. Little beads of water catch in the smallest lobes after rain. The fluffy plumes of pale green flowers cover the clump from early summer. Cut these off as they darken and form seeds if the seedlings become a nuisance. About 18 in (45 cm) tall.*

Rodgersia podophylla *Big striking leaves divided into narrowly fan-shaped sections with jagged edges and on 2 ft (60 cm) stalks make this a distinguished foliage plant. The coppery colour of the young leaves returns in late summer. The puffs of small pinkish flowers don't add very much when they appear in summer.*

1F. **Herbaceous perennials which form clumps**

Geranium renardii *The neat, rounded leaves are lobed and puckered, have a greyish tinge and form a neat clump about a foot (30 cm) high. The white flowers over the leaves appear briefly in early summer and are lightly veined with violet blue. Tolerates a little shade.*

Euphorbia polychroma *(or epithymoides or pilosa) This spurge shoots up to 18 in (45 cm) high in spring and quickly forms bright yellow bracts on top of a neat dome of foliage. The bracts fade to green as summer advances and the leaves go yellow in autumn. Very attractive in spring and nice and leafy in summer. More ground covering in habit but best in the garden as an individual clump. The sap is poisonous.*

Meconopsis cambrica (Welsh poppy) *A clump of soft green foliage covered by striking clear yellow flowers in late spring/early summer, with some flowers later. The orange variety has equally clear coloured flowers. There are double forms of both which do not have the simple elegance of single poppy flowers. Reaches a foot (30 cm) or so high and seeds about a bit.*

Malva moschata *The native musk mallow is a very lovely plant with straight stems, deeply cut leaves and rose pink flowers in summer. 'Alba' is a very beautiful white-flowered form. Both seed themselves gently about the garden.*

Anemone japonica (hybrida) (Japanese Anemone) *There are a number of varieties with deep pinkish to white flowers which grow 18 in – 5 ft (45 cm – 1.5 m) tall. They are especially good in shade but also thrive on sun. The usual white 'Honorine Jobert' has big, open anemone flowers in late summer and autumn, on long stems. 'Prinz Heinrich' is much shorter, with pink and red flowers which have extra, narrower petals. The common pink is usually called Anemone tomentosa and spreads extensively. It starts to flower in late summer and the pink petals have a darker reverse. All these*

anemones are very welcome for their late flowering.

Polemonium caeruleum (Jacob's ladder) *Another native that seeds about the place and is very easy to grow. The 2 ft (60 cm) spires of clear blue flowers (or white in* album*) in early summer appear above a clump of neat leaves with a lot of leaflets. If you come across* foliosissimum *it is neater, with darker blue flowers and a longer flowering season.*

1G. **Climbers**

Rosa 'Albertine' *A strong-growing rose that has healthy, dark foliage and a big display of richly scented, coppery pink flowers in June and July. Can also be grown as a weeping standard as suggested for the front garden. Although often called a rambler it should be pruned as a climber. Allow 12 ft (3.5 m) by 12 ft (3.5 m) if grown as a climber.*

Rosa 'Albéric Barbier' *Rather like 'Albertine' but with smaller and glossier leaves. The double creamy yellow flowers in June and July are repeated on a smaller scale in autumn.*

Rosa 'New Dawn' *Delicately scented, pale pink flowers in June and July and a big second flowering late August onwards. Fairly vigorous, growing to 10 ft (3 m) by 10 ft (3 m). Good healthy pale green leaves.*

Rosa 'Félicité et Perpétue' *A rambler with small dark green leaves and flexible stems up to 15 ft (4.5 m) long. The flowers, in June and July (though mine have flowered in November), form a neat white rosette opening in clusters from red-tinted buds. The leaves stay evergreen in a mild winter. Cut out old flowered stems right to the ground.*

Rosa 'Zéphirine Drouhin' (the thornless rose) *Not only is it thornless, but 'Zéphirine' has a long succession of magenta pink, sweet-scented, semi-double flowers. It will grow in a part shaded site but unless it has good soil and adequate moisture in the summer it can suffer from black spot and mildew. If you think the colour is too bright, then a sport of it called 'Kathleen Harrop' is a clear, pale pink. Slightly stronger coloured, without the magenta, is 'Martha' which is just becoming available, having been re-discovered recently.*

Rosa 'Mermaid' *A rather vigorous and very thorny rose; only a little pruning is desirable, but luckily not essential. The glossy foliage is almost evergreen and beautifully sets off the single creamy yellow flowers, with a boss of reddish anthers, which continue from*

June to the autumn. A very classy-looking rose.

Rosa 'Bobbie James' *There are a number of wild roses of very vigorous growth with masses of big clusters of small single white flowers in June and July and a sweet fragrance that carries on the breeze. 'Bobbie' is a seedling of one of these and has semi-double white flowers; it needs 25 ft (7.5 m) to develop in or the support of an old tree or a big, dull conifer.*

Jasmine *The old cottage garden jasmine is* Jasminum officinale. *It is a vigorous climber with small pinnate leaves and sweetly scented tubular white flowers in summer. Train it a bit in its early years or it will get in a hopeless tangle. The variety* affine *has slighly larger, pink tinted flowers.*

Jasminum stephanense *is unusual in having pale pink flowers in June and July and some leaves pinnate, while some are undivided.*

Jasminum nudiflorum *is the winter flowering one with yellow flowers but no scent. The shoots are green all winter. Needs tying up as it is not self-supporting. Prune after it has flowered. It reaches 10 ft (3 m) or so. If grown as a shrub, do not bother to prune.*

Honeysuckles *A wonderful plant, but beware, there is a wide range of species and some do not have scented flowers.*

Lonicera periclymenum 'Serotina' *Our native woodbine has yellow flowers but Serotina has them flushed reddish purple on the outside. The flowers are borne from June to September, with the characteristic sweet scent in summer evenings (to attract night flying moths). A very vigorous twiner, so keep it away from young trees or shrubs.*

Lonicera japonica 'Halliana' *This Japanese is evergreen and rampant. Ideal for a bare wall or fence – if trained, or on a trellis. The small white flowers age to yellow and are not very conspicuous but are scented. 'Aureoreticulata' has leaves netted with golden veins and is a good foliage plant but seldom flowers.*

Lonicera 'Dropmore Scarlet' *Non-scented but with striking hanging scarlet flowers in July and into the autumn. Good on a background wall where the scent will not be missed.*

Forsythia suspensa *Not really a climber but a forsythia with long flexible shoots easily trained on a wall where its summer dullness can be covered by frontal planting. The usual striking yellow flowers in*

spring. Shorten the shoots after flowering.

Clematis macropetala *A moderate growing clematis that can reach 12 ft (3.5 m) if exceptionally well placed. Besides liking its roots in the shade, like all clematis, this one will tolerate some shade where it grows. In spring the plant is covered with many-petalled violet blue bells which are followed by feathery seed heads. Flowers on old wood so does not need pruning.*

2. PLANTS FOR SUN

2A. **Shrubs – evergreen – dense weed suppressing**

Santolina chamaecyparissus (incana) (Cotton lavender) *A mound of intensely silver grey dissected and felty branches. The flowers are in lemon yellow pompoms in July. Keep it neat with an annual trim in spring. About 18 in (45 cm) high and wide.*

Osteospermum ecklonis *Soft wooded plant with a profusion of white, slaty grey-backed flowers all summer and autumn. Not very hardy, so root a few cuttings to keep on the window sill over winter.*

Lavandula (Lavender) *Lovely blue grey foliage and spikes of lavender flowers in July and through the summer. Three compact varieties for the trouble free garden, 1–2 ft (30–60 cm) high and a little wider, are 'Hidcote', of typical colour; 'Twickel Purple', lavender blue; and 'Munstead', slightly more blue. They all need a trim over in spring to keep them shapely but don't cut into old wood.*

Cytisus kewensis (Broom) *A low-growing broom with long, slender, weeping branches, small leaves and a profusion of yellow flowers in May. Very good for draping over a low wall. The green stems are effective in winter. Grows about a foot (30 cm) high and spreads up to 4 ft (1.2 m). Trim after flowering if necessary.*

Hebe andersonii 'Variegata' *A striking variegated evergreen with a broad creamy white margin to the leaves. Plumes of flowers from the leaf axils in August and September which are pale blue fading to white. Not very hardy but it is very easy to root cuttings in summer.*

Hebe albicans *A hardy species with rather rounded grey-green leaves and small spikes of white flowers in June/July. A good foliage shrub when out of flower, with a 2 ft (60 cm) height and spread. A number of hebes are available from garden centres, so you can choose the foliage that appeals to you.*

Hebe 'Great Orme' *Amid the bewildering array of variety names, this one is distinctive with narrow leaves and pink flowers in long plumes. Fairly hardy.*

Hebe pinguifolia 'Pagei' *Small leaved and very hardy. A little greyer than albicans and with a sprawling habit, making it good on the edge of a bed.*

Cistus 'Silver Pink' (Sun rose) *One of the best Cistus with a neat habit, grey leaves and pink flowers in June and July. Grows about 2–3 ft (60–90 cm) by 3 ft (90 cm) and is one of the hardiest.*

Ceanothus thyrsiflorus 'Repens' (Californian lilac) *Shiny dark green leaves and a spreading habit up to 3 ft (90 cm) high and 8 ft (2.5 m) wide make this a valuable foliage shrub. In May and June it is lit up with little powder puffs of blue flowers. It may be damaged in a cold winter; if so, cut out any dead wood in spring.*

Phlomis fruticosa (Jerusalem Sage) *This grows very thickly making it an excellent weed-suppressing plant. It has grey green felted leaves up to 4 in (10 cm) long and yellow flowers in whorls above the foliage in early summer. A very reliable shrub up to 3 ft (90 cm) high and 5 ft (1.5 m) wide but can be kept smaller if pruned after flowering.*

Carpenteria californica *Much hardier than usually supposed, this does very well at the foot of a south wall. 4 in (10 cm) long shiny dark green leaves and long clusters of large white flowers with golden anthers in July. Can be pruned hard if necessary to keep it below its natural 6–8 ft (1.8–2.5 m) height and width.*

2B. Shrubs – evergreen – need underplanting

Escallonia 'Apple Blossom' *This is one of several named varieties of this valuable summer flowering evergreen with shiny leaves. The attractive pink and white flowers of 'Apple Blossom' are borne all along the branches. It grows to about 3 ft (90 cm) high and a little wider. 'Crimson Spire' is a taller red flowered variety (up to 6 ft/1.8 m) for a background.*

Ceanothus 'Autumnal Blue' *Some ceanothus, including this one, flower in autumn. The plentiful blue powder puffs are borne from late summer against a background of small dark green leaves. About 6 ft (1.8 m) high with rather upright growth.*

Magnolia grandiflora 'Goliath' *Best on a wall, this magnolia has magnificent shiny mid-green leaves with a rusty felt underneath. Very large (up to 9 in/22.5 cm across) flowers, in summer and autumn, with a tangy citrus scent. It can reach 20 ft (6 m) or so but is not very fast growing and can be pruned if necessary.*

2C. Shrubs – deciduous – dense, weed suppressing.

Hypericum moserianum 'Tricolor' *Green leaves with a white edge which have a red tinge make this a striking mound of foliage about 12–18 in (30–45 cm) high with a wider spread. The bright yellow flowers from June to September clash a bit with this colouring.*

Philadelphus 'Manteau d'Hermine' (Mock orange) *This dwarf only reaches 2–3 ft (60–90 cm) high and wide and has proportionately small leaves. The small double scented flowers have a true orange scent with a slight overtone of pineapple.*

Hydrangea 'Lanarth White' *This hydrangea is a lace cap and needs sun to stay compact and flower well. It keeps up its display of white outer flowers and tiny blue fertile flowers in the centre from July to October. (It is easy to identify as 'Lanarth' lacks the brown spots on the young stems that all other hydrangeas have.) Usually about 3 ft (90 cm) high and wide.*

Philadelphus 'Beauclerk' *Can reach 8 ft (2.5 m) high and 5–6 ft (1.5–1.8 m) wide but is a dense growing shrub. Wide open milk white flowers in June and July. Prune after flowering.*

Philadelphus 'Sybille' *is smaller growing and compact and has more cup-shaped flowers with a purple stain at the base of the petals. Very attractive with a powerful fragrance.*

2D. Shrubs – deciduous – need underplanting

Daphne × burkwoodii *A very neat shrub which can grow to 3 ft (90 cm) high with a 4 ft (1.2 m) spread in the open or become rather upright if enclosed by other plants. It has small light green leaves and terminal clusters of tiny light pink tubular flowers in May and June; the flowers have a very sweet fragrance that is carried by a light breeze. A few late flowers come in summer.*

Fuchsia 'Lady Thumb' *Most hardy fuchsias flower best in sun. This one is compact and its flowers have pink sepals and a violet skirt. 'Mrs Popple' is large flowered with red sepals and a purple skirt. 'Rufus' is all red and unusual. They grow to between 18 in and 4 ft (45 cm – 1.2 m) high depending on the climate. Cut them back to near the base each spring.*

Acer palmatum dissectum 'Atropurpureum' *Japanese maples need a neutral or acid soil and some extra humus. The long name disguises a small growing foliage shrub of great elegance. The finely divided leaves are a pleasing purple all summer. It slowly builds up to a lacy mound about 3 ft (90 cm) high and 5 ft (1.5 m) wide.*

Rosa gallica 'Versicolor' (Rosa mundi) *A really old rose that forms a solid clump and is topped by the palest blush pink flowers striped with a splash of crimson. Flowers in June and July. It can be pruned after flowering or in spring, when it can even be sheared over.*

Rosa 'Old Blush China' *A very old rose imported from China two hundred years ago but its history goes back a thousand years. It is a neat shrub with dainty mid-pink flowers that carry on from June until December in a mild autumn. Easy to grow from autumn cuttings and very compact grown on its own roots. Usually reaches 3 ft (90 cm) in height and spread.*

Rosa virginiana *This wild rose from North America is bushy and has shiny foliage that changes to brilliant reds and oranges in autumn to go with the round red hips. The single pink flowers are borne from June to August. It reaches 5 ft (1.5 m) or so high and not quite so wide.*

Rosa alba 'Maiden's Blush' *Another very old rose with lots of neatly placed and folded petals in a rather flat flower that is a very delicately blush pink, handsome until the petals drop. It reaches 5 ft (1.5 m) in height and spread. Prune as for 'Versicolor' above.*

Lavatera olbia 'Rosea' *A soft wooded shrub with softly furry maple-like leaves which contrast attractively with the long succession of mallow-like pink flowers through late summer and autumn. Cut it back hard in spring to keep it bushy. It will shoot up to 6 ft (1.8 m) high and wide with ease.*

Chaenomeles speciosa 'Cardinalis' (Flowering quince *or* japonica) *An early flowering shrub that is best trained on a wall or fence so that it does not grow too vigorously at the expense of flowers. Crimson, saucer-shaped flowers with yellow stamens appear from January (in warm gardens) till April or May. It reaches 6 ft (1.8 m) and can spread to 6 ft (1.8 m) on a wall. There are a number of other*

varieties to choose from.

Acer palmatum 'Senkaki' *A quietly elegant plant, this is the coral bark Japanese maple which is so striking in winter. In spring the leaves open very pale green and slowly darken as they age, contrasting with the new growth. In autumn they turn clear yellow. Rather vase-shaped, it can grow slowly to 12 ft (3.5 m) with a 6 ft (1.8 m) spread. Needs a neutral or acid soil with extra humus.*

Lilacs *The common lilac, flowering in May, has many colour varieties. Choose the one to suit your planting scheme.* Syringa vulgaris 'Katherine Havemeyer' *is a little darker lilac in colour and double, which means that there are no seed pods forming after flowering. It is fairly bushy with a height of 8–12 ft (2.5–3.5 m) and a spread of 5–8 ft (1.5–2.5 m). Much more upright in habit is* 'Charles Joly' *with double deep red flowers. This is probably the most useful in a narrow border.* 'Vestale' *is a very fine white but single so cut the seed pods off after flowering or there will not be so many flowers next year.*

Syringa microphylla *is quite different, much more bushy, growing to about 5 ft (1.5 m) by 4 ft (1.2 m). It has small leaves and more open clusters of pink flowers, just as fragrant. A few extra flowers form in late summer and autumn.* Syringa persica *gives the same effect as the common lilac but is much more dainty and restrained, with small leaves, twiggy growth and lilac flowers.*

2E. Herbaceous perennials – ground cover.

Stachys lanata (Lambs' ears) *Felted, almost deep-pile, leaves of silvery sheen. Similarly woolly spikes of small blue flowers in July. A very good edging plant especially in the form* 'Silver Carpet' *which does not flower and stays neater. The leaves only rise 6 in (15 cm) or so and the plant spreads well.*

Anthemis cupaniana *A mat of finely dissected, aromatic, grey leaves and rather large white daisy flowers June to August. Needs a well drained spot and reaches 9 in (22.5 cm) or so with a good spread.*

Nepeta faassenii (mussinii) (Catmint) *Small bluish grey leaves are topped by sprays of lavender coloured flowers from June to early autumn. Cats love it and will roll in it. Mixes with almost anything and is an excellent border edging. About 18 in (45 cm) high and spreading.* 'Six Hills Giant' *is twice as big and more of a border plant.*

Convolvulus mauritanicus *A leafy mass of pointed leaves of a soft green and bindweed flowers in lavender blue. It does not behave like bindweed and can be killed in a cold winter. It reaches 1 ft (30 cm) in height and can spread 2 ft (60 cm).*

Diascia rigescens *These Diascias have been recently introduced from South Africa but are fairly hardy. Rigescens has stiff but arching growth from a central crown with leaves all the way along the stem and terminal clusters of flowers of striking deep pink all summer.*

Diascia vigilis *is of softer, more bushy growth and has masses of pale pink flowers. Both grow to about 1 ft (30 cm) high and 2 ft (60 cm) wide.*

Artemisia 'Lambrook Silver' (Wormwood) *A silvery variety of our native wormwood with the same pungent smell when the leaves are crushed. It grows up to 3 ft (90 cm) high and wide and is topped by small greyish flowers that tone gently in with the silver leaves. Slightly woody at the base and needs cutting back in spring to keep it bushy.*

2F. Herbaceous perennials – clump forming

Festuca glauca (Fescue grass) *A little tufted grass with intense blue grey narrow foliage making it resemble a bristly hedgehog. Grassy flowers in June and July. Distinct in form and colour. Reaches 6 in (15 cm) high.*

Sedum × 'Autumn Joy' *A fleshy leaved perennial like our native rose root Sedum roseum. Straight stems up to 2 ft (60 cm) with fleshy, jagged edged leaves and plates of hundreds of tiny pink flowers in early autumn. Sedum spectabile is very similar but a sharper, paler pink. Sedum maximum 'Atropurpureum' has intense maroon purple leaves and off-white and reddish flowers in the same flat heads. Butterflies love them.*

Dianthus 'Mrs Sinkins' (Pink) *An old-fashioned pink with double white flowers and a strong clove scent. Grey green narrow, evergreen leaves set them off. Countless other varieties in red, pink and white have been raised but this old one is special. Gets to be around a foot (30 cm) high and wide. Needs well drained soil.*

Aster frikartii (Michaelmas daisy) *In fact, this branches freely and so is less stiff than the true Michaelmas daisy. It flowers from July to October if well looked after and has pale lavender-blue flowers with a pale orange yellow centre. Mixes with anything in the same way as catmint. Reaches 3 ft (90 cm) high and about half as wide.*

Salvia nemorosa 'East Friesland' *A bushy perennial sage with spikes of purple flowers over a leafy clump from July to September. A compact plant, it grows about 2 ft (60 cm) high and wide. Lubeca is similar and 'Superba' is taller.*

Iris germanica 'Solid Mahogany' (Bearded Iris) *Broad blade-like evergreen greyish leaves. Deep red-brown mahogany flowers, which are scented, in May. There is a large range of different coloured forms of bearded iris growing about 2–3 ft (60–90 cm) tall. 'Mahogany' was chosen for a special colour scheme in the paved garden.*

Ranunculus aconitifolius *A buttercup but a very refined one. It springs from a tuberous root and has mid-green divided leaves with delicate small white flowers well above the leaves in May and June. 2 ft (60 cm) high and 1 ft (30 cm) wide. Rather unusual.*

Paeonia officinalis 'Rosea-plena' (Peony) *This is one of the old double cottage garden peonies that flower in May and June, with big globular flowers full of petals from a woody rootstock. This has fat buds on it which must be planted only just below the soil surface or the plant won't flower. Nice divided leaves with rounded lobes offset other plants in later summer. The deep red form 'Rubra-plena' is more common and there is a very pale pink 'Alba-plena'. Easily divided by carefully cutting the woody root stock with a knife in October before they die down completely.*

Eryngium oliverianum (Sea holly) *Something unusual is always arresting in a bed of plants. This sea holly has greyish spiky holly-like leaves in a rosette. From this springs one or more stems topped by round blue thistle-like flower heads to 2 ft – 2 ft 6 in (60–75 cm) in July and August with a ruff of leaves like the basal ones. The flowers dry well.*

Althaea rosea (Hollyhock) *This tall upright plant is fairly perennial but needs renewing now and then. Wide open flowers, with a cone of stamens in the middle, all the way up the stem in shades of pink and red from July to September. There are double ones too. Easy from seed.*

2G. Climbers

Clematis 'Nelly Moser' *One of the large flowered hybrid clematis, Nelly has pale pinky flowers with a purple-red stripe on each petal. Flowers from May to*

September if the roots are in the shade and the stems in the sun. With light pruning it will achieve 12 ft (3.5 m). The well-known purple jackmanii flowers only on young wood so should be cut back hard each spring.

Clematis viticella 'Abundance' *More subtle than the large flowered types the viticella varieties ramble happily over other shrubs or climbers. 'Abundance' has double deep red flowers in a pompom all summer. 'Royal Velours' has single flowers of a glowing deep red. C. viticella itself is mauve. These need light pruning only and can reach 10 ft (3 m).*

Clematis armandii *An evergreen clematis with long shoots that do not branch much. It will seek out a shrub or tree to climb in rather than be trained on a wall. White flowers in spring are beautiful against the dark green leaves. 'Snow Drift' is a selected form and 'Apple Blossom' has a pink tint. Can in theory grow to 30 ft (9 m) but rarely does so.*

Rosa 'Pink Perpétue' *An easy, reliable and repeat flowering rose with deep to light pink flowers July to September. Can reach 15 ft (4.5 m) and is bushy.*

Rosa 'Aloha' *Half way between a tall shrub and a short climber at 8–10 ft (2.5–3 m). Good foliage, shiny green and very full petalled flowers, rich pink and strongly perfumed.*

Wisteria floribunda 'Alba' *The white wisteria was chosen for the Georgian garden. They are vigorous climbers once established. The long hanging clusters of white scented flowers come in April and May. They may reach 25–30 ft (7.5–9 m) but can be kept smaller by reducing the length of the shoots regularly. The usual mauve one is Wisteria sinensis. There are also named varieties.*

Passiflora caerulea (Passion flower) *A soft wooded climber that can cover a fence or wall, evergreen in mild winters or sheltered gardens. Shiny deeply divided leaves and extraordinary flowers with blue petals, a corona of blue threads and three stigmas sitting on the top. In a warm summer these mature to oval orange fruits. Can reach 20 ft (6 m) but usually less.*

Trachelospermum jasminoides *An evergreen with dark green leathery leaves and dense growth. The white flowers in July and August are very like jasmine but have wavy edges. The sweet perfume carries on the wind. The green and creamy white leaved 'Variegata' is a spectacular foliage plant but*

neither is reliably hardy in very cold areas. Slowly grows to 12 ft (3.5 m).

3. PLANTS FOR SHADE

3A. Shrubs – evergreen – dense and weed suppressing

Vinca minor *A low creeping evergreen that grows up to 6 in (15 cm) high and thrives in shade. Blue star-shaped flowers in spring with a few on into summer. 'Alba plena' is a double white and 'Miss Jekyll' an improved blue. There is also a variety with burgundy coloured flowers and others with white or yellow variegated foliage.*

Pachysandra terminalis 'Variegata' *Each upright shoot is crowned with a ruff of beautifully white variegated leaves making an even carpet in good soil. Reaches about 6 in (15 cm) and has pale green flowers in spring.*

Skimmia *These excellent dome-shaped shrubs have rounded leathery leaves and pale green flowers at the end of each shoot in spring. They are very fragrant. On female plants very showy red berries develop which may hang on until the next crop of flowers. Skimmia japonica 'Rubella' is compact and has red tinted buds. 'Fragrans' is another male which is a little taller at 3–4 ft (90 cm–2 m) with a 4–5 ft (1.2–1.5 m) spread. 'Foremanii' is a good female and 'Nymans' is more compact and perhaps the best berrying kind.*

Daphne odora 'Aureomarginata' *A nicely domed shrub, best in some shade. The powerfully scented rose pink flowers are whitish inside and open from January or February through to April. The glossy leaves have a thin yellow variegation. Can reach 4 ft (1.2 m) high and wide.*

Prunus laurocerasus 'Zabeliana' (Laurel) *This is quite unlike the usual laurels. The dark evergreen leaves are much narrower and the branches spread out horizontally, building up in tiers. Candles of greenish white flowers appear all along the branches in spring. It can grow 5 ft (1.5 m) high and 10 ft (3 m) wide but can be kept smaller by pruning. To keep the shape, take out whole branches rather than cutting the whole plant back.*

Garrya elliptica (Silk tassel bush) *A robust shrub good on a shady wall or fence where it can reach 12 ft (3.5 m). In winter the 9 in (22.5 cm) long pale green catkins hang down all over the shrub. If you can find 'James Roof', it will have catkins over 12 in*

(30 cm) long. Vulnerable to cold winters.

3B. Shrubs – evergreen – need underplanting.

Itea ilicifolia *An unusual shrub with glossy holly-like leaves and masses of hanging catkins of pale green flowers up to 10 in (25 cm) long. Rather like a summer flowering Garrya. Worth looking out for for a shady wall. Can reach 8 ft (2.5 m) high but is usually shorter.*

Camellia *Very noble trouble free shrubs with dark green leathery, glossy leaves and spectacular flowers in spring. They must have acid soil with plenty of humus, free draining but never drying out in summer. Camellia × williamsii and its varieties are a little easier to grow than the japonica types and tolerate a little more sun. 'Francis Hanger' is a beautiful single white, 'J.C. Williams' is a lovely single pale pink. Choose them by colour and form of flower. They can reach 6 ft (1.8 m) (a lot more in the south-west). Camellia japonica has even more varieties and is a more upright shrub, to 8 ft (2.5 m). Again, choose them in flower if possible. They are all worth extra soil preparation and are also good in tubs with lime-free soil.*

3C. Shrubs – deciduous – dense, weed suppressing

Hydrangea macrophylla 'Blue Bird' *A very good lace cap hydrangea. It starts to flower in July and goes on, with pale blue sterile flowers, until September. Reaches about 4 ft (1.2 m) by 5 ft (1.5 m) in good conditions.*

Hydrangea macrophylla 'Blue Wave' *A much lusher plant to 5 ft (1.5 m) by 7 ft (over 2 m) and larger leaves and lace cap flower heads. Despite its name the sterile flowers are rich pink in all but the most acid soils, when they are a lovely pale blue.*

3D. Shrubs – deciduous – need underplanting

Clethra alnifolia (Sweet pepper bush) *Often overlooked, this shrub has sweet scented candles of small white flowers in late summer. It is rather upright but suckers a little to form a clump up to 6 ft (1.8 m) high. Pleasant pale green leaves.*

Hydrangea villosa *A stately upright growing hydrangea with big, rough leaves and thick stems with peeling bark. Large domed lace cap flower heads in late summer with blue sterile flowers in the centre. Doesn't like the soil to dry out in summer. Reaches 8 ft (2.5 m) by 4 ft (1.2 m). A very good late summer shrub if underplanted skilfully.*

3E. Herbaceous perennials for ground cover

Ajuga reptans 'Atropurpurea' (Bugle) *The bugle is a native plant of shady places with a mat of fresh green leaves 4 in (10 cm) high and 8 in (20 cm) high spires of blue flowers. 'Atropurpurea' has burnished purple coppery and green leaves and is a wonderful low growing plant under shrubs. For a brighter effect 'Burgundy Glow' is well named with splashes of burgundy, white and purple.*

Lamium maculatum 'Roseum' (Striped deadnettle) *A lively and rather rampageous ground cover, grows to 6 in (15 cm) high with a central stripe of white down each leaf. The clusters of light pink flowers in spring and a few through the summer are very fresh. The common variety has purple flowers and is more sombre. 'Album' has white flowers and paler green leaves, while in 'Beacon Silver' the central stripe has spread to cover all but the very edge of the leaf. The purple flowers are better against the more silvery leaf. 'White Nancy' is the same but has white flowers and rather weak growth.*

Convallaria majalis (Lily of the valley) *This delightful May flowering (majalis in Latin) perennial may do well for you or it may not. If it doesn't romp away, try it around the garden in various places. It is easier to establish when grown in a pot or in a clump taken from another garden (even in summer) than from the 'pips' you can buy in bundles wrapped in moss. The dark green leaf is rather paddle-shaped and in a vigorous clump they are packed together and reach about 6 in (15 cm) high. The well-known clusters of ivory bells are on stalks a little taller and have the intoxicating sweet scent. Grow a patch big enough to cut for your house and you'll never want to be without them. Don't plant them under delicate shrubs like Japanese maples as their roots form a mat.*

Tiarella cordifolia (Foam flower) *Where lily of the valley can become a solid mat of roots when doing well, the foam flower is a complete but gentle ground cover that can go anywhere in shade. The furry mid-green maple-shaped leaves are topped by 9–12 in (22.5–30 cm) little feathery spires. A mass of them is a delicate foam.*

Pulmonaria saccharata (Lung wort) *Most herbaceous plants for shade are woodlanders and flower in spring before the trees come into leaf. Lung worts are no exception. This is a fairly coarse one with big hairy*

leaves specked with white spots and forming a 9 in
(22.5 cm) high ground cover. The bell-shaped flowers
are red and blue or purple, changing colour as they
age. In the variety 'Argentia' the spots have spread
to cover the whole leaf making it a striking foliage
plant.

Pulmonaria rubra *has red flowers and unspotted leaves,
rather pale green, while* Pulmonaria angustifolia *is
a little more compact and has rich blue flowers from
very early spring. It is often called 'Azurea' or
'Munstead Variety'.*

Helleborus orientalis (Lenten rose) *This is much
easier to grow than the Christmas rose, which is not
a low maintenance plant. For ground cover, plant
them at about 1 ft (30 cm) spacing and they form
ever-broadening clumps of big fingered leaves. The
bowl shaped flowers come on 1 ft (30 cm) stalks from
February to April, depending on the climate. They
are especially welcome at that time of the year.
Mixed seedlings are the cheapest but at some special
nurseries (like Washfield Nursery, Hawkhurst,
Kent) you can select them in flower and take them
away. The colours range from white, pink and deep
red (all of which can have maroon spots) or deepest
grape purple.*

3F. Herbaceous perennials that need underplanting

Helleborus foetidus (Stinking hellebore) *Native on
chalk downs and don't be put off by the threat of
'stinking', which I have never noticed. Rather
upright growth with even more deeply fingered leaves
with narrower segments than the Lenten rose, making
it a good evergreen foliage plant. Each of these 12 in
(30 cm) shoots is topped by a spire of yellow green
flowers from February to April. If you let these seed
you will get extra plants all over the garden. At
some stage cut away the shoots to the ground and
new ones appear as the old ones die away after
flowering. Needs underplanting as it is not quite
weed-proof and the plants can die after three years or
so and need replacing from your stock of seedlings.*

Digitalis purpurea (Foxglove) *Another short-lived
perennial although the selected strains from seedsmen
mostly die after they have flowered in the second
year. Cut down the spires immediately they have
flowered and the clump will usually live on – or let
them seed themselves. The felted leaf rosettes are
quite low but the flowering shoots can reach 6 ft*

(1.8 m) *in good conditions.*

Smilacina racemosa *An unusual clump-forming
perennial that is becoming more widely available.
The leaves, rather like Solomon's Seal, shoot up fast
in spring and by May are tipped with a fluffy spray
of tiny ivory white scented flowers. Very charming
and reaches about 2 ft 6 in (75 cm).*

3G. Climbers

Hedera helix (Ivy) *There is a wide range of varieties
with green or variegated leaves and different vigour.
'Cristata' has a rounded leaf with crisped and
scalloped edges. Quite vigorous. Much smaller is
'Glacier', a cool silvery effect of mottled white silver
and green. 'Gold Heart' is the popular dark green
leafed variety with a golden heart to the centre of the
leaf. Also less vigorous but even this can reach 10 ft
(3 m) on a shady wall unless pruned, which is easily
done.*

Hedera colchica 'Dentata Variegata' *This is the
aristocrat of variegated ivies. Big, handsome
burnished leaves with lovely yellow and pale green
variegations round the edge of the dark green leaf.
Can reach 20–30 ft (6–9 m) on a shady wall but
easily pruned to keep it smaller.*

Hydrangea petiolaris (Climbing hydrangea) *A self-
clinging climber for a shady wall where it can reach
15 ft/4.5 m (much taller in nature). Nice evenly
disposed leaves and flat heads of white flowers, with
a few rather small white sterile florets, in summer. If
the wall is dry and cement rather than lime mortar,
give it a permanent fixing every couple of years or
so, or it can all peel off rather alarmingly. Treat and
feed it well or it can be slow to get away in the early
years. An evergreen version called* Hydrangea
seemanii *is a new introduction from Mexico. The
smaller leathery leaves are very handsome and it is
also self-clinging.*

4. ACCENT PLANTS – SHRUBS

Yucca filamentosa *Tufts of spiky evergreen leaves up
to 3 ft (90 cm) high with peeling threads from the
edges. Towards the end of summer a magnificent 4–
5 ft (1.2–1.5 m) spike of ivory coloured bells
emerges. Don't crowd the plant in or the effect is
lost. The clump slowly spreads by suckers. Even
more dramatic is* Yucca gloriosa *(Adam's needle)
which has broader leaves, with no threads, and a more
spiky appearance. It slowly forms a short trunk on
which new rosettes appear. May not flower every year.*

Cordyline australis (Cabbage palm) *Not really a palm but a sheaf of narrow spiky leaves on a rugged trunk and related to lilies. Can be grown out of doors in the extreme south-west counties where it makes a small tree. It is also very useful as a pot and tub plant with a strong contrast to the rounded line and form of the pot. The leaves need tying up in winter to protect the 'heart' from the frost. The variety 'Atropurpurea' has rather coppery purple leaves for where a dark accent is needed or against a whitewashed wall. They can both be kept in a pot for several years before they get too big.*

Phormium tenax (New Zealand flax) *Like a huge evergreen iris, New Zealand flax can be used to break up a monotonous border to great effect. The green one reaches 8 ft (2.5 m) high in a warm climate but 'Purpureum' has bronzy-purple leaves with a bloom on the back and is shorter growing. There are countless variegated varieties coming on the market but they may not be fully hardy. Strange heads of bronzy-red flowers can tower over the foliage but the coloured leaved varieties rarely flower.*

Fatsia japonica *A handsome big-leaved evergreen shrub of rounded form that is especially good in shade. The fingered, pointed leaves can reach a foot (30 cm) across and are deep glossy green. The big open clusters of small, creamy white flowers come in autumn and lighten up the bush as the days get duller. Dramatic as an accent on its own in a shady corner or as a contrast to small leaved plants.*

Laurus nobilis (Bay) *More of an accent for the shapes it can be pruned into than for the plant itself. Left to its own devices it makes a big multi-stemmed shrub, not fully hardy in cold areas. Planted in a tub or in the ground it can be clipped into a formal pompom shape, a pyramid, a cone, a cylinder or whatever shape you fancy. The leathery dark green leaves can also be used in stews. Small white flowers in spring.*

Juniperus virginiana 'Skyrocket' *This juniper is naturally upright and rocket-shaped. It makes a striking exclamation mark of slightly bluish foliage and stays slim without pruning. Up to 10 ft (3 m) high.*

Arundinaria viridistriata (Variegated bamboo) *In contrast to the juniper, bamboos are evergreen grasses with broad leaves. This one only grows about 2–3 ft (60–90 cm) high and has startlingly yellow and green longitudinally striped foliage, if grown in sun.*

Can be cut down to the ground each spring for a fresh crop of variegated shoots. (Don't try this with other bamboos or they will die.) There is a wide choice of bamboos which are better than the plant most people call 'bamboo'. Perhaps the best that is reasonably easy to obtain is Arundinaria murielae *which can get 12 ft (3.5 m) tall and become a feathery plume of foliage as the leaves are rather small. Quite upright for the first few years, so does not take much space. (Watch out for some of the others which are extremely rampageous.)*

Ficus carica (Fig) *There are a few deciduous accent plants and one of these is the fig. The big lobed leaves can reach a foot (30 cm) across and are borne on stout shoots which make a very robust winter skeleton. Small figs form on these in late autumn and only ripen into figs after a mild winter. Can be trained flat on a south wall or grow it on a 1 ft – 4 ft (30 cm – 1.2 m) stem; otherwise it will become a mass of unmanageable shoots from the base. The most reliable variety is called 'Brown Turkey'.*

Paeonia lutea ludlowii (Tree peony) *Where the fig leaves are big and rounded, these are big with pointed divisions creating a sharper effect. Several very stout stems grow from the base and create the same robust winter skeleton. There are also the true tree peonies with big flowers in May but these are not usually easy plants to grow. Ludlow's peony has large, slightly drooping yellow cups just above the foliage in May. It grows up to 10 ft (3 m) tall in an open 'V' shape in sun or shade.*

5. ACCENT PLANTS – HERBACEOUS PERENNIALS

Polygonatum multiflorum (hybridum) (Solomon's Seal) *A quiet accent plant for shade with gracefully arching stems set with rounded leaves and hung all along with white, green tipped bells in May. 2–3 ft (60–90 cm).*

Osmunda regalis (Royal Fern) *This is a tall dramatic fern that can reach 6 ft (1.8 m) in moist soil in sun or half-shade. The young unfolding fronds are brownish and the autumn colour yellow. A magnificent foliage plant well worth seeking out.*

Fritillaria imperialis (Crown imperial) *This is a large bulb formed of a lot of small overlapping scales and has a foxy smell. The accent it creates is due to its reaching 4 ft (1.2 m) by the time it flowers in mid-spring. There are large drooping cups of yellow, orange or dullish red arrayed at the top of the stem around a tuft of leaves. In all but very well drained soils they need planting on their sides as soon as possible after they have died down in summer. Heavy soils need lightening with compost and 2 or 3 in (6– 7.5 cm) of grit under the bulb. They prefer full sun when growing (mine only get late afternoon sun and have survived).*

Rheum palmatum 'Atrosanguineum' (ornamental rhubarb) *This species has even bigger leaves than ordinary rhubarb and the lobes are sharply pointed. The young leaves are deep red and this colour stays on the undersides of the leaves into summer. The leaves can reach 3–4 ft (90 cm–1.2 m) across and from the centre of the clump 6 ft (1.8 m) plumes of tiny reddish flowers rise in summer. These can be cut off if they interfere with your scheme. Grow in sun or light shade.*

Acanthus spinosus (Bears' breeches) *The acanthus is the plant woven into the leaf pattern on classical Corinthian columns. The long dark green leaves are very divided and each division ends in a sharp point. They make a dense cover about 3 ft (90 cm) high and the flower spikes rise two feet (60 cm) or so above them. Each flower is protected by a spiny hood. Needs full sun.*

Iris pallida dalmatica *One of the wild bearded irises, this one has broad leaf blades that are grey all through the summer and need to be in full sun. The pale blue flowers are scented and reach about 3 ft (90 cm) in May and June. In 'Variegata' the leaves are broadly striped white or pale yellow in beautiful soft colouring against the grey leaf. In fact there are two different forms that don't seem to have separate names.*

Iris sibirica *The Siberian iris is an easy-to-grow leafy tuft of straight sword-shaped leaves up to 2 ft (60 cm) high. The flowers are in shades of blue, white or red and come in May and June and named varieties should be chosen by colour. They thrive best in a moist soil in sun or light shade.*

Miscanthus sinensis *This grass is a stately 6 ft (1.8 m) clump of leafy stems. 'Silver Feather' is a plain green form that flowers in autumn. 'Zebrinus' is the zebra grass that has regular yellow bands across the leaf. 'Gracillimus' has very narrow, long leaves, very elegant. All reach 4–6 ft (1.2–1.8 m) and the pale brown dead stems can be left in winter or cut*

down in autumn.

6. TREES
6A. **Trees – evergreen**

Eucalyptus niphophila (Snow gum) *There are few evergreen trees hardy in Britain, even fewer that are fast growing. The snow gum is about the best of these for the low maintenance gardener as it does not get so large as the other hardy gum tree, the blue gum, Eucalyptus gunnii. The pale, mottled trunk and blue/grey green leaves are a striking combination. It is fairly upright in growth and may reach 30 ft (9 m) but can be pruned to keep it smaller.*

Arbutus unedo (strawberry tree) *This one is a slow-growing evergreen that makes a multi-stemmed tree up to 20 ft (6 m) tall after many years. Very handsome dark green, leathery, tooth-edged leaves offset the small ivory bells in autumn. These slowly develop into red strawberry-like fruits by the time the next flowering comes around. May not fruit well until it is several years old. If you spot the hybrid Arbutus andrachnoides, this could be an even better choice as the trunks and older branches are a beautiful shining cinnamon brown.*

6B. **Trees – deciduous**

Cercis siliquastrum (Judas tree) *This is a low branching tree with distinctive round glaucous green leaves and clusters of pinky lilac flowers, just before the leaves open in April and May, even on the trunk. May reach 20 ft (6 m) in a warm garden.*

Magnolia × soulangiana *This is the commonest magnolia and fairly easy to grow. It has the same low-branching habit as the Judas tree, with large goblet-shaped flowers on the bare branches in spring and a few late flowers after the leaves open in May. They are white with a purplish stain at the base of each petal but can be rosy purple all over the outside in the variety 'Lennei'. 'Rustic Rubra' is redder in colour. In 'Alba Superba' the flowers are pure white. In a good soil these can reach 15 ft (4.5 m) with a 12 ft (3.5 m) spread but can be pruned after flowering with careful thought to the shape of the tree. The varieties 'Picture' and 'Sundew' are naturally more upright growing and have very fine flowers with a purple and rosy pink stain respectively.*

Gleditsia triacanthos 'Sunburst' (Honey locust) *A North American tree that needs warm summers to grow well. The finely divided pinnate leaves are a* striking yellow in spring and mature to pale green. The young leaves are yellow throughout the summer. It slowly reaches 15 ft (4.5 m) and the growth is rather twiggy. The branches are brittle so it needs shelter from the wind.

Sorbus 'Joseph Rock' and 'Embley' (Mountain ash or rowan) *Two excellent and interesting trees for the small garden. Both grow 15– 25 ft (4.5– 7.5 m) and have a neat upright habit. The pinnate leaves (like an ash tree) are mid-green and turn splendid shades of red, yellow and orange in autumn. 'Joseph Rock' has yellow berries and 'Embley' orange-red ones. The smallest rowan that forms a real tree is Sorbus cashmiriana which is a slender tree to 12 ft (3.5 m) or so and has large round white berries that hang for a few months. Good against a dark evergreen. The leaves fall a month earlier than most trees.*

Sorbus 'Wilfred Fox' (Whitebeam) *The whitebeams have simple greyish leaves but are rather too round crowned for small gardens. Two are slim crowned, this one and Sorbus thibetica, but both are hard to find in nurseries. The lovely greyish foliage is gently set off by creamy white flowers in May and sombre brown-speckled berries in autumn. Both grow slowly to 20 ft (6 m).*

Prunus hillieri 'Spire' (Flowering Cherry) *A full-sized Japanese flowering cherry may swamp your garden with its broad crown and dull summer leaves. However, there are a few cherries with an upright habit and smaller, daintier leaves which turn orange and scarlet in autumn. The flowers are smaller and single but as they only last two or three weeks this is a small sacrifice for a better garden tree. 'Spire' has pale pink flowers in mid spring and can reach 25 ft (7.5 m). 'Pandora' is similar but a little earlier and shorter in growth. 'Kursar' is even earlier and even smaller, while 'Shosar' is paler pink, a little taller and a little later flowering. 'Amanogawa' is closest to a big flowered cherry, very upright and with double pale pink flowers. Let it branch from near the ground or it looks like a besom.*

Betula jacquemontii (Himalayan birch) *For a really white trunk this is the one to choose – even the branches are dazzling white. Fairly upright habit and leaves that turn gold in autumn. Usually under 20 ft (6 m) high. Our native birch has a selection Betula pendula 'Tristis' with a straight white trunk*

and fairly horizontal branches with drooping branchlets. A very elegant outline growing up to 30 ft (9 m).

Ginkgo biloba (Maidenhair tree) *An unusual tree, in fact a primitive conifer found fossilised in coal measures hundreds of millions of years old. A few survived in China and so we can grow it for its fan-shaped pale green leaves (like a maidenhair fern). Slow-growing with a stout winter outline. May reach 50 ft (15 m) after many many years and has quite a narrow habit. Lovely autumn foliage.*

Metasequoia glyptostroboides (Dawn redwood) *Another primitive conifer found in China. Very ferny foliage and a slender conical habit. The leaves, at first light green, often have a burnished tinge and turn soft brown with a tinge of pink in autumn. Grows to 30 ft (9 m), quite fast in moist conditions. Orange bark with red/brown tinge.*

Malus floribunda (Flowering crab) *If you need a tree with a low, wide-spreading crown, what could be more enchanting than the soft cloud of deep pink buds and pale pink to white flowers of this spring-flowering tree. A little dull after it has flowered but the small leaves mean that it is not so oppressive. Reaches about 15 ft (4.5 m) and can spread about as much.*

Pyrus salicifolia 'Pendula' (Willow leaved pear) *Fully dome-shaped with weeping branches to the ground, this popular tree has narrow silvery leaves. Should be trained up a stout stake or it will tend to sprawl. Can reach 12 ft (3.5 m) or so.*

Standard Roses *Neat miniature trees but need a permanent stake and tie. Weeping standards have a climbing or rambling rose budded on top of the stem and some people prefer to train them over a wire dome to make them graceful. Prune as for bush roses, climbers or ramblers respectively.*

7. BULBS

Galanthus nivalis (Snowdrops) *Well-known early-flowering bulb with greyish leaves. What is not so well known is that they only move well when 'in the green', that is in full leaf. Dry bulbs take years to flower. Specialist nurseries sell green snowdrops; or you could beg a few from a friend with a large clump or two and they will multiply. Good under deciduous shrubs as they die down before the shrub leafs out.*

Endymion non-scriptus (Bluebell) *The true bluebell with narrow deep blue bells. Always let the leaves* die down naturally and never cut them off green. The Spanish bluebell is more common with taller stems of more open bells in blue, pink or white. True bluebells recall an English wood in spring and have a delightful scent.

Ranunculus ficaria 'Plena' (Lesser celandine) *This little native woodlander has small tubers and is best bought grown in a pot. The leaves come up very early and are followed by perfect rosettes of buttercup yellow flowers (it is related to buttercups) in spring. Dies down early, so good under a deciduous shrub. 'Primrose' is very pale yellow and 'Cuprea' is coppery orange. Both are single and grow up to 6 in (15 cm) high.*

Daffodils *There is a very large choice of daffodils (all Narcissus in Latin) but for a smaller garden it is worth choosing the smaller-growing but easy ones which have less foliage to cover up after they have flowered. Leave the foliage until at least mid-June before you cut it off. 'Charity May' is pure yellow with swept back petals in April and May. 'February Gold' is very easy and in a very mild winter may flower at the end of February. Otherwise it often flowers for six weeks and spreads rapidly. Narrower, slightly less reflexed petals than 'Charity May' and a little paler yellow, 'Jack Snipe' is a little shorter at 8 in, with a pale yellow cup and white petals. 'Dove Wings' is a little darker and a little taller. These are just some of the ones to choose if the big daffodils like 'King Alfred' are out of scale.*

Muscari botryoides (Grape hyacinth) *Clusters of tubby blue bells on 6 in (15 cm) stems in May. 'Album' is white and makes a good contrast to the blue. Spreads easily.*

Tulipa turkestanica *A nice compact wild species from Central Asia which grows 8 in (20 cm) high and has narrow grey leaves. The white flowers have a green and bronze flush on the outside of the petals. There are many tulip species, much easier to handle than the large flowered ones, in a sunny, well-drained position. A very bright one is Tulipa praestans 'Fusilier' with military red flowers on 6 in (15 cm) stalks. Of the tall ones 'Schnoord' is a good double white used in the Georgian garden.*

Ornithogalum umbellatum (Star of Bethlehem) *A vigorous bulb with starry white flowers on 4 in (10 cm) stems and quite attractive leaves with a central white stripe.*

Lilium candidum (Madonna lily) *Loves you or hates you but well worth a try in a dryish, sunny spot. Only just cover the bulb with soil and plant in August. Tall spires of pure white beautifully scented flowers in May and June. Can grow to 5 ft (1.5 m) if the bulbs are happy.*

Gladiolus byzantinus (Hardy gladiolus) *In a sunny well-drained place it will produce ribbed leaves and spikes of screaming magenta flowers in June and July. Good for the adventurous. 'The Bride' is a demure white.*

Cyclamen neapolitanum hederifolium (Hardy cyclamen) *The little 4 in (10 cm) high cyclamen flowers are pink and come in early September. Beautifully marbled leaves follow them and make a wonderful ground cover under a tree or in front of a hedge until they die down in July. They seed themselves when they are happy and white ones often appear. Buy the flat corms in August only if they are nice and firm if you squeeze them, or buy them grown in pots. Plant the corm rounded side down just under the surface of the soil and sprinkle a little compost on top each autumn. They sometimes take time to get established.*

Crocus speciosus (Autumn flowering crocus) *This is the best crocus for autumn. The Colcicums have crocus-like flowers but big tufts of leaves follow them and can be rather obtrusive in the garden. The blue crocus flowers of C. speciosus are followed in spring by narrow grassy leaves, with a central white stripe, only 4 in (10 cm) tall. There are masses of other crocus, often called winter or species crocus, that are much more dainty than the later flowering Dutch crocus. They grow 4–6 in (10–15 cm) high and can be chosen by colour. Ideal for the sunny front of a border or shrub group.*

8. ALPINES

Easy alpines are those that grow in ordinary garden soil and form a good weed-free mat that can be used to drape a rock or low wall. These are in order of flowering.

Arabis albida *The well known arabis is a vigorous plant 6 in (15 cm) high with masses of white flowers in spring.*

Dryas octopetala (Mountain avens) *This forms a neat mat of oak-shaped dark green leaves. Above it, in May, eight petalled white flowers rise to about 4 in (10 cm). The stems elongate as a fluff of leathery seeds form by June.*

Phlox subulata (Moss phlox) *A mossy mat of foliage 5 in (12.5 cm) high and studded with flowers of various colours, depending on the variety, in May and June.*

Saponaria ocymoides (Trailing soapwort) *Another vigorous mat former with shiny leaves and pink flowers with a puffy little calyx in June.*

Dianthus 'Little Jock' (Pink) *One of the alpine pinks that grows 4–6 in (10–15 cm) tall. A mound (which spreads with age) of narrow grey leaves with double pink flowers above the foliage. All have a strong sweet clove scent. Other good varieties are 'Pikes Pink' with darker flowers, 'Hidcote' with deep red single flowers and 'Waithman's Beauty' with single pink flowers.*

Geranium 'Ballerina' *Beautiful pink flowers with darker veins over a neat 4 in (10 cm) clump of round, dissected leaves. Geranium cinereum is a deep magenta with black eye, also flowering in June and July, with a few flowers later.*

Campanula portenschlagiana (Alpine bluebell) *There are a number of species and varieties and this is a vigorous one that can be invasive. Blue rather open flowers in June and July. Campanula carpatica flowers through the summer with open bowl-shaped flowers over the mounds of foliage. 'Blue Chip' is a nice blue, 'White Star' is a good white. They can seed themselves around a bit.*

Thymus × citriodorus (Lemon scented thyme) *A 6 in (15 cm) cover of tiny leaves that is fairly weed-free. Needs a well drained soil and has small pink flowers in summer. 'Aureus' has golden leaves and 'Silver Queen' has grey leaves, edged in white. The crushed leaves have a lemony tang.*

Polygonum affine 'Dimity' *The long leaves form a good cover about 3 in (7.5 cm) high and above them in summer 6 in (15 cm) pokers of pink flowers spring up. These mature to deep red as the seeds ripen so the combination of the colours is very good right into the autumn.*

9. HERBS *These herbs are all decorative shrubs or perennials and can be used in with other ornamental plants. They all prefer well drained soil and full sun.*

Camomile *A low mat of feathery foliage with daisy flowers in summer. 'Treneague' does not flower and is good for a camomile 'lawn' or seat. The crushed leaves have a spicy fragrance.*

Hyssop *Another tangy fragrance, hyssop is a low, spreading evergreen shrub with narrow leaves and blue, pink or white flowers according to variety. Needs a light clipping in spring to keep it neat.*

Lavender *Fragrant grey leaves and lavender flowers on a 1–2 ft (30–60 cm) evergreen shrub. Must be trimmed in spring to keep it bushy, but not into the old wood. Three compact varieties, all flowering in summer, are 'Hidcote' with dark violet flowers, 'Twickel Purple' with rather mauve flowers and 'Munstead' with deep lavender flowers.*

Mint *Needs containing by paving or a sunken bucket without a bottom. Spearmint has rather long narrow leaves, Apple Mint has rounded hairy leaves and has a handsomely white variegated variety.*

Rosemary *A shrub with long narrow deep green leaves and a variable habit. The common one sprawls a bit and has pale blue flowers in spring and a few all through the year. 'Severn Sea' is particularly spreading but 'Miss Jessops Upright' is a column of foliage that can reach 6 ft (1.8 m) if tied in gently with green string to stop its branches arching out.*

Sage *Broad grey green leaves on a mounded shrub about 18 in (45 cm) high. The non-flowering form is very useful and compact but does not seem to have a name. 'Purpurea' has purple tinged foliage and is a rich colour combination. 'Tricolor' is the same with a few splashes of white. 'Icterina' has gold variegated foliage. They are all wonderful foliage plants. Cut off the flowers after flowering.*

Thyme *The shrubby culinary thyme can grow 8 in (20 cm) tall and is the right flavour for stuffings. Small pale blue flowers in summer and tiny leaves on a twiggy bush.*

Accent Plant *A plant that is a different shape, colour or height and therefore provides a contrast to the other plants.*

Acid Soil *Soil that has no free lime. The acid quality of soil can change the appearance of plants grown in it; for instance hydrangeas grown in acid soil have blue flowers, and hydrangeas grown in alkaline soil have pink flowers. Plants that require acid soil will die in an alkaline one.*

Algae *A green scum that grows on damp surfaces, or in stagnant water.*

Alkaline *Soils that contain a great deal of lime or chalk are alkaline and are usually described as limey or chalky.*

Alpine *A plant native to high mountains, e.g. the Alps. Small plants suitable for growing in a rock garden, garden troughs or old sinks.*

Annual *A bedding plant or a plant that grows from seed, flowers and dies in the same year.*

Aphid *Small insects such as greenfly and blackfly that suck the juices from plants. They do a lot of harm in the garden, are virus carriers, and reproduce at a rapid rate.*

Arbour *A group of plants or small trees, or climbing plants grown over trellis work, creating a sheltered area in which to sit.*

Bare-root *A tree or shrub that has no soil around the roots and should be planted between November and March.*

Bedding plant *An annual or non-hardy perennial plant usually planted in borders and tubs to give summer colour.*

Biennial *A plant that grows in the first year and flowers and dies during the next (such as sweet william and honesty).*

Blackfly *A tiny plant aphid (see* Aphid*).*

Black spot *A plant disease which produces black spots or patches on the leaves; mostly on roses.*

Blight *A disease that causes the plant to wither.*

Bog garden *A garden used for growing water-loving plants that like a permanently moist soil.*

Bonemeal *An organic (phosphate and potassium) fertiliser made of crushed or ground bone.*

Canopy *(of a tree) The spread of a tree's branches.*

Carpet bedding *A specialised form of planting or bedding out where dwarf and flat-growing plants are planted and produce a carpet-like appearance.*

Catkin *A pendulous flower. Willow, garrya, hazel and birch trees all have catkins in spring.*

Climber *Any plant that climbs up a firm surface, tree or shrub. Honeysuckle, ivy, clematis and jasmine officinale are true climbers. Roses have to be trained against walls and do not actually attach themselves to the wall or they can scramble in other plants.*

Conifer *Mostly evergreen trees and shrubs (such as pine and spruce) whose seeds are in cones.*

Coppice *A system of cutting back a tree to a 6–12 in (15–30 cm) stump so that it sends up a mass of stems. These can then be cut down every few years.*

Corm *The rounded thick underground stem of plants such as crocus.*

Creeper *A plant that spreads over the ground, rooting as it goes.*

Cut back *Shorten by cutting the length of a branch on trees and shrubs.*

Dead-head *Remove dead flowers from a rose or any other plant.*

Deciduous *A plant that loses all its leaves each winter.*

Double dig *To dig soil to a depth of 2 ft (60 cm). Mainly soil under trees that has been neglected and is in need of feeding and organic matter. Double digging is essential before planting in poor soil.*

Drainage trench *A deep, narrow trench dug in the garden to take the excess water from a certain area of the garden.*

Evergreen *Tree or shrub that has green leaves throughout the year.*

Fern *Flowerless, seedless plants which reproduce by spores.*

Fertiliser *Compost, manure or chemical mixture which provides nutrients in the soil to help feed plants.*

Festoon *Training a fruit tree by bending its leader over in an arch and tying it to the stem when it is a maiden, and repeating the process in following years. Festooning keeps the tree small and encourages early fruiting.*

Floribunda *Cultivated hybrid roses with large clusters of flowers. (See* Hybrid Tea*.)*

Foliage plant *A plant grown for its interesting foliage.*

Frond *A leaf, especially of a palm or fern.*

Germinate *When a seeds begins growing.*

Grass *Any of large family (Gramineae, the grass family) of plants having jointed stems sheathed by slender leaves and bearing tiny flowers in spikelets.*

Greenfly *Green-coloured sticky aphids that carry plant virus and are very destructive to plants.*

Ground-cover plant *Low-growing plant that covers the soil under trees or between bushes and keeps* down weeds.

Habit *The particular manner in which the branches and leaves form and characterise the growth of a plant, i.e. bushy, sprawling.*

Half-hardy *A plant able to withstand moderately low temperatures but not frost-resistant.*

Half-standard *A plant or tree resembling a standard, but with a shorter length of bare stem.*

Hard prune *To cut back growing shoots to a few dormant buds above ground. See* Prune.

Hardy *A plant that does not die from frost during a normal winter.*

Head back *To prune (trees or shrubs) by cutting back some or all of the branches above well-developed dormant buds. Usually applied to fruit trees.*

Heel-in *Temporarily cover the roots of plants with soil before planting in the final growing position. Plants can remain in good condition for several weeks.*

Herbaceous *Plants that do not have woody stems. Usually applied to perennials that grow again from their roots for many years.*

Herbaceous border *A flower bed for herbaceous plants.*

Herb garden *An area of the garden used for growing herbs.*

Hybrid *A plant derived from the crossing of two different species, either in the same genus or from different genera.*

Hybrid tea *Cultivated hybrid roses which flower in mid-summer and autumn and have larger flowers than old roses.*

Insecticide *Substances used for killing garden insects.*

John Innes compost *A standard potting compost developed at the John Innes Horticultural Institute. There are three varieties, all a mixture of seven parts sterilised loam, three parts sphagnum peat and two parts coarse sand. No. 1 contains ground limestone or chalk, base fertiliser made from superphosphate of lime, Hoof and Horn meal, sulphate of potash. No. 2 has twice the amount of added fertiliser and No. 3 three times the amount. Choose the strength of compost depending on the size of the plants to be planted. Nos 2 and 3 are suitable for more substantial plants.*

Kitchen garden *A part of the garden used for growing vegetables for the house.*

Larva *An insect in the first stage of its life after emerging from the egg. Some larvae, e.g. those of the chafer beetle, can cause damage to garden plants.*

Lateral *(Of a stem, bud or shoot) branching out from the side of the leader or from the main branch. This term is usually applied to fruit trees to explain where to prune.*

Lawn rake *A fan-shaped rake designed especially for use on grass lawns.*

Lawn sand *A prepared sand and chemicals mixture used for killing weeds and moss on lawns.*

Leaf mould *A compost made of decayed leaves. It is rich in humus and extremely valuable when added to poor soil, or to help lighten clay soil. It can be used as a mulch.*

Leaf spot *Dark circular spots on a plant's leaves caused by fungi.*

Leatherjacket *The larva of daddy longlegs which damages plants by feeding on their roots.*

Leggy *(Of a plant) spindly and having a bare lower stem.*

Light pruning *Pruning of a tree or shrub by cutting back old growth moderately in early spring before the new growing season begins; and the removal of dead flowers from a plant.*

Lop *To prune a tree by drastically cutting back its upper branches.*

Maintenance pruning *Systematically cutting branches of old fruit to encourage new growth.*

Manure *Organic matter or animal excrement from stables and farmyard that is used to fertilise the land after it has been composted, usually with straw, for a few months.*

Meadow grass *Long grass that likes moist areas.*

Mildew *A plant disease which leaves a whitish deposit on the surface of the plant. It usually occurs when the atmosphere is moist and the soil dry.*

Mineral deficiency *The condition or result of having too little of one or more of the mineral elements necessary for normal growth.*

Moss *Non-flowering primitive plant with tiny tufted leaves.*

Mulch *Compost, manure, peat, bark chippings or other organic matter spread on the ground to control weeds, preserve moisture and enrich the soil.*

Offset *A shoot that grows out of the base of a plant and produces its own new shoots and roots; often happens with roses. A small bulb coming from the base of another bulb.*

Orchard *A section of the garden where fruit trees are grown.*

Organic *Composed of plant or animal matter.*

Organic fertiliser *Any fertiliser that is made from animal or plant matter.*

Organic manure *Manure made from materials containing animal or plant matter.*

Organic matter *A substance consisting of decayed living organisms, e.g. compost, manure made from plants.*

Ornamental *(Of a plant) grown for beauty or pleasure rather than for use as timber or food.*

Parterre *Bedding scheme in a garden best viewed from above, ornamental planting separated by a pattern of walks.*

Patio *A paved area usually adjoining the house used for sitting outdoors. An ideal place for plants in containers.*

Peat *Half-decomposed (in water) mosses and sedge, found in large bogs and used for planting and to lighten and improve soil. Also used as a mulch.*

Perennial *A plant that lives for several years.*

Pesticide *A chemical, be it fungicide or insecticide, used to deter or destroy insects and other garden pests, also applied now to weed killers.*

Pinch back *Taking out the young shoots of trees and shrubs by nipping off with the nails of forefinger and thumb the soft tips of the plant, to encourage the development of the remaining buds.*

Pinch out *Removing the tips of unwanted shoots in order to encourage new growth to grow from the side shoots.*

Planter *A container in which plants are grown.*

Pollination *The first step in fertilisation in which a bee or other insect or wind carries pollen from an anther to a stigma of one plant to another.*

Potash *A substance usually used in fertilisers that contains potassium and can be used to supply or increase potassium in the soil.*

Pot-bound *(of plant in a pot) Having little or no space for further growth as the pot is too small.*

Pot-grown *A plant that has been grown in a container.*

Pot plant *Any plant placed in a flower pot or container filled with soil usually to be grown inside.*

Potting compost *Sterilised materials including perlite, soil, peat, sand and other ingredients, for potting plants. Soilless compost is composed mainly of peat and perlite.*

Propagation *The creation of a new plant from an existing plant by dividing, cutting, layering or seed.*

Prune *To cut or trim woody growth on plants to help future growth of the shrub, tree, climber or vine.*

Raised bed *A place for growing plants above ground level. Raised beds can be held in position with stone,* brick or wood, or can just be soil raised 1 ft (30 cm) or more above the level of the ground. Raised beds are often used to help vegetables and alpines grow with better drainage.*

Rhizome *A long thick horizontal plant stem, underground or on the soil surface (like bearded iris). It is distinguished from a real root by the buds that are attached to it and scale-like leaves.*

Rockery *A natural or artificial arrangement of rocks and earth to grow alpines and small plants.*

Rock garden *A garden of the same.*

Rock plant *A small plant, usually an alpine, that grows happily among rocks.*

Root pruning *Cutting back strong, thick roots in order to check growth, and prepare for planting, for instance when planting bare-rooted roses or other bare-rooted plants.*

Root rot *Root decay caused by the attack of fungi or other diseases.*

Root run *The place in the soil in which the roots of a plant choose to grow.*

Runner *A weak, usually horizontal shoot that roots at the joints to form new plants. Strawberries and violets are among the plants which produce runners.*

Sap *The liquid in a plant's stems, shoots and branches.*

Seedling *A germinated young plant grown from seed (rather than from a cutting).*

Selective weedkiller *A weedkiller that kills a particular unwanted plant while leaving other plants unharmed. Weed Out, for example, only kills couch and other grass.*

Self-fertile *Capable of fertilising with its own pollen.*

Semi-evergreen *A tree or shrub that retains most of its leaves during the winter, although it may shed all of them in a severe winter.*

Shingle *Small water-worn pebbles which come from the sea, as opposed to gravel which comes from pits.*

Shrub *A usually several-stemmed woody plant that does not develop a trunk.*

Shrubbery *An area in the garden where a collection of shrubs are planted.*

Side shoot *A lateral growth, branching from the main stem.*

Single dig *To dig the soil 1 ft (30 cm) deep.*

Slow-release *(fertiliser) A fertiliser that releases nutrients into the ground over a long period of time, e.g. bone meal, hoof and horn meal.*

Slug *A slimy, elongated, ground-living gastropod mollusc without shell that likes dark damp areas of the garden. Slugs feed on young shoots of plants.*

Slug pellets *Ready-made poison which kills slugs (usually containing concentrated metaldehyde) and is potentially destructive to wildlife and pets.*

Soil testing *Means of determining the nutritional value of the soil, its pH (acidity and alkalinity) and drainage characteristics.*

Sprout *To produce a young shoot.*

Stake *A piece of wood, often a bamboo cane or a thick straight length of wood, used to support a plant. It is placed in the hole alongside the stem of the plant or trunk of a small tree to which it is then tied.*

Standard *A tree or shrub having a bare main stem and in which the growth is concentrated in a terminal crown of foliage and blooms.*

Sucker *A shoot arising from below ground at the base of a plant, usually directly from the roots.*

Summer pruning *A system of pruning in the summer months, used particularly on fruit trees.*

Support *Providing a plant support such as stake or bamboo poles, a means of growing upright.*

Tender annual *An annual that requires greenhouse cultivation and then planting out in May, not suitable for a low-maintenance garden.*

Thin out *To reduce the number of shoots and branches on trees to prevent overcrowding.*

Thorn *A tiny sharply pointed piece of wood that protrudes from the woody part of a bush or shrub, usually found on roses and brambles.*

Tie *A material which fastens a plant to its support. Most ties are made of garden twine, plastic-covered wire or raffia. Tree ties are made of plastic like a very small belt with a buckle.*

Tip cutting *A stem cutting from the uppermost growth of a non-flowering plant shoot.*

Top dress *A layer of compost, peat, soil or mulch, laid on the top of borders, beds, containers or round the base of a tree. See also Mulch.*

Topiary *The art of training, cutting and trimming trees or shrubs into an ornamental shape.*

Total weedkiller *A weedkiller which destroys all vegetable matter that it touches.*

Trace element *A chemical element important to the growth of a plant, usually only deficient on very light soils. These chemicals are only needed in minute quantities. (They include boron, iron and manganese.) An excess can be harmful.*

Train *To 'persuade' plants by placing and tying them in such a way as to make them grow in a certain direction.*

Transplant *To move a plant that is growing in one place to another. Always water well for at least a week before doing this. Do not transplant in summer.*

Trimmer *A tool, powered either by an electric motor or a petrol engine, for cutting back small hedges.*

Tropical *Originating in the tropics. Tropical plants need to be grown in warm conditions inside or in a greenhouse, with a minimum temperature of 64°F (18°C) and they usually need a great deal of moisture in the air.*

Trug *A long shallow basket made of flat bits of wood, as opposed to woven, used for carrying small plants, garden tools, vegetables and flowers.*

Truncate *To shorten a plant part by cutting off a part.*

Tuber *A thickened or swollen underground stem that stores food and is potentially able to produce a new plant, e.g. a potato.*

Underplant *To plant smaller plants, often bulbs, beneath taller plants. (Usually deciduous plants that are not in flower or leaf when the bulb or other plant that has been underplanted is in flower.)*

Variegated *A leaf or flower that is marked with a contrasting colour, so the leaf is two-tone.*

Vegetative *The non-flowering growth of a plant.*

Virus disease *A large variety of plant diseases usually carried from one plant to another by aphids. (See Aphids).*

Water garden *A part of the garden that has a (usually man-made) pond, lake or fountain.*

Weeping *A tree or shrub that has slender drooping branches; of pendulous habit.*

Weevil *Small beetles that tend to eat the roots of houseplants or plants in window boxes.*

Whitefly *Any of numerous small white insects that are injurious plant pests.*

Wildlife garden *A garden that does not use any chemicals or insecticides and is devoted to growing mostly wild native plants which provide a refuge for insects, birds and wild animals, in a garden that is similar to their natural habitat.*

Windbreak *Trees, hedge or fence grown especially to break the wind.*

Winter pruning *The cutting back of deciduous trees (especially fruit trees) in the dormant season, usually from November onwards.*

Woody *A tough, fibrous plant that is not soft to the touch.*

39: *Recommended books*

Expert Series by D. G. Hessayon (pbi Publications)

The Vegetable Grower's Directory by Susan Conder (Macdonald)

The Gardening Year (Readers Digest Association)

Herbs, New Guidelines by Jack Harvey (Macdonald Optima)

Natural Pest and Disease Control by Jim Hay (Century)

Encyclopaedia of Garden Plants and Flowers (Readers Digest Association)

How to Make a Wildlife Garden by Chris Baines (Elm Tree Books)

The Heritage of the Rose by David Austin (Antique Collectors' Club)

Classic Roses by Peter Beales (Harvill Press)

The Makers of Heavenly Roses by Jack Harkness (Souvenir Press)

ORNAMENTS

Stapeley Water Gardens Ltd, Stapeley,
Nantwich, Cheshire CW5 7LH, Tel: Nantwich
623868
*(Large range of fountains, and statues and ornaments
that associate well with water)*

T Crowther & Sons Ltd, 282 North End Road,
Fulham, London SW6, Tel: 01 385 1375
(Dealers in antique garden statuary and ornaments)

Crowthers of Syon Lodge, Syon Lodge, Busch
Corner, London Road, Isleworth, Middlesex
TW7 5BH
(Dealers in antique garden statuary and ornaments)

David Bridgwater, 14 Fountain Buildings, Bath
BA1 5DX, Avon, Tel: 0225 69288/63652
(Stone troughs, statues and garden antiques)

Brookbrae Ltd, 53 St Leonard's Road, London
SW14 7NQ, Tel: 01 876 4370
*(Sundials. Original creations made to order if you
want)*

Chilstone Garden Ornaments, Sprivers Estate,
Horsmonden, Kent TN12 8DR, Tel: Brenchley
3553
(A wide range of reconstituted stone ornaments)

Haddonstone Ltd, The Forge House, East
Haddon, Northampton NN6 8DB, Tel:
Northampton 770711
(A wide range of reconstituted stone ornaments)

Jim Keeling Flowerpots, Whichford Pottery,
Whichford, Shipston-on-Stour, Warwickshire
CV36 5PG, Tel: Shipston-on-Stour 84416
(Clay pots and some ornaments, hand-made)

Minsterstone (Wharf Lane) Ltd, Ilminster,
Somerset TA19 9AS, Tel: Ilminster 2277
(Reconstituted stone garden ornaments)

Renaissance Casting, 102 Arnold Avenue,
Styvechale, Coventry CV3 5NE, Tel: Coventry
27275
(Lead ornaments in traditional styles)

MAIL ORDER SPECIALISTS

Begonias, Geraniums, Ivies:
Fibrex Nurseries Ltd, Honeybourne Road,
Pebworth, Nr Stratford on Avon CV37 8XT,
Tel: 0789 720788

Bulbs:
Walter Blom and Son Ltd, Coombelands
Nurseries, Leavesden, Watford, Herts
WD2 7BH, Tel: 09273 72071

Van Tubergen, PO Box 74, Hull HU9 1PQ,
Tel: 01031 2521 19030

Broadleigh Gardens, Bishops Hull, Taunton,
Somerset TA4 1AE, Tel: 0823 86231

Peter Nyssen Ltd, Railway Road, Urmston,
Manchester, Tel: 061 748 6666

Wallace and Barr, The Nurseries, Marden,
Tonbridge, Kent.

Fuchsias:
Jackson's Nurseries, Clifton Campville, Nr
Tamworth, Staffs B79 0AP, Tel: 082786 307.

Roses, Hardy Plants and Shrubs (*David
Austin roses*):
David Austin, Bowling Green Lane,
Albrighton, Wolverhampton WV7 3HB, Tel:
090722 2141

John Mattock, Nuneham Courtney, Oxford
OX9 9PY, Tel: 086738 285

Roses:
Peter Beales, London Road, Attleborough,
Norfolk, Tel: 0953 454707

R Harkness and Co Ltd, The Rose Gardens,
Hitchen, Herts SG4 0JT, Tel: 0462 34027

Herbaceous, Conifers and Shrubs:
Bressingham Gardens, Diss, Norfolk IP22 2AB,
Tel: 037988 464

Highfield Nurseries (Western Forestry Co Ltd), Whitminster, Gloucester GL2 7PL, Tel: 0452 740266

Hillier Nurseries, Winchester, Hants, Tel: 0794 68733

Notcutts, Woodbridge, Suffolk IP12 4AE, Tel: 03943 3344

Unusual Plants:
Beth Chatto, Whitebarn House, Elmstead Market, Colchester, Essex

Seed Companies:
J Arthur Bowers, Horticultural Advisory Service, Wigford House, Brayford Pool, Lincoln LN5 7BL

J W Boyce, 67 Station Road, Soham, Ely, Cambs CB7 5ED

D T Brown & Co Ltd, Poulton Le Fylde, Blackpool FY6 7HX

John Chambers, 15 Westleigh Rd, Barton Seagrave, Kettering, Northants NN15 5AJ
(excellent for wild flowers)

Chase Seeds UK Ltd, Coomsland House, Coomsland Lane, Addlestone, Weybridge, Surrey KT15 1HY
(excellent for vegetables)

Chelsea Choice Seeds, Folly Farm, Stortford Road, Dunmow, Essex CM6 1SG

Chiltern Seeds, Bortree Stile, Ulverston, Cumbria LA12 7PB

Samuel Dobie & Son Ltd, Upper Dee Mills, Llangollen, Clywd LL20 8SD

Emorsgate Seeds, Emorsgate, Torrington St Clement, Kings Lynn, Norfolk
(excellent for wild flowers)

Mr Fothergills Seeds, Kentford, Newmarket, Suffolk CB8 7QB

Heritage Seeds, DRA Sales, Ryton on Dunsmoor, Coventry CV8 3LG

S E Marshall & Co Ltd, Regal Road, Wisbech, Cambs PE13 2RF

Seeds by Post, Suffolk Herbs, Sawyers Farm, Little Cornard, Sudbury, Suffolk CO10 0NY
(unusual and oriental vegetables)

Suttons Seeds, Head Office, Hele Road, Torquay, Devon TQ2 7QJ

Thompson & Morgan, London Road, Ipswich, Suffolk IP2 0BA

Unwins Seeds Ltd, Histon, Cambridge CB4 4LE

MISCELLANEOUS

Pea Shingle:
Mid Essex Gravel Pits (Chelmsford) Ltd, Broomfield, Chemlsford, Essex CM3 3PZ, Tel: 0245 440621
(or your local supplier)

Graded Bark Flakes:
Melcourt Industries, Three Cups House, Tetbury, Glos GL8 8JG, Tel: 0666 52711/53919
(or your local supplier)

Gardening from Which (Magazine):
Castlemead, Gascoyne Way, Hertford SG14 1LH

Redland Bricks:
Redland Bricks Ltd, The Gables, 17 Massetts Road, Horley, Surrey RH6 7DQ, Tel: 0293 786688

The Brick Advisory Centre:
The Building Centre, Store St, London WC1 7BT

Tiles:
Reed Harris Tiles, Riverside House, Carnwath Road, London SW6 3HS

Pest Control (Moles):
Chase Centre, Rugeley Road, Hednesford,
Staffs WS12 5TB, Tel: 0785 21 49946/46731

Renardine (Rabbits):
Gilberton & Page Ltd, Corrys, Roestock Lane,
Colney Heath, St Albans, Herts HL4 0QW

Trellis:
Anthony Christie & Robin Macloskey, Lloyds
Christie Garden Architecture, Unit 10, Acorn
Production Centre, 105 Blundell Street, London
N7, Tel: 01 609 3667

Pavilions:
Machine Designs Ltd, Ransomes's Dock,
Parkgate Road, London SW11 4NP, Tel:
01 350 1581

Walton Conservatories Ltd, Unit 26, Lyon Rd,
Hersham Industrial Estate, Walton-on-Thames,
Surrey, KT12 3PU. Tel: 0932 242579

Ollerton Gazebos, Ollerton Engineering
Services Ltd, Samlesbury Bottoms, Preston,
Lancs. Tel: 025 485 2127

Conservation Organisations:

Royal Society for Nature Conservation, The
Green, Nettleham, Lincoln LN2 2NR

Botanical Society of the British Isles, c/o
Department of Botany, British Museum
(Natural History), Cromwell Road, London
SW7 5BD

Wild Flower Society, 68 Outwoods Road,
Loughborough, Leicester LE11 3LY

Conservation Association of Botanical Societies,
323 Norwood Road, London SE24 9AQ

Conservation Foundation, Lowther Lodge,
1 Kensington Gore, London SW7

Royal Society for the Protection of Birds, The
Lodge, Sandy, Bedfordshire, Tel: 0767 80551

As they appear in the garden plans (pp. 13–84) and the plant lists (pp. 166–182)

Acanthus spinosus 57, 179
Acer palmatum 28, 173
Ajuga reptans 48, 57, 176
Alchemilla mollis 57, 83, 169
Althaea rosea 56, 174
Anemone japonica 83, 170
Anthemis cupaniana 57, 173
Arabis albida 181
Arbutus andrachnoides 179
Arbutus unedo 179
Artemisia absinthium 'Lambrook Silver' 57, 174
Arundinaria murielae 178
Arundinaria viridistriata 178
Aster frikartii 29, 57, 174
Astilbe arendsii 34

Bay Tree see Laurus nobilis
Bergenia cordifolia 19, 29, 36, 169
Betula jacquemontii 31, 180
Betula pendula 77, 180
Buddleia alternifolia 68

Camellia japonica 176
Camellia williamsii 34, 81, 176
Camomile 57, 182
Campanula 57, 83, 182
Carpenteria californica 80, 172
Ceanothus 'Autumnal Blue' 42, 172
Ceanothus thyrsiflorus 'Repens' 28, 172
Centaurea montana 36, 169
Cercis siliquastrum 39, 179
Chaenomeles speciosa 'Cardinalis' 54, 173
Choisya ternata 18, 42, 54, 167
Cistus 'Silver Pink' 42, 47, 172
Clematis armandii 48, 56, 175
Clematis macropetala 81, 171
Clematis 'Nelly Moser' 29, 48

Clematis viticella 29, 175
Clethra alnifolia 176
Convallaria majalis 75, 83, 176
Convolvulus mauritanicus 174
Cordyline australis 42, 81, 178
Cotoneaster 'Autumn Fire' 18, 167
Cotoneaster franchettii 167
Crocus speciosus 181
Cyclamen neapolitanum 181
Cytisus kewensis 74, 171

Daffodils 75, 181
Daphne burkwoodii 56, 172
Daphne mezereum 18, 47, 168
Daphne odora 'Aurçomarginata' 43, 175
Dianthus 'Little Jock' 182
Dianthus 'Mrs Sinkins' 57
Diascia rigescens 174
Diascia vigilis 174
Digitalis purpurea 57, 177
Dryas octopetala 181

Endymion non-scriptus 34, 180
Eryngium oliverianum 36, 174
Escallonia 'Apple Blossom' 28, 172
Escallonia 'Crimson Spire' 172
Eucalyptus gunnii 179
Eucalyptus niphophila 77, 179
Euonymus fortunei 'Silver Queen' 80, 167
Euphorbia polychroma 170
Euphorbia wulfenii 31, 83, 167

Fatsia japonica 34, 178
Festuca glauca 36, 174
Ficus carica 77, 178
Forsythia suspensa 75, 171
Fritillaria imperialis 75, 178

Fuchsia 'Lady Thumb' 43, 172
Fuchsia magellanica 28, 54, 168

Galanthus nivalis 180
Garrya elliptica 31, 80, 175
Geranium 'Ballerina' 182
Geranium endressii 'Wargrave Pink' 29, 169
Geranium 'Johnson's Blue' 42, 48, 84, 169
Geranium 'Kashmir White' 169
Geranium magnificum 169
Geranium macrorrhizum 169
Geranium renardii 170
Ginkgo biloba 77, 180
Gladiolus byzantinus 29, 181
Gleditsia triacanthos 'Sunburst' 74, 179

Hebe albicans 47, 171
Hebe andersonii 'Variegata' 80, 171
Hebe 'Great Orme' 17, 172
Hebe pinguifolia 'Pagei' 172
Hedera colchica 81, 177
Hedera helix 19, 34, 74, 75, 177
Helleborus foetidus 34, 36, 177
Helleborus niger 84
Helleborus orientalis 177
Heuchera sanguinea 57, 168
Hosta crispula 36, 169
Hosta fortunei 83, 169
Hosta lancifolia, 169
Hosta sieboldiana 19, 29, 34, 83, 169
Hosta ventricosa 'Variegata' 169
Hydrangea 'Blue Bird' 18
Hydrangea macrophylla 80, 176
Hydrangea 'Lanarth White' 18, 172
Hydrangea petiolaris 17, 31, 81, 177
Hydrangea seemanii 177

Hydrangea villosa 80, 176
Hypericum moserianum 'Tricolor' 74, 172
Hyssop 28, 182

Iris germanica 48, 174
Iris pallida 48, 57, 179
Iris sibirica 84, 179
Iris unguicularis 34
Itea ilicifolia 80, 176

Jasminum nudiflorum 17, 75, 171
Jasminum officinale 17, 48, 81, 171
Jasminum stephanense 48, 56, 171
Juniperus virginiana 43, 178

Lamium maculatum 48, 176
Laurus nobilis 39, 43, 178
Lavandula 42, 47, 56, 81, 171, 182
Lavatera olbia 'Rosea' 54
Lilium candidum 36, 181
Lonicera 'Dropmore Scarlet' 29, 171
Lonicera japonica 17, 48, 56, 171
Lonicera periclymenum 171

Magnolia grandiflora 77, 172
Magnolia liliifolia 168
Magnolia soulangiana 179
Mahonia aquifolium 74, 167
Mahonia japonica 17, 167
Mahonia pinnata 167
Mahonia undulata 28, 167
Malus floribunda 68, 180
Malva moschata 56, 170
Meconopsis cambrica 170
Metasequoia glyptostroboides 180
Mint 182
Miscanthus sinensis 36, 179
Muscari botryoides 43, 181

Nepeta faassenii 57, 83, 173

Nicotiana *34, 43, 119*

Olearia haastii *167*
Ornithogalum umbellatum *34, 181*
Osmunda regalis *36, 178*
Osteospermum ecklonis *171*

Pachysandra terminalis 'Variegata' *175*
Paeonia lutea ludlowii *178*
Paeonia officinalis *48, 57, 174*
Passiflora caerulea *34, 175*
Philadelphus 'Beauclerk' *47, 54, 172*
Philadelphus 'Manteau d'Hermine' *75, 172*
Philadelphus 'Sybille' *172*
Phlomis fruticosa *56, 172*
Phlox subulata *48, 182*
Phormium tenax *178*
Polemonium caeruleum *170*
Polygonatum multiflorum *83, 178*
Polygonum affine *48, 182*
Potentilla 'Elizabeth' *28, 168*
Potentilla 'Longacre' *74, 168*
Prunus hillieri *180*

Prunus laurocerasus 'Zabeliana' *175*
Prunus 'Pandora' *74*
Pulmonaria angustifolia
Pulmonaria rubra *177*
Pulmonaria saccharata *42, 84, 176*
Pyracantha 'Soleil d'Or' *167*
Pyracantha watereri *168*
Pyrus salicifolia 'Pendula' *39, 180*

Ranunculus aconitifolius *174, 181*
Ranunculus ficaria *75*
Rheum palmatum 'Atrosanguineum' *79*
Rodgersia podophylla *36, 170*
Rosa alba 'Maiden's Blush' *56, 173*
Rosa 'Albéric Barbier' *170*
Rosa 'Albertine' *39, 56, 170*
Rosa 'Aloha' *17, 175*
Rosa 'Bobbie James' *81, 171*
Rosa 'Félicité et Perpétue' *81, 170*
Rosa gallica 'Versicolor' *54, 173*

Rosa 'Mermaid' *74, 170*
Rosa 'New Dawn' *48, 170*
Rosa 'Old Blush China' *54, 173*
Rosa 'Pink Perpétue' *48, 175*
Rosa rubrifolia *42, 168*
Rosa 'The Fairy' *84*
Rosa virginiana *56, 173*
Rosa 'Zéphirine Drouhin' *29, 170*
Rosemary *42, 56, 182*

Sage *19, 182*
Salix lanata *168*
Salvia nemorosa 'East Friesland' *29, 174*
Santolina chamaecyparissus *56, 171*
Saponaria ocymoides *182*
Saxifraga umbrosa *169*
Sedum 'Autumn Joy' *29, 174*
Sedum maximum 'Atropurpureum' *174.*
Sedum roseum *174*
Sedum spectabile *19, 174*
Senecio 'Sunshine' *28, 167*
Skimmia japonica *28, 80, 175*
Smilacina racemosa *177*
Sorbus 'Joseph Rock' *28, 180*

Sorbus 'Wilfred Fox' *180*
Stachys lanata *42, 48, 57, 83, 173*
Standard rose *180*
Syringa microphylla *173*
Syringa persica *173*
Syringa vulgaris *80, 173*

Thyme *57, 182*
Thymus citriodorus *182*
Tiarella cordifolia *75, 176*
Tolmiea menziesii 'Taffs Gold' *169*
Trachelospermum jasminoides *56, 175*
Tulipa turkestana *83, 181*

Viola tricolor *75*
Viburnum burkwoodii *18, 168*
Viburnum plicatum tomentosum *80, 168*
Vinca minor *43, 74, 175*

Weigela florida *19, 28, 168*
Wisteria floribunda *81, 175*

Yucca filamentosa *42, 177*
Yucca gloriosa *177*

Zantedeschia aethiopica *83*